MYTHOLOGY

MYTHOLOGY
THE VOYAGE OF THE HERO

Second Edition

DAVID ADAMS LEEMING

University of Connecticut, Storrs

1817

HARPER & ROW, PUBLISHERS, New York
Cambridge, Hagerstown, Philadelphia, San Francisco,
London, Mexico City, São Paulo, Sydney

Sponsoring Editor: Phillip Leininger
Project Editor: Eleanor Castellano
Designer: T. R. Funderburk
Production Manager: Marion A. Palen
Compositor: Ruttle, Shaw & Wetherill, Inc.
Printer and Binder: Halliday Lithograph Corporation

Cover Photo: Navajo sand-painting from Gladys A. Reichard and F. J. Newcomb's
Sandpaintings of the Navajo Shooting Chant.

MYTHOLOGY: THE VOYAGE OF THE HERO, Second Edition
Copyright © 1981 by David Adams Leeming

Library of Congress Cataloging in Publication Data

Leeming, David Adams, 1937-
  Mythology, the voyage of the hero.

  Bibliography: p.
  Includes index.
  1. Mythology—Collected works. I. Title.
BL311.L326   1981   291.1'3   80-12703
ISBN 0-06-043942-4

ACKNOWLEDGMENTS

Grateful acknowledgment is made for use of the following materials:

PAGE 11: Reprinted with permission of The Macmillan Company from *The Collected Poems of W. B. Yeats* by W. B. Yeats. Copyright 1928 by The Macmillan Company, renewed 1956 by Georgia Yeats.

PAGES 12–13, 55–56, 59, 118, 124, 145–148, 279: Reprinted with permission of Penguin Books Inc., Baltimore, Maryland, from *The Greek Myths* by Robert Graves.

PAGES 14–18, 71–72, 290–291: Reprinted by permission of the publishers from Henry Clarke Warren, *Buddhism in Translations* (Cambridge, Mass.: Harvard University Press, 1896).

PAGES 19, 304: From *The Masks of God: Primitive Mythology* by Joseph Campbell. Copyright © 1959 by Joseph Campbell. Reprinted by permission of The Viking Press, Inc.

PAGES 20–21, 22: Reprinted with permission of Alfred A. Knopf, Inc., from *The Myth of the Birth of the Hero* by Otto Rank, edited by Philip Freund. Copyright 1932, 1936, © 1959 by Alfred A. Knopf, Inc. Copyright renewed 1960, 1964 by Alfred A. Knopf, Inc.

PAGES 23–24: From C. V. Narasimhan, trans., *The Mahabharata* (New York: Columbia University Press, 1964), VIII, pages 19–20.

PAGES 25, 166–171, 239–245: From *Myths and Legends of the Polynesians* by Johannes Andersen. Reprinted by permission of Charles E. Tuttle Company, Inc. of Tokyo, Japan, pp. 192, 268–278, 280–283.

PAGE 28: Reprinted with permission of Harvard University Press from *Diodorus of Sicily*, translated by C. H. Oldfather. The Loeb Classical Library.

PAGES 29, 39, 40, 203 (lines 1–9), 219, 280, 283 (lines 23–29), 284: Reprinted by permission of the publisher, The Vanguard Press, from *Gods of the Greeks* by C. Kerényi.

PAGES 30–32: Reprinted with permission of the American Folklore Society from *Indian Tales of North America*, edited by T. P. Coffin.

PAGES 33–35, 149–153, 222, 253, 294: Reprinted with permission of the University of Nebraska Press from *Blackfoot Lodge Tales* by George Bird Grinnell.

PAGES 36, 62–63: Reprinted with permission of Cooper Square Publishers, Inc., from *The Mythology of All Races*, edited by Louis Gray.

PAGE 37: From *Larousse World Mythology*, edited by Pierre Grimal. Reprinted by permission of Hamlyn Publishing Group, Ltd.

PAGES 38, 203 (lines 12–27), 204, 207 (lines 4–26), 208, 209–212, 292–293, 298–299: Reprinted by permission of S. G. Phillips, Inc., from *The New Golden Bough* by Sir James Frazer and Theodor H. Gaster. Copyright © 1959 by S. G. Phillips, Inc.

PAGES 41, 73: Reprinted from *Myth and Ritual in Christianity* by Alan Watts by permission of the publisher, Vanguard Press, Inc. Copyright, 1954, by Alan W. Watts. Pp. 115–116, 116, 111–112.

PAGES 53–54, 316–317: Reprinted with permission of Dover Publications, Inc., from *Myths of the Hindus and Buddhists* by A. K. Coomaraswamy and Sister Nivedita.

PAGES 57–58, 266–270: From *The Odyssey of Homer* translated by T. E. Shaw. Copyright 1932 by Bruce Rogers. Renewed 1960 by A. W. Lawrence. Reprinted by permission of Oxford University Press, Inc.

PAGES 60–61, 155–156 (lines 1–20), 320–321: Reprinted with permission of the New American Library, Inc., from *Bulfinch's Mythology: The Age of Chivalry* by Thomas Bulfinch.

PAGES 64–66, 112, 157–158: From *Romances and Epics of Our Northern Ancestors* by W. Wagner. London: Norroena Society, 1907.

PAGES 74–75: From *Butler's Lives of the Saints*, edited by Herbert Thurston and Donald Attwater. Reprinted with permission of Search Press Ltd.

PAGES 78–80, 263–265, 312–313, 314–315: Reprinted with permission of the Jewish Publication Society of America from *The Legends of the Jews* by Louis Ginzberg.

PAGES 81–82, 193–196, 247: From *Crowell's Handbook of Classical Mythology*, edited by Edward Tripp. Copyright © 1970 by Edward Tripp. With permission of Thomas Y. Crowell Company, Inc.

PAGES 87–92: Reprinted with permission of George G. Harrap & Company Ltd. from *Buddha and the Gospel of Buddhism* by A. K. Coomaraswamy.

PAGES 92–95, 101 (lines 19–36), 102, 319: From *Technicians of the Sacred,* edited by Jerome Rothenberg. Copyright © 1968 by Jerome Rothenberg. Reprinted by permission of Doubleday & Company, Inc.

PAGES 100, 101 (lines 1–18): Source: The National Museum of Man of the National Museums of Canada, Bulletin 152, Medicine Men of the North Pacific Coast, by Marius Barbeau. Reproduced by permission of Information Canada.

PAGES 103–106: From *The Myth of Hiawatha and Other Oral Legends Mythologic and Allegoric of the North American Indians,* by Henry R. Schoolcraft. Copyright 1856 by Henry R. Schoolcraft. Reprinted by courtesy of J. B. Lippincott Company.

PAGES 107–111: From *Myths and Legends of the Australian Aboriginals,* by W. Ramsay Smith. London: George G. Harrap, 1970.

PAGES 113–115: Reprinted with permission of John Grant, Publisher, from *The Life of Mohammad* by Sir William Muir.

PAGES 116–117: Excerpted from Homer, *The Odyssey,* translated by Robert Fitzgerald. Copyright © 1961 by Robert Fitzgerald. Reprinted by permission of Doubleday & Company, Inc.

PAGES 119–123, 323 (lines 16–28) 326: Reprinted with permission of the authors from *The Golden Legend* by Jacobus De Voragine, adapted from the Latin by William Granger Ryan and Helmut Ripperger.

PAGES 131–138, 139–144, 251–252, 318: Reprinted with permission of Granada Publishing Limited from *The Stories of the Greeks* by Rex Warner.

PAGE 154: Reprinted with permission of Princeton University Press from *The Hero with a Thousand Faces,* by Joseph Campbell, Bollingen Series XVII, copyright © 1949 by Bolllingen Foundation.

PAGES 160–165, 285–287: From *The Oldest Stories in the World* by

Theodor H. Gaster. Copyright 1952 by Theodor H. Gaster. Reprinted by permission of The Viking Press, Inc.

PAGES 172–173: Reprinted with permission of The University of Chicago Press from *The Quest of Seth* by E. C. Quinn. © 1962 by The University of Chicago. All rights reserved.

PAGES 174–176: Reprinted with permission of Emmet M. Greene, executor, Estate of Padraic Colum, from *Myths of the World* by Padraic Colum.

PAGES 185–193: From *Greek Tragedy and Comedy* edited by F. L. Lucas. © Elna Lucas 1967. Reprinted by permission of The Viking Press, Inc.

PAGES 205–206, 213–218, 220–221, 239–243, 254–257, 271–272, 273, 281–282, 283 (lines 1–22) 344–349: From *Ovid: The Metamorphoses* translated by Horace Gregory. Copyright © 1958 by The Viking Press, Inc. Reprinted by permission of The Viking Press, Inc.

PAGES 223–224, 246, 303: From *African Folktales and Sculpture,* edited by Paul Radin and James J. Sweeney.

PAGE 230: From *Myth and Religion of the North* by E. O. G. Turville-Petre. Copyright © 1964 by E. O. G. Turville-Petre. Reprinted by permission of Holt, Rinehart and Winston, Inc.

PAGES 237–238: Reprinted with permission of Harper and Row, Publishers, from *Sumerian Mythology* by S. N. Kramer.

PAGES 248–250: From *The Bible of the World* edited by Robert O. Ballou. Copyright 1939, © 1967 by Robert O. Ballou. Reprinted by permission of The Viking Press, Inc.

PAGE 258: Reprinted with permission of the author from *The North American Indian Orpheus Tradition* by Åke Hultkrantz.

PAGES 259–260: Reprinted by permission of the publisher, The Vanguard Press, from *Gods of the North* by Brian Branston.

PAGES 261–262, 288–294: From *Mythologies of the Ancient World* by Samuel Noah Kramer, ed. Copyright © 1961 by Doubleday & Company, Inc. Reprinted by permission of the publisher.

PAGES 271–274: From *Mythology* by Edith Hamilton, by permission of Little, Brown and Co. Copyright 1942, by Edith Hamilton, copyright renewed © 1969 by Dorian Fielding Reid, copyright renewed © 1969 by Doris Fielding Reid, executrix of the will of Edith Hamilton.

PAGES 295–297: From *Myths of the Cherokee* by James Mooney, reprinted by Johnson Reprint Corporation, 1970.

PAGES 309–311: From *Sophocles' Oedipus at Colonus,* translated by Robert Fitzgerald, copyright, 1941, by Harcourt Brace Jovanovich, Inc.; renewed, 1969, by Robert Fitzgerald. Reprinted by permission of the publishers.

QUOTATIONS FROM CARL GUSTAV JUNG ON PAGES 329, 330, 331, 332: From *Memories, Dreams, Reflections* by C. G. Jung, edited by Aniela Jaffe, translated by Richard and Clara Winston. Copyright © 1963 by Random House, Inc. Reprinted by permission of Pantheon Books, a division of Random House, Inc.

PAGES 334–335, 336, 337–338, 339–340, 341, 342, 343, 350: From *Gods, Goddesses and Myths of Creation* by Mircea Eliade. Reprinted by permission of Harper & Row.

For
Marion Stancioff

CONTENTS

PREFACE

The subject of mythology is much too complex to be covered in a single book, and no attempt has been made to do so here. There are as many mythic stories as there are dreams, and numerous ways in which these stories might be arranged for study. There are as many mythic traditions as there are races, tribes, or villages; and equally many ways to experience myth.

This book is arranged in sections according to theme. Each section ends with a commentary which is designed to assist the reader in his discovery of the basic myth which underlies the stories of the section. The purpose of this inversion of the usual pattern of introduction followed by literary text is to encourage the reader to develop his own insights before reading the commentaries, which then may serve as catalysts for deeper understanding. A brief headnote precedes each story, supplementing the commentaries, outlining essential motifs, and suggesting connections between the stories.

Since its original publication in 1973 *Mythology: The Voyage of the Hero* has been used successfully as a textbook for courses in mythology. It has also been used as a freshman English text, as a supplementary text for anthropology, religion, and upper-level English courses, and as a general reference book on world mythology.

The revisions made in this edition reflect the needs and suggestions of those students and teachers who have used the book in the past. The addition of several heroine myths, several myths from Africa and Polynesia, and appendixes on the Creation and the Flood make this a more comprehensive volume.

The book is directed, finally, to any reader with an interest in the study of human nature. The record of that nature is reflected in the myths collected here, and to study those myths is to study the quest for self that concerns us all.

David Adams Leeming

MYTHOLOGY

INTRODUCTION
The Meaning of Myth

Myth comes via *mythos* from the Greek root μυ (*mu*) meaning to make a sound with the mouth and is thus basic to human existence as we know it: "In the beginning was the Word." To the orthodox believer what we call myth is the word of God – the metaphorical, symbolical, or direct expression of the "unknown": "and the Word was with God, and the Word was God."

If we put aside the commonplace definition of myth as story with no basis in fact, we will have made a necessary first step toward a meaningful definition of our subject. The next step involves the choice of a path. Individual temperament and inclination will be the major factors in this choice. No longer is mythology approached primarily in conjunction with the study of classical or other literatures. Mythologists are now anthropologists, philologists, etiologists, ethnologists, and perhaps most of all, psychologists. And crossing these disciplines are ritualists, diffusionists, structuralists, Jungians, Freudians, and culturalists, who, in turn, are not always mutually exclusive. The modern student of mythology might be helped in his choice of an approach by making himself aware of some of the major theorists and their theories. A brief review here will serve as a beginning.

E. B. Tylor (*Primitive Culture*), Sir James Frazer (*The Golden Bough*), and Adolf Bastian with his theory of "elementary ideas" common to all mankind were major pioneers in the modern study of myth. Each believed that the comparing of myths from various cultures would reveal certain laws of human life. Few mythologists now would disagree with this general assumption, but just as few would agree on what to do with the assumption. There are the culturalists – Emile Durkheim, Franz Boas, and Bronislaw Malinowski, for example – who see society as the shaping force behind the mythology of a given culture. Diffusionism is more popular today. Its father is Leo Frobenius, and its essential tenet is that certain vast areas of the world are united by cultural affinities and that the explanation for this fact lies in the diffusion of cultures, including myths, from certain "mythogenetic zones." Others – perhaps they should be called parallelists or in some cases Jungians, after C. G. Jung – have stressed cultural similarities which appear to be the result of

1

neither society nor diffusion. The argument here is that just as certain physical traits are common to man wherever he lives, so are certain psychological ones. Humans eat because they have to; they have myths of survival after death for the same reason. There are those who would say that as far as mythology is concerned, all of these approaches are false. Claude Lévi-Strauss, who has been called a "structuralist," finds meaning in the structure of a tale—in the relationship between its various components rather than in the components themselves. Earlier, Sir James Frazer saw in mythology simply an attempt to explain the natural world. His followers—particularly Jane Harrison (*Themis*)—became known as the "Cambridge school" or the "myth-ritual school." For them myth was the narrative correlative of the ritual act, meaningful only when considered in the context of the ritual. One valuable result of the work of this school was the development of the theory of the ritualistic origins of drama. Giorgio de Santillana and Hertha von Dechend in their controversial *Hamlet's Mill* see myth as an ancient astrological language.

Much has been done—especially through the psychological approach—to make myth relevant to modern man. Sigmund Freud (*Totem and Taboo*) applied the principles of psychoanalysis to myth and found parallels between myth and neurosis. He and others—Norman O. Brown, for example—have done a great deal with the connection between language and myth as they relate to human psychology. Jung, following Bastian, contributed his theories of archetypes and the collective unconscious and his belief that myth could better be associated with the process of education—of individuation—than with neurosis. Jung has had many followers and associates who have made major contributions. The work of Paul Radin on the Trickster myth owes something to Jung, as does that of Mircea Eliade, who has done so much to relate myth and ritual to modern man. Erich Neumann, too, has been influenced by the theory of archetypes. Most of all, Jung broke the path into regions scientists had feared to explore —regions which had been labeled "mystical" and therefore unworthy of attention. He provided a certain respectability for those who, like him, carried myth into the realm of metaphysics— thinkers such as Alan Watts and Ananda Coomaraswamy. Coomaraswamy could go so far as to see in myth "the penultimate truth, of which all experience is the temporal reflection.

The mythical narrative is of timeless and placeless validity, true nowhere and everywhere."[1]

The list of mythologists by no means ends here. A. A. Aarne and Stith Thompson have done invaluable work in the indexing and classifying of mythic themes and motifs. Robert Graves, C. Kerényi, Theodor Gaster, S. N. Kramer, Rex Warner, and others have collected the myths. Many literary critics have become mythologists. Northrop Frye especially has applied myth to literature with great perception and has, therefore, added significantly to our understanding of myth.

In this long list I have not yet mentioned Joseph Campbell, who has perhaps done more than anyone else to revive the study of myth with his now standard works, *The Hero with a Thousand Faces* and the four-part *The Masks of God*. Campbell is particularly important because he makes the next step in our approach to mythology much simpler by demonstrating that mythology is the property of no single theorist or theory. It finally does not matter whether one is a diffusionist or a Jungian or a structuralist. Any honest path will lead to the beginning of an understanding of mythology. Campbell has written, ". . . when scrutinized in terms not of what it is but of how it functions, of how it has served mankind in the past, of how it may serve today, mythology shows itself to be as amenable as life itself to the obsessions and requirements of the individual, the race, the age."[2]

Each of us, then, must make the next step on his own, making use when possible of the discoveries and perceptions of others. What follows here is necessarily one individual's path, and it must be stated at the outset that his views have been colored by the works he has found most compatible and, therefore, most useful—those particularly of Jung, Campbell, Eliade, and Coomaraswamy. The search which forms the body of this book is of a general enough sort, however, to be of interest to the student of mythology, whatever his views on the subject. The basic questions we must ask are: What makes something mythic, and what do mythic events and narratives have to do with us?

C. G. Jung wrote: "the primitive mentality does not invent *myths*, it *experiences* them. Myths are original revelations of

[1] Ananda Coomaraswamy, *Hinduism and Buddhism*, p. 6. See the bibliography for complete documentation of this and all footnotes.

[2] Joseph Campbell, *The Hero with a Thousand Faces*, p. 382.

3

the pre-conscious psyche, involuntary statements about unconscious psychic happenings. . . ."[3] The point is not to search for the physical or historical correlative of myth, but for the meaning which is intrinsic in the myth itself, for myths, like dreams, are psychically real. Indeed, myths might be called the dreams of mankind. Dreams serve as escape valves for individuals. They represent wishes and fears. Myths serve whole societies and, as we shall see, many societies at once in much the same manner. The priests or medicine men or shamans who feel and convey the myths are, as Géza Róheim has written, "the lightning conductors of common anxiety. They fight the demons so that others can hunt the prey and in general fight reality."[4]

Most of us have had dreams of falling from a great height, dreams of being lost or left behind, dreams of conquest—sexual, athletic, or whatever. Nearly every society has myths which express these themes on the group level. To be sure, dreams are in part products of the individual's personality and environment, but Jung has shown that the individual's psyche cannot be divorced from the psyche of the human race as a whole. Dreams are also products of inherited themes which are buried in the very depths of the human psyche. These are themes—archetypes—which, when we come across them, in literature, for instance, "strike a chord" for no apparent reason. So myths spring from the particular problems and concerns of a given race or tribe, but on a deeper level their source is the universal soul of the human race itself. The myths of the Aztecs reflect the particular reality of Mexico—the veil of a culture—but when seen in conjunction with the myths of Iceland or Egypt or Greece, the Aztec myths reveal concerns which are common to all of us as a species. Whether a man's dream is the result of the way his parents treated him or of a neurosis is of limited importance. Whether a myth of the Aztecs was inherited from the Japanese is of secondary importance to the fact that the Aztecs incorporated the Japanese theme because it "struck a chord" already present in their group psyche.

In the same way a Christian or a Jew or a Buddhist need not feel threatened upon being told that his religion—his ritual or

[3] Carl Gustav Jung and C. Kerényi, *Introduction to a Science of Mythology*, p. 101.
[4] Géza Róheim, *The Origin and Function of Culture*, p. 51.

mythology—resembles that of the worshipper of Osiris or Attis. Rather he might find satisfaction in the thought that the myth he has experienced has been experienced universally. Myth is as real as human concerns are real. It is when we lose our ability to feel the mythic that we lose contact with that which is most basically and universally human. In a real sense a society loses its soul when it can no longer experience myth. And as we interpret dreams to gain insight into the individual psyche, we can study myths to better understand the human psyche.

We must move now from the general to the specific. How do we approach the particular story or tale? How do we determine what is myth and what is simply local color or "fill"? We make use of comparison—of comparative mythology. We search, as we do in dreams, for recurrent themes and patterns. We attempt to take the myth out of the context of Egyptian or Greek or Norse society and try to consider it in the context of human society as a whole. The Grail legend is a good example of a story which has been told in many forms and which is clearly a mixture of essential myth and local or national elements added in innumerable retellings. When Jessie Weston conducted her now classic search for the true Grail myth (*From Ritual to Romance*), she made use of the comparative method and discovered that vegetation myths and rituals—those of Tammuz, Osiris, Attis, Adonis, and even Jesus—could tell us much about the Grail hero and the Fisher King. She found that what was basic to the Grail legend was not the personality of Percival or the many exploits of Galahad but the hope of regeneration that is common to all the stories of the hero in relation to the Fisher King. Here lies the myth—as the ritualists would say, the correlative to the ritual, which is essentially the same ritual enacted around the ancient god-heroes mentioned above.

Doubtless there are those who will still ask what all of this has to do with us. The answer is that it has everything to do with us. The search for life is the search for the self—for the personal myth which is veiled in the local and the immediate but which, on a deeper level, is but an expression of the world myth. James Joyce, Joseph Campbell, and others have called this myth the "monomyth." To understand the monomyth—to relate to it meaningfully—is to create a mythic consciousness and by so doing to rejoin the real forces from which our modern age of reason and technocracy has done so much to remove us.[5] As individuals and groups we need to put our personal myths into proper relationship with the human myth. We need to rediscover the magic or "unknown" in life.

The monomyth itself is an expression of the journey of the hero figure, of our own journey through physical and psychic life, and of the evolutionary path of humanity to full consciousness. "The hero," writes Joseph Campbell, "is the man or woman who has been able to battle past his personal and local historical limitations to the generally valid, normally human forms."[6] The hero does what we would all like to do; he literally "finds himself." For Campbell.

the agony of breaking through personal limitations is the agony of spiritual growth. Art, literature, myth and cult, philosophy and ascetic disciplines are instruments to help the individual past his limiting horizons into spheres of ever-expanding realization. As he crosses threshold after threshold, conquering dragon after dragon, the stature of the divinity that he summons to his highest wish increases until it subsumes the cosmos.[7]

We must go with the hero through his rites of passage. We must lose ourselves to find ourselves in the overall pattern of the cosmos. We must discover the image of man within the self. To study myth is to listen to "the wonderful song of the soul's high adventure."[8]

This book of myths is built upon a simplified form of the monomyth. The monomyth is divided into eight basic events, which will be considered individually. They are supreme mythic events in the life of the hero. Admittedly this is not an ideal arrangement, as myths found in one section might be applicable to another as well. The story of the Buddha and the Tree is a myth of withdrawal and meditation, but it is also a quest myth and in some ways a descent myth. The story of Gawain is a quest myth and a rebirth myth. In a large mythic event elements of many or all of the basic rites of passage are apt to be found. The story of Aeneas's descent to the underworld itself moves from initiation to a descent to a kind of rebirth. And in a sense all mythic events are initiatory. The events of the monomyth, as I have arranged them, are not meant to be final. They are isolated here to be

[5] See the appendix on Jung.
[6] Joseph Campbell, *The Hero with a Thousand Faces*, pp. 19–20.
[7] Ibid., p. 190.
[8] Ibid., p. 22.

studied before being released into the cosmic flow which is their natural habitat. Hopefully, the isolation of similar myths from various cultures and the implicit and explicit comparing of these myths will make the essential reality and importance of mythology obvious.

The monomyth is arranged here as follows: In Part 1 the hero (and each of us) begins his "high adventure" by being born. The conception or the birth or the events immediately following the birth (or all three) are miraculous or unusual in the extreme. This is not surprising. For all humans birth is the first experience of trauma and the first miracle of life. For the hero who will burst through the limitations of the local and historical, this first event, like all the events in his life, must be special. Part 2 is childhood —a stage of basic initiation. The child is suddenly aware of forces infinitely larger than himself which he cannot fully comprehend. In myth this is expressed by struggles with wild animals or with giants (in a sense, to little children, all adults must be giants— friendly or cruel). To get through this stage the child often requires outside assistance—a sense of security based in a more powerful being. Mythically this often becomes the divine sign. The modern individual seeking to achieve a mythic consciousness must work his way through this primitive but idyllic stage of his existence.

In Part 3 the initiated hero withdraws for meditation and preparation. Anyone in search of personal destiny must use intellect and spirit to find the god within the self. This is a major step in the losing of the self to find the self. Often the hero, like any individual in this stage, is tempted by "the world," which is represented mythically by a devil figure who attempts to disrupt the lonely vigil. Next, in Part 4 comes the quest or trials—the agony and rewards of adult life. For the hero this might be a quest for a Golden Fleece or a Holy Grail, or it might be the labors of a Heracles or a Christ. The source of these myths is man's need to cope with the externals of life, as he has coped with the internals in his stage of meditation.

The labors or the quest continue essentially in Part 5, where the hero must confront physical death. For the hero, death, like birth, is miraculous or unusual. As his birth is definitive in the extreme, so is his death apparently so. Often he is dismembered. In death the hero acts, psychologically, for all of us; he becomes a scapegoat for our fear and our guilt. Of course he also serves as a reminder that we all must follow. In any case it is important that his death be memorable – especially when we consider what follows.

In Part 6 the hero continues in his role as scapegoat and in his role as quester or laborer. He is now the representative of the wish that death might somehow be known and understood. So he descends to the underworld to confront the forces of death. Sometimes he goes as one who has suffered physical death, sometimes as a living being who in his descent suffers a symbolic death. In a sense this stage is a more dramatic expression of the withdrawal stage. It is the final confrontation of the self – now on a cosmological level – with its depths. But the dismemberment and the descent into the earth hold promise of a new life. Fertility and death are inseparable in the cycle of nature, whether that cycle be expressed by the seasons, the moon, or the sun. And logically enough the hero, usually with the help of a woman – woman representing both fertility and the hope of the eventual union of all things – ascends from the underworld and, in Part 7, continuing in his role as scapegoat, rises from the dead. He thus acts out man's most elementary desire – he overcomes death physically and is united with the natural cycle of birth, death, and rebirth.

In Part 8 the hero reflects a later desire, to be given special treatment by being taken out of the cycle and placed in a permanent state in relation to the cosmos and to the creator-father god. Man longs for eternal life, for immortality. Thus the hero in Part 8 ascends to heaven, achieves atonement, or is made a god himself if he was not one already. In a purely psychological sense this is the individual's final step. Having dealt with his childhood, his inner self, his adult life, and the problem of death, he is prepared to discover God once and for all. The "wonderful song of the soul's high adventure" is complete.

Mythology, then, as the term is used in this book, is the expression in symbols and images of the most basic level of the human psyche. That we be concerned with this level is of crucial importance. As Jung wrote, "it is possible to live the fullest life only when we are in harmony with these symbols; wisdom is a return to them. It is a question neither of belief nor knowledge, but of the agreement of our thinking with the primordial images of the unconscious."[9]

[9] Carl Gustav Jung, *Modern Man in Search of a Soul*, p. 129.

1

THE MIRACULOUS CONCEPTION AND BIRTH AND THE HIDING OF THE CHILD

This modern "great mother," appropriately oversized, points as madonnas of the past do to the child miraculously visible in a mandalic womb. By so doing she reminds us that the child hero—the Self within—can provide meaningful focus to the otherwise disparate activities of a distorted world. [Marc Chagall, *Maternity* (1913), Stedelijk Museum, Amsterdam. Reproduced with permission.]

LEDA AND HELEN
Greek

The hero, the agent of divinity on earth, is often born of immortal god and mortal woman. Divine purpose is sometimes achieved by the god in the form of an animal.

Zeus, in the form of a swan, raped Leda beside the river Eurotas.

A sudden blow: the great wings beating still
Above the staggering girl, her thighs caressed
By the dark webs, her nape caught in his bill,
He holds her helpless breast upon his breast.   5

How can those terrified vague fingers push
The feathered glory from her loosening thighs?
And how can body, laid in that white rush,
But feel the strange heart beating where it lies?

A shudder in the loins engenders there   10
The broken wall, the burning roof and tower
And Agamemnon dead.
                    Being so caught up,
So mastered by the brute blood of the air,
Did she put on his knowledge with his power   15
Before the indifferent beak could let her drop? [1]

    After being ravished by Zeus, Leda laid an egg from which were hatched Helen and, according to some versions, Clytemnestra and/or Castor and Polydeuces. She was then deified as Nemesis.

---

[1] William Butler Yeats, "Leda and the Swan."

AETHRA AND THESEUS
Greek

The god may visit the woman of his choice by night and leave the parentage of the child hero in question.

Now, while Pittheus was still living at Pisa, Bellerophon had asked to marry his daughter Aethra, but had been sent away to Caria in disgrace before the marriage could be celebrated; though still contracted to Bellerophon, she had little hope of his return. Pittheus, therefore, grieving at her enforced virginity, and in- 5
fluenced by the spell which Medea was casting on all of them from afar, made Aegeus drunk, and sent him to bed with Aethra. Later in the same night, Poseidon also enjoyed her. For, in obedience to a dream sent by Athene, she left the drunken Aegeus, and waded across to the island of Sphaeria, which lies close to 10
the mainland of Troezen, carrying libations to pour at the tomb of Sphaerus, Pelops's charioteer. There, with Athene's connivance, Poseidon overpowered her, and Aethra subsequently changed the name of the island from Sphaeria to Hiera, and founded on it a temple of Apaturian Athene, establishing a rule that every 15
Troezenian girl should henceforth dedicate her girdle to the goddess before marriage. Poseidon, however, generously conceded to Aegeus the paternity of any child born to Aethra in the course of the next four months.

Aegeus, when he awoke and found himself in Aethra's bed, 20
told her that if a son were born to them he must not be exposed or sent away, but secretly reared in Troezen. Then he sailed back to Athens, to celebrate the All-Athenian Festival, after hiding his sword and his sandals under a hollow rock, known as the Altar of Strong Zeus, which stood on the road from Troezen to 25
Hermium. If, when the boy grew up, he could move this rock and recover the tokens, he was to be sent with them to Athens. Meanwhile, Aethra must keep silence, lest Aegeus's nephews, the fifty children of Pallas, plot against her life. The sword was an heirloom from Cecrops. 30

At a place now called Genethlium, on the way from the city to the harbour of Troezen, Aethra gave birth to a boy. Some say that she at once named him Theseus, because the tokens had been *deposited* for him; others, that he afterwards won this name at Athens. He was brought up in Troezen, where his guardian Pittheus discreetly spread the rumour that Poseidon had been his father; and one Connidas, to whom the Athenians still sacrifice a ram on the day before the Thesean Feasts, acted as his pedagogue. But some say that Theseus grew up at Marathon.[1] 5

[1] Robert Graves, *The Greek Myths*, vol. 1, pp. 324–325.

MAHA-MAYA AND BUDDHA
Indian

In this story the white elephant is the agent by which the spirit of divinity enters the world of flesh. The divine nature of the hero is indicated by the purity of his mother's thoughts, her early removal to heaven, the miraculous events surrounding the birth, and the adult qualities possessed by the infant.

It is related that at that time the midsummer festival had been proclaimed in the city of Kapilavatthu, and the multitude were enjoying the feast. And queen Maha-Maya, abstaining from strong drink, and brilliant with garlands and perfumes, took part in the festivities for the six days previous to the day of full moon. And when it came to be the day of full moon, she rose early, bathed in perfumed water, and dispensed four hundred thousand pieces of money in great largess. And decked in full gala attire, she ate of the choicest food; after which she took the eight vows, and entered her elegantly furnished chamber of state. And lying down on the royal couch, she fell asleep and dreamed the following dream:

The four guardian angels came and lifted her up, together with her couch, and took her away to the Himalaya Mountains. There, in the Manosila table-land, which is sixty leagues in extent, they laid her under a prodigious sal-tree, seven leagues in height, and took up their positions respectfully at one side. Then came the wives of these guardian angels, and conducted her to Anotatta Lake, and bathed her, to remove every human stain. And after clothing her with divine garments, they anointed her with perfumes and decked her with divine flowers. Not far off was Silver Hill, and in it a golden mansion. There they spread a divine couch with its head toward the east, and laid her down upon it. Now the future Buddha had become a superb white elephant, and was wandering about at no great distance, on Gold Hill. Descending thence, he ascended Silver Hill, and approaching from the north, he plucked a white lotus with his silvery trunk, and trumpeting loudly, went into the golden mansion. And three times he walked round his mother's couch, with his right side towards it, and striking her on her right side, he

14

seemed to enter her womb. Thus the conception took place in the midsummer festival.

On the next day the queen awoke, and told the dream to the king. And the king caused sixty-four eminent Brahmanas to be summoned, and spread costly seats for them on ground festively 5 prepared with green leaves, dalbergia flowers, and so forth. The Brahmanas being seated, he filled gold and silver dishes with the best of milk-porridge compounded with ghee, honey, and treacle; and covering these dishes with others, made likewise of gold and silver, he gave the Brahmanas to eat. And not only with 10 food, but with other gifts, such as new garments, tawny cows, and so forth, he satisfied them completely. And when their every desire had been satisfied, he told them the dream and asked them what would come of it.

"Be not anxious, great king!" said the Brahmanas; "a child 15 has planted itself in the womb of your queen, and it is a male child and not a female. You will have a son. And he, if he continue to live the household life, will become a universal monarch; but if he leave the household life and retire from the world, he will become a Buddha, and roll back the clouds of sin and folly 20 of this world." . . .

Now the instant the future Buddha was conceived in the womb of his mother, all the ten thousand worlds suddenly quaked, quivered, and shook. And the thirty-two prognostics appeared, as follows: an immeasurable light spread through ten 25 thousand worlds; the blind recovered their sight, as if from desire to see this his glory; the deaf received their hearing; the dumb talked; the hunchbacked became straight of body; the lame recovered the power to walk; all those in bonds were freed from their bonds and chains; the fires went out in all the hells; 30 the hunger and thirst of the departed ancestors were stilled; wild animals lost their timidity; diseases ceased among men; all mortals became mild-spoken; horses neighed and elephants trumpeted in a manner sweet to the ear; all musical instruments gave forth their notes without being played upon; bracelets and 35 other ornaments jingled; in all quarters of the heavens the weather became fair; a mild, cool breeze began to blow, very refreshing to men; rain fell out of season; water burst forth from the earth and flowed in streams; the birds ceased flying through the air; the rivers checked their flowing; in the mighty ocean the 40 water became sweet; the ground became everywhere covered with lotuses of the five different colours; all flowers bloomed, both those on land and those that grow in the water; trunk-lotuses bloomed on the trunks of trees, branch-lotuses on the branches, and vine-lotuses on the vines; on the ground, stalk-lotuses, as they are called, burst through the overlying rocks and came up by sevens; in the sky were produced others, called hanging-lotuses; a shower of flowers fell all about; celestial music was heard to play in the sky; and the whole ten thousand worlds became one mass of garlands of the utmost possible magnificence, with waving chowries, and saturated with the incense-like fragrance of flowers, and resembled a bouquet of flowers sent whirling through the air, or a closely woven wreath, or a superbly decorated altar of flowers.

From the time the future Buddha was thus conceived, four angels with swords in their hands kept guard, to ward off all harm from both the future Buddha and the future Buddha's mother. No lustful thought sprang up in the mind of the future Buddha's mother; having reached the pinnacle of good fortune and of glory, she felt comfortable and well, and experienced no exhaustion of body. And within her womb she could distinguish the future Buddha, like a white thread passed through a transparent jewel. And whereas a womb that has been occupied by a future Buddha is like the shrine of a temple, and can never be occupied or used again, therefore it was that the mother of the future Buddha died when he was seven days old, and was reborn in the Tusita heaven.

Now other women sometimes fall short of and sometimes run over the term of ten lunar months, and bring forth either sitting or lying down; but not so the mother of a future Buddha. She carries the future Buddha in her womb for just ten months, and then brings forth while standing up. This is a characteristic of the mother of a future Buddha. So also queen Maha-Maya carried the future Buddha in her womb, as it were oil in a vessel, for ten months; and being then far gone with child, she grew desirous of going home to her relatives, and said to king Suddhodana,

"Sire, I should like to visit my kinsfolk in their city Devadaha."

"So be it," said the king; and from Kapilavatthu to the city of Devadaha he had the road made even, and garnished it with plantain-trees set in pots, and with banners, and streamers; and, seating the queen in a golden palanquin borne by a thousand of his courtiers, he sent her away in great pomp.

Now between the two cities, and belonging to the inhabitants of both, there was a pleasure-grove of sal-trees, called Lumbini Grove. And at this particular time this grove was one mass of flowers from the ground to the topmost branches, while amongst the branches and flowers hummed swarms of bees of the five different colours, and flocks of various kinds of birds flew about warbling sweetly. Throughout the whole of Lumbini Grove the scene resembled the Chittalata Grove in Indra's paradise, or the magnificently decorated banqueting pavilion of some potent king.

When the queen beheld it she became desirous of disporting herself therein, and the courtiers therefore took her into it. And going to the foot of the monarch sal-tree of the grove, she wished to take hold of one of its branches. And the sal-tree branch, like the tip of a well-stemmed reed, bent itself down within reach of the queen's hand. Then she reached out her hand, and seized hold of the branch, and immediately her pains came upon her. Thereupon the people hung a curtain about her, and retired. So her delivery took place while she was standing up, and keeping fast hold of the sal-tree branch.

At that very moment came four pure-minded Maha-Brahma angels bearing a golden net; and, receiving the future Buddha on this golden net, they placed him before his mother and said,

"Rejoice, O queen! A mighty son has been born to you."

Now other mortals on issuing from the maternal womb are smeared with disagreeable, impure matter; but not so the future Buddha. He issued from his mother's womb like a preacher descending from his preaching-seat, or a man coming down a stair, stretching out both hands and both feet, unsmeared by any impurity from his mother's womb, and flashing pure and spotless, like a jewel thrown upon a vesture of Benares cloth. Notwithstanding this, for the sake of honouring the future Buddha and his mother, there came two streams of water from the sky, and refreshed the future Buddha and his mother.

Then the Brahma angels, after receiving him on their golden net, delivered him to the four guardian angels, who received him from their hands on a rug which was made of the skins of black antelopes, and was soft to the touch, being such as is used on state occasions; and the guardian angels delivered him to men who received him on a coil of fine cloth; and the men let

17

him out of their hands on the ground, where he stood and faced the east. There, before him, lay many thousands of worlds, like a great open court; and in them, gods and men, making offerings to him of perfumes, garlands, and so on, were saying,

"Great Being! There is none your equal, much less your superior."

When he had in this manner surveyed the four cardinal points, and the four intermediate ones, and the zenith, and the nadir, in short, all the ten directions in order, and had nowhere discovered his equal, he exclaimed, "This is the best direction," and strode forward seven paces, followed by Maha-Brahma holding over him the white umbrella, Suyama bearing the fan, and other divinities having the other symbols of royalty in their hands. Then, at the seventh stride, he halted, and with a noble voice he shouted the shout of victory, beginning,

"The chief am I in all the world."

Now at the very time that our future Buddha was born in Lumbini Grove there also came into existence the mother of Rahula, and Channa the courtier, Kaludayi the courtier, Kanthaka the king of horses, the great Bo-tree, and the four urns full of treasure. Of these last, one was a quarter of a league in extent, another a half-league, the third three-quarters of a league, and the fourth a league. These seven are called the connate ones.

Then the inhabitants of both cities took the future Buddha, and carried him to Kapilavatthu.[1]

---

[1] From the introduction to the *Jataka*, in Henry Clarke Warren, *Buddhism in Translations*, pp. 183–187.

CHIMALMAN AND QUETZALCOATL
Toltec and Aztec

The disguised god, the mother's early removal to heaven, and the hero's adult qualities at birth are the significant characteristics of this story. The importance of the events is confirmed by the fact that the impregnation is somehow spiritual rather than carnal; the hero is born of a virgin.

. . . the great high priest and monarch of the Golden Age in the Toltec city of Tula, the City of the Sun, in ancient Mexico, whose name, Quetzalcoatl, has been read to mean both "the Feathered Serpent" and "the Admirable Twin," and who was fair of face and white of beard, was the teacher of the arts to 5 the people of pre-Columbian America, originator of the calendar, and their giver of maize. His virgin mother, Chimalman—the legend tells—had been one of three sisters to whom God, the All-Father, had appeared one day under his form of Citlallatonac, "the morning." The other two had been struck by fright, but upon 10 Chimalman God breathed and she conceived. She died, however, giving birth, and is now in heaven, where she is revered under the honorable name of "the Precious Stone of Sacrifice," Chalchihuitzli.

Quetzalcoatl, her child, who is known both as the Son of the 15 Lord of the High Heavens and as the Son of the Lord of the Seven Caves, was endowed at birth with speech, all knowledge, and all wisom. . . .[1]

[1] Joseph Campbell, *The Masks of God: Primitive Mythology*, pp. 457–458.

DUGHDA AND ZOROASTER (ZARATHUSHTRA)
Persian

The hero is threatened even before his birth by evil forces. Only miracles preserve him from destruction.

[Zoroaster's] mother, Dughda, dreams, in the sixth month of her pregnancy, that the wicked and the good spirits are fighting for the embryonic Zoroaster; a monster tears the future Zoroaster from the mother's womb; but a light god fights the monster with his horn of light, re-encloses the embryo in the mother's womb, blows upon Dughda, and she becomes pregnant again. On awakening, she hurries in her fear to a wise dream-interpreter, who is unable to explain the wonderful dream before the end of three days. He then declares that the child she is carrying is destined to become a man of great importance; the dark cloud and the mountain of light signify that she and her son will at first have to undergo numerous trials, through tyrants and other enemies, but at last they will overcome all perils. Dughda at once returns to her home and informs Pourushacpa, her husband, of everything that has happened. Immediately after his birth, the boy was seen to laugh; this was the first miracle through which he drew attention to himself. The magicians announce the birth of the child as a portent of disaster to the prince of the realm, Duransarun, who betakes himself without delay to the dwelling of Pourushacpa, in order to stab the child. But his hand falls paralyzed, and he must leave with his errand undone; this was the second miracle. Soon after, the wicked demons steal the child from his mother and carry him into the desert, in order to kill him; but Dughda finds the unharmed child, calmly sleeping. This is the third miracle. Later on, Zoroaster was to be trampled upon, in a narrow passageway, by a·herd of oxen, by command of the king. But the largest of the cattle took the child between his feet and preserved it from harm. This was the fourth miracle. The fifth is merely a repetition of the preceding: what the cattle had refused to do, was to be accomplished by horses. But again the child was protected by a horse from the hoofs of the other horses. Duransarun thereupon had the cubs in a wolf's den killed during the absence of the old wolves, and Zoroaster was laid down in their place. But a god closed the jaws of the furious wolves, so that they could not harm the child. Two divine cows arrived instead and presented their udders to the child, giving it to drink. This was the sixth miracle through which Zoroaster's life was preserved.[1]

[1] Otto Rank, *The Myth of the Birth of the Hero*, pp. 55–56.

SIEGFRIED

German and Norse

To protect the child from the evil forces the mother frequently hides him in a makeshift vessel and entrusts him to the river. The child is then adopted by animals or common people.

King Sigmund of Tarlungaland, on his return from an expedition, banishes his wife Sisibe, the daughter of King Nidung of Hispania, who is accused by Count Hartvin, whose advances she has spurned, of having had illicit relations with a menial. The king's counselors advise him to mutilate the innocent queen, [5] instead of killing her, and Hartvin is ordered to cut out her tongue in the forest, so as to bring it to the king as a pledge. His companion, Count Hermann, opposes the execution of the cruel command, and proposes to present the tongue of a dog to the king. While the two men are engaged in a violent quarrel, Sisibe gives [10] birth to a remarkably beautiful boy; she then took a glass vessel, and after having wrapped the boy in linens, she placed him in the glass vessel, which she carefully closed again and placed beside her. Count Hartvin was conquered in the fight, and in falling kicked the glass vessel, so that it fell into the river. When [15] the queen saw this she swooned, and died soon afterwards. Hermann went home, told the king everything, and was banished from the country. The glass vessel meantime drifted downstream to the sea, and it was not long before the tide turned. Then the vessel floated onto a rocky cliff, and the water ran off so that [20] the place where the vessel was was perfectly dry. The boy inside had grown somewhat, and when the vessel struck the rock, it broke, and the child began to cry. The boy's wailing was heard by a doe, which seized him with her lips, and carried him to her litter, where she nursed him together with her young. After the [25] child had lived twelve months in the den of the doe, he had grown to the height and strength of other boys four years of age. One day he ran into the forest, where dwelt the wise and skillful smith Mimir, who had lived for nine years in childless wedlock. He saw the boy, who was followed by the faithful doe, took him [30] to his home, and resolved to bring him up as his own son. He gave him the name of Siegfried.[1]

[1] Otto Rank, *The Myth of the Birth of the Hero*, pp. 56–57.

KUNTI AND KARNA
Indian

Karna is miraculously conceived and born of a virgin. He is hidden in the river and adopted by ordinary people.

The chief of the Yadus, named Sura, had a son, Vasudeva, and a daughter, Prtha, whose beauty was matchless on earth. As had been promised, Sura gave Prtha in adoption to his childless cousin and close friend, the high-souled Kuntibhoja. Hence she also came to be known as Kunti. In her adopted father's 5 house Kunti's duties were to worship the family deities and look after the guests.

One day, by her solicitude, she pleased the terrible and notoriously short-tempered sage Durvasa, who was learned in the mysteries. Through his foresight, Durvasa could see that Kunti 10 would have difficulty in conceiving sons. He therefore taught her an invocatory spell, saying to her, "Through the radiance of those celestials whom you invoke by this spell, you will obtain progeny."

After a while the virtuous Kunti out of curiosity tried the spell and invoked the sun god. That brilliant deity the Sun, who sees 15 everything in the world, immediately appeared before her, and the beautiful Kunti was overcome by astonishment at this wondrous sight. The light of the universe, the Sun, got her with child. Thus was born the hero of divine ancestry, known all over the world by the name of Karna, the foremost of warriors. He was 20 born wearing armour and earrings. Thereafter the Sun restored Kunti's maidenhood and returned to heaven.

Afraid of her friends and relatives, Kunti resolved to hide her transgression. She accordingly threw her handsome son into the river, from which he was rescued by a charioteer. He and his 25 wife Radha brought up the infant as their own son, giving him the name of Vasusena, because he was endowed with wealth even at birth, namely armour and earrings. Vasusena grew up to be very strong and energetic, and adept in the use of all weapons. He used to worship the Sun until the afternoon sun scorched his 30 back. When he was thus engaged in worship, the heroic, truthful, and high-souled Vasusena would give away to the Brahmanas anything on earth which they requested of him.

Once Indra, the protector of all living things, came to him for alms, adopting the guise of a Brahmana, and asked him for his armour and the earrings. Perplexed though he was at Indra's request, he cut off the armour from his body, and also his earrings from his ears, and gave them, dripping with blood, to Indra with joined hands. Greatly surprised at his generosity, Indra gave him 5 the Sakti weapon, saying, "Be your foe a celestial, asura, human being, Gandharva, Naga, or Raksasa, if you hurl this missile at him, it will certainly kill him." The son of Surya, who till then was known by the name of Vasusena, came to be called Karna [the cutter] after this act of unequalled generosity.[1] 10

[1] C. V. Narasimhan, trans., *The Mahabharata*, VIII, pp. 19–20.

24

MAUI
Polynesian

The familiar theme of miraculous birth, the hiding of the child in water, and his adoption are present in the story of this trickster figure — the most important of the Polynesian demigods.

Maui' the demigod was the sixth generation in descent from Niwa-reka and Mata-ora. His father was Makea-tutara, his mother Taranga, and there were born four sons and a daughter before Maui' appeared. He was born prematurely as Taranga one day walked by the seashore; and she rolled up the unformed being in a wisp of her hair and cast it into the sea, lest it should become a malignant spirit through never having associated with kindly human kindred.

The sea-deities took the immature child, and hiding it among the long sea-tangles they nourished and preserved it; but storms tearing away the kelp, it was cast ashore, the growing child lying as it were swathed in a jellyfish, about which flies and other devouring creatures swarmed. Seeing this, a sea-ancestor, Tama-nui-ki-te-rangi, hastened to see what the thing was about which so many creatures were gathered. He found a man-child, and, taking him home, wakened him to life.

Maui' dwelt with his ancestor, with Tama'rangi, who related tales, and sang songs, whereby he acquainted the child with the lore of his ancestors; he also described to him the dances and games that went on in the meeting-house not far distant. The boy listened, first with wonder, then with curiosity; and he determined to go and see for himself the things of which he had heard.[1]

---

[1] Johannes Andersen, *Myths and Legends of the Polynesians*, p. 192.

MOSES
Judaic

Moses' very name is derived from his having been found in the bulrushes of the river. He, too, is adopted.

Now these are the names of the children of Israel, which came into Egypt; every man and his household came with Jacob. Reuben, Simeon, Levi, and Judah, Issachar, Zebulun, and Benjamin, Dan, and Naphtali, Gad, and Asher. And all the souls that came out of the loins of Jacob were seventy souls: for Joseph was in Egypt already. And Joseph died, and all his brethren, and all that generation. And the children of Israel were fruitful, and increased abundantly, and multiplied, and waxed exceeding mighty; and the land was filled with them.

Now there arose up a new king over Egypt, which knew not Joseph. And he said unto his people, Behold, the people of the children of Israel are more and mightier than we: come on, let us deal wisely with them; lest they multiply, and it come to pass, that, when there falleth out any war, they join also unto our enemies, and fight against us, and so get them up out of the land. Therefore they did set over them taskmasters to afflict them with their burdens. And they built for Pharaoh treasure cities, Pithom and Raamses. But the more they afflicted them, the more they multiplied and grew. And they were grieved because of the children of Israel. And the Egyptians made the children of Israel to serve with rigor: and they made their lives bitter with hard bondage, in mortar, and in brick, and in all manner of service in the field: all their service, wherein they made them serve, was with rigor.

And the king of Egypt spake to the Hebrew midwives, of which the name of the one was Shiphrah, and the name of the other Puah; and he said, When ye do the office of a midwife to the Hebrew women, and see them upon the stools, if it be a son, then ye shall kill him; but if it be a daughter, then she shall live. But the midwives feared God, and did not as the king of Egypt commanded them, but saved the men children alive. And the king of Egypt called for the midwives, and said unto them, Why have ye done this thing, and have saved the men children alive? And the midwives said unto Pharaoh, Because the Hebrew women are not as the Egyptian women; for they are lively, and are delivered ere the midwives come in unto them. Therefore God dealt well with the midwives: and the people multiplied, and waxed very mighty. And it came to pass, because the midwives feared God, that he made them houses. And Pharaoh charged all his people, saying, Every son that is born ye shall cast into the river, and every daughter ye shall save alive.

And there went a man of the house of Levi, and took to wife a daughter of Levi. And the woman conceived, and bare a son: and when she saw him that he was a goodly child, she hid him three months. And when she could not longer hide him, she took for him an ark of bulrushes, and daubed it with slime and with pitch, and put the child therein; and she laid it in the flags by the river's brink. And his sister stood afar off, to wit what would be done to him. And the daughter of Pharaoh came down to wash herself at the river; and her maidens walked along by the river's side: and when she saw the ark among the flags, she sent her maid to fetch it. And when she had opened it, she saw the child: and, behold, the babe wept. And she had compassion on him, and said, This is one of the Hebrews' children. Then said his sister to Pharaoh's daughter, Shall I go and call to thee a nurse of the Hebrew women, that she may nurse the child for thee? And Pharaoh's daughter said to her, Go. And the maid went and called the child's mother. And Pharaoh's daughter said unto her, Take this child away, and nurse it for me, and I will give thee thy wages. And the woman took the child, and nursed it. And the child grew, and she brought him unto Pharaoh's daughter, and he became her son. And she called his name Moses: and she said, Because I drew him out of the water.[1]

---

[1] Exodus 1 and 2.

CYBELE (THE GREAT MOTHER)
Phrygian

The great Phrygian mother, Cybele, is exposed to the elements, nourished by beasts, and adopted by common folk.

. . . an account is handed down also that this goddess was born in Phrygia. For the natives of that country have the following myth: In ancient times Meion became king of Phrygia and Lydia; and marrying Dindyme he begat an infant daughter, but being unwilling to rear her he exposed her on the mountain which was called Cybelus. There, in accordance with some divine providence, both the leopards and some of the other especially ferocious wild beasts offered their nipples to the child and so gave it nourishment, and some women who were tending the flocks in that place witnessed the happening, and being astonished at the strange event took up the babe and called her Cybele after the name of the place. The child, as she grew up, excelled in both beauty and virtue and also came to be admired for her intelligence; for she was the first to devise the pipe of many reeds and to invent cymbals and kettledrums with which to accompany the games and the dance, and in addition she taught how to heal the sicknesses of both flocks and little children by means of rites of purification; in consequence, since the babes were saved from death by her spells and were generally taken up in her arms, her devotion to them and affection for them led all the people to speak of her as the "mother of the mountain."[1]

---

[1] C. H. Oldfather, trans., *Diodorus of Sicily*, vol. 2, book 3.

NANA AND ATTIS
Phrygian

Attis is the son of Cybele in her form as the virgin, Nana, who is
impregnated by the divine force in the form of a pomegranate.
Like his mother and so many other heroes, he is exposed to the
elements and nourished by a beast.

The Agdos rock—so the story runs—had assumed the shape
of the Great Mother. [The Phrygian sky-god, Papas] . . . fell asleep
upon it. As he slept, or as he strove with the goddess, his semen
fell upon the rock. In the tenth month the Agdos rock bellowed
and brought forth an untamable, savage being, of twofold sex   5
and twofold lust, named Agdistis. With cruel joy Agdistis plun-
dered, murdered and destroyed whatever it chose, cared for neither
gods nor men, and held nothing mightier on earth or in heaven than
itself. The gods often consulted together as to how this insolence
could be tamed. When they all hesitated, Dionysos took over the   10
task. There was a certain spring to which Agdistis came to assuage
its thirst when it was overheated with sport and hunting. Dionysos
turned the springwater into wine. Agdistis came running up, im-
pelled by thirst, greedily drank the strange liquor and fell per-
force into deepest sleep. Dionysos was on the watch. He adroitly   15
made a cord of hair, and with it bound Agdistis's male member
to a tree. Awakened from its drunkenness, the monster sprang up
and castrated itself by its own strength. The earth drank the
flowing blood, and with it the torn-off parts. From these at once
arose a fruit-bearing tree: an almond-tree or—according to an-   20
other tale—a pomegranate-tree. Nana, the daughter of the king
or river-god Sangarios (Nana is another name for the great goddess of Asia Minor), saw the beauty of the fruit, plucked it and
hid it in her lap. The fruit vanished, and Nana conceived a child
of it. Her father imprisoned her, as a woman deflowered, and   25
condemned her to death by starvation. The Great Mother fed her
on fruits and on the foods of the gods. She gave birth to a little
boy. Sangarios had the child left out in the open to perish. A he-
goat tended the suckling, who, when he was found, was fed upon
a liquor called "he-goat's milk." He was named Attis, either be-   30
cause *attis* is Lydian for a handsome boy or because *attagus*
was Phrygian for a he-goat.[1]

[1] C. Kerényi, *The Gods of the Greeks*, pp. 89–90.

WATER JAR BOY
Tewa Indian

This hero's mother receives the god as a piece of clay, the traditional substance of life. The "illegitimate" child is miraculously protected by his temporary form as a water jar.

The people were living at Sikyatki. There was a fine looking girl who refused to get married. Her mother made water jars all the time. One day as she was using her foot to mix some clay, she told her daughter to go on with this while she went for water. The girl tried to mix the clay on a flat stone by stepping on it. Some- 5 how some of it entered her. This made her pregnant, and after a time she gave birth. The mother was angry about this, but when she looked she saw it was not a baby that had been born, but a little jar. When the mother asked where it came from the girl just cried. Then the father came in. He said he was very glad his 10 daughter had a baby. When he found out that it was a water jar, he became very fond of it.

He watched it and saw it move. It grew, and in twenty days it had become big. It could go about with the other children and was able to talk. The children also became fond of it. They found 15 out from his talk that he was Water Jar Boy. His mother cried, because he had no legs or arms or eyes. But they were able to feed him through the jar mouth.

When snow came the boy begged his grandfather to take him along with the men to hunt rabbits. "My poor grandson, you can't 20 hunt rabbits; you have no arms or legs."

"Take me anyway," said the boy. "You are so old, you can't kill anything." His grandfather took him down under the mesa where he rolled along. Pretty soon he saw a rabbit track and followed it. Then a rabbit ran out, and he began to chase it. He 25 hit himself against a rock. The jar broke, and up jumped a boy.

He was very glad his skin had been broken and that he was a big boy. He had lots of beads around his neck, earstrings of turquoise, a dance kilt and moccasins, and a buckskin shirt. He was fine-looking and handsomely dressed. He killed four jack- 30 rabbits before sunset, because he was a good runner.

His grandfather was waiting for him at the foot of the mesa, but did not know him. He asked the fine looking boy, "Did you see my grandson anywhere?"

"No, I did not see him."

"That's too bad; he's late."

"I didn't see anyone anywhere," said the boy. Then he said, "I am your grandson." He said this because his grandfather looked so disappointed.

"No, you are not my grandson."

"Yes, I am."

"You are only teasing me. My grandson is a round jar and has no arms and legs."

Then the boy said, "I am telling you the truth. I am your grandson. This morning you carried me down here. I looked for rabbits and chased one, just rolling along. Pretty soon I hit myself on a rock. My skin was broken, and I came out of it. I am the very one who is your grandson. You must believe me." Then the old man believed him, and they went home together.

When the grandfather came to the house with a fine looking man, the girl was ashamed, thinking the man was a suitor. The old man said, "This is Water Jar Boy, my grandson. The grandmother then asked how the water jar became a boy, and the two men told her. Finally, the women were convinced.

The boy went about with the other boys of the village. One day he said to his mother, "Who is my father?"

"I don't know," she replied. He kept on asking, but it just made her cry. Finally he said, "I am going to find my father, tomorrow."

"You can't find him. I have never been with any man so there is no place for you to look for a father," she said.

"But I know I have one," the boy said. "I know where he lives. I am going to see him."

The mother begged him not to go, but he insisted. The next day she fixed food for him, and he went off toward the southwest to a place called Horse Mesa Point. There was a spring at this place. As he approached he saw a man walking a little way from the spring. He said to the boy, "Where are you going?"

"To the spring," the boy answered.

"Why are you going there?"

"I want to see my father."

"Who is your father?"

"He lives in this spring."

"Well, you will never find your father," said the man.

"Well, I want to go to the spring. My father is living in it," said the boy.

"Who is your father?" asked the man again. 5

"Well, I think you are my father."

"How do you know that?"

"I just know, that's all."

Then the man stared hard at the boy, trying to scare him. The boy just kept on saying, "You are my father." At last the 10 man said, "Yes, I am your father. I came out of the spring to meet you." He put his arms around the boy's neck. He was very glad his boy had come, and he took him down to the spring.

There were many people living there. The women and the girls ran up to the boy and put their arms around him, because 15 they were glad he had come. This way he found his father and his father's relatives. He stayed there one night. The next day he went to his own home and told his mother he had found his father.

Soon his mother got sick and died. The boy thought to him- 20 self, "It's no use for me to stay with these people," so he went to the spring. There he found his mother among the other women. He learned that his father was Red Water Snake. He told his boy that he could not live over at Sikyatki, so he had made the boy's mother sick so she would die and come to live with him. After 25 that they all lived together.[1]

[1] T. P. Coffin, ed., *Indian Tales of North America*, pp. 99–101.

KUTOYIS
Blackfoot Indian

The agent of impregnation here is a clot of blood—like the clay, a symbol of the source of life. The young hero quickly achieves adult status and recognition.

Long ago, down where Two Medicine and Badger Creeks come together, there lived an old man. He had but one wife and two daughters. One day there came to his camp a young man who was very brave and a great hunter. The old man said: "Ah! I will have this young man to help me. I will give him my daugh- 5 ters for wives." So he gave him his daughters. He also gave this son-in-law all his wealth, keeping for himself only a little lodge, in which he lived with his old wife. The son-in-law lived in a lodge that was big and fine.

At first the son-in-law was very good to the old people. When- 10 ever he killed anything, he gave them part of the meat, and furnished plenty of robes and skins for their bedding and clothing. But after a while he began to be very mean to them.

Now the son-in-law kept the buffalo hidden under a big log jam in the river. Whenever he wanted to kill anything, he would 15 have the old man go to help him; and the old man would stamp on the log jam and frighten the buffalo, and when they ran out, the young man would shoot one or two, never killing wastefully. But often he gave the old people nothing to eat, and they were hungry all the time, and began to grow thin and weak. 20

One morning, the young man called his father-in-law to go down to the log jam and hunt with him. They started, and the young man killed a fat buffalo cow. Then he said to the old man, "Hurry back now, and tell your children to get the dogs and carry this meat home, then you can have something to eat." And the 25 old man did as he had been ordered, thinking to himself: "Now, at last, my son-in-law has taken pity on me. He will give me part of this meat." When he returned with the dogs, they skinned the cow, cut up the meat and packed it on the dog travois, and went home. Then the young man had his wives unload it, and told his 30 father-in-law to go home. He did not give him even a piece of liver. Neither would the older daughter give her parents anything to eat, but the younger took pity on the old people and stole a piece of meat, and when she got a chance threw it into the lodge to the old people. The son-in-law told his wives not to give the old people anything to eat. The only way they got food was when the younger woman would throw them a piece of meat unseen by her husband and sister. 5

Another morning, the son-in-law got up early, and went and kicked on the old man's lodge to wake him, and called him to get up and help him, to go and pound on the log jam to drive out the buffalo, so that he could kill some. When the old man pounded on the jam, a buffalo ran out, and the son-in-law shot it, but only 10 wounded it. It ran away, but at last fell down and died. The old man followed it, and came to where it had lost a big clot of blood from its wound. When he came to where this clot of blood was lying on the ground, he stumbled and fell, and spilled his arrows out of his quiver; and while he was picking them up, he picked 15 up also the clot of blood, and hid it in his quiver. "What are you picking up?" called out the son-in-law. "Nothing," said the old man; "I just fell down and spilled my arrows, and am putting them back." "Curse you, old man," said the son-in-law, "you are lazy and useless. Go back and tell your children to come with the 20 dogs and get this dead buffalo." He also took away his bow and arrows from the old man.

The old man went home and told his daughters, and then went over to his own lodge, and said to his wife: "Hurry now, and put the kettle on the fire. I have brought home something 25 from the butchering." "Ah!" said the old woman, "has our son-in-law been generous, and given us something nice?" "No," answered the old man; "hurry up and put the kettle on." When the water began to boil, the old man tipped his quiver up over the kettle, and immediately there came from the pot a noise as of a 30 child crying, as if it were being hurt, burnt or scalded. They looked in the kettle, and saw there a little boy, and they quickly took it out of the water. They were very much surprised. The old woman made a lashing to put the child in, and then they talked about it. They decided that if the son-in-law knew that it was a boy, he 35 would kill it, so they resolved to tell their daughters that the baby was a girl. Then he would be glad, for he would think that after a while he would have it for a wife. They named the child Kutoyis (Clot of Blood).

The son-in-law and his wives came home, and after a while 40 he heard the child crying. He told his youngest wife to go and

find out whether that baby was a boy or a girl; if it was a boy, to
tell them to kill it. She came back and told them that it was a girl.
He did not believe this, and sent his oldest wife to find out the
truth of the matter. When she came back and told him the same
thing, he believed that it was really a girl. Then he was glad, for   5
he thought that when the child had grown up he would have another wife. He said to his youngest wife, "Take some pemmican
over to your mother; not much, just enough so that there will be
plenty of milk for the child."

Now on the fourth day the child spoke, and said, "Lash me in   10
turn to each one of these lodge poles, and when I get to the last
one, I will fall out of my lashing and be grown up." The old
woman did so, and as she lashed him to each lodge pole he could
be seen to grow, and finally when they lashed him to the last pole,
he was a man.[1]   15

---

[1] George Bird Grinnell, *Blackfoot Lodge Tales*, pp. 29–32.

COATLICUE AND HUITZILOPOCHTLI
Aztec

In the story of Huitzilopochtli a ball of feathers is equivalent to the divine animals, the piece of clay, the clot of blood, and the pomegranate. The hero, like Buddha and Quetzalcoatl, is born with adult qualities; he can, thus, defend himself against the powers which immediately attack him.

The myth of the birth of Huitzilopochtli . . . throws light upon the character of the divinity. His mother, Coatlicue ("She of the Serpent-Woven Skirt"), dwelling on Coatepec ("Serpent Mountain"), had a family consisting of a daughter, Coyolxauhqui ("She whose Face is Painted with Bells"), and of many sons, [5] known collectively as the Centzonuitznaua ("the Four Hundred Southerners"). One day, while doing penance upon the mountain, a ball of feathers fell upon her, and having placed this in her bosom; it was observed, shortly afterward, that she was pregnant. Her sons, the Centzonuitznaua, urged by Coyolxauhqui, [10] planned to slay their mother to wipe out the disgrace which they conceived to have befallen them; but though Coatlicue was frightened, the unborn child commanded her to have no fear. One of the Four Hundred, turning traitor, communicated to the still unborn Huitzilopochtli the approach of the hostile brothers, and [15] at the moment of their arrival the god was born in full panoply, carrying a blue shield and dart, his limbs painted blue, his head adorned with plumes, and his left leg decked with humming-bird feathers. Commanding his servant to light a torch, in shape a serpent, with this Xiuhcoatl he slew Coyolxauhqui, and destroying her [20] body, he placed her head upon the summit of Coatepec. Then taking up his arms, he pursued and slew the Centzonuitznaua, a very few of whom succeeded in escaping to Uitztlampa ("the Place of Thorns"), the South.[1]

---

[1] Louis Gray, ed., *The Mythology of All Races*, vol. 11, *Latin-American*, p. 60.

LITUOLONE
Bantu African

This African god-hero is born miraculously of an old woman. He immediately achieves adulthood and destroys the forces of evil that would devour him. Lituolone is a savior who reminds us in his childhood of Herakles, Kutoyis, and Buddha.

There is a Sesuto tale that tells of a monster that used to devour humans; eventually the only person left on earth was an old woman who had gone into hiding, and who, without the aid of a man, gave birth to a child bedecked with amulets, to whom she gave the name of the god Lituolone. On the very day he was born, [5] the child attained adult stature. He asked his mother where other men were, and, being told of the monster Kammapa, he took hold of a knife and prepared to fight it. He was swallowed by the fabulous animal, and this allowed him to tear the beast's entrails to pieces and bring forth from its stomach thousands of human be- [10] ings.[1]

[1] *Larousse World Mythology*, p. 522.

ISIS AND HORUS
Egyptian

The conception of Horus by way of the dead Osiris is appropriate to a religion which placed so much emphasis on the resurrection. The presence of the evil Set is in keeping with the tradition of the dangers surrounding the hero's infancy.

[Isis conceived a son in a swamp] while she fluttered in the form of a hawk over the corpse of her dead husband [Osiris]. The infant was the younger Horus, who in his youth bore the name of Harpocrates, that is, the child Horus. Him Buto, the goddess of the north, hid from the wrath of his wicked uncle Set. Yet she could not guard him from all mishap; for one day when Isis came to her little son's hiding-place she found him stretched lifeless and rigid on the ground: a scorpion had stung him. Then Isis prayed to the sun-god Ra for help. The god hearkened to her and staid his bark in the sky, and sent down Thoth to teach her the spell by which she might restore her son to life. She uttered the words of power, and straightway the poison flowed from the body of Horus, air passed into him, and he lived. Then Thoth ascended up into the sky and took his place once more in the bark of the sun, and the bright pomp passed onward jubilant.[1]

---

[1] Sir James Frazer, *The New Golden Bough*, edited by Theodor H. Gaster, p. 385.

PERSEPHONE (PROSERPINA) AND DIONYSOS (DIONYSUS)

Greek

This version of the birth of Dionysos contains the familiar motif of the god in animal form. Also significant is the maternal cave, which is related to the grove in the Buddha story, the wolf-den in the Zoroaster story, the swamp in the Horus story, the kettle in the Kutoyis story, and the stable in the Christian nativity.

Demeter came from Crete to Sicily, where, near the springs of Kayane, she discovered a cave. There she hid her daughter Persephone, and set as guardians over her two serpents that at other times were harnessed to her chariot. In the cave the maiden worked in wool—the customary occupation for maidens under 5 the protection of Pallas Athene, in her sacred citadel at Athens. Persephone began weaving a great web, a robe for her father or her mother, which was a picture of the whole world. While she was engaged in this work Zeus came to her in the shape of a serpent, and he begat by his daughter that god [Dionysos] who, in 10 the Orphic stories, was to be his successor, the fifth ruler of the world. . . . The birth of the son and successor to the throne actually took place in the maternal cave. A late ivory relief shows the bed in the cave: the bed in which the horned child—the horns signify that he is the son of Persephone—had just been born to 15 the goddess.[1]

[1] C. Kerényi, *The Gods of the Greeks*, pp. 252–254. The more common Dionysian birth story appears as a rebirth story in Part 7.

MYRRHA AND ADONIS
Babylonian and Greek

In this unusual story the maternal cave and hiding place is the bark of a tree. Trees play important roles in the lives of several heroes, including Buddha, Jesus, Attis, Osiris, and Odin.

The story of the lord and loved one of the great Goddess of Love was connected—amongst us, and presumably also in the eastern countries where it was adopted, in Syria, Cyprus and Asia Minor—with the story of a tree, of that Arabian shrub whose strongly fragrant gum the peoples of antiquity prized most of all their congealed saps. The gum was called "myrrh" or "smyrna."

The tale goes that Myrrha (or Smyrna) was a king's daughter; a daughter of King Theias of Lebanon, or of King Kinyras of Cyprus, founder of Paphos—or variously a daughter of other kings whom I need not mention. Myrrha fell mortally in love with her father. (Various reasons were given for this: the wrath of the sun-god, or the wrath of Aphrodite. Myrrha was supposed to have thought her hair lovelier than that of the goddess; and there are other similar stories.) The daughter succeeded in deceiving her father, or in making him drunk—an occurrence also found in a Biblical tale. She slept with him as an unknown wench for twelve nights, or for less. At last her father discovered, by the light of a hidden lamp, who his bedmate was, and pursued her with a drawn sword. Myrrha had already conceived a child of this forbidden love, and was full of shame. She prayed to the gods that she might be nowhere, neither amongst the living nor amongst the dead. Some deity, possibly Zeus or Aphrodite, took pity on her, and she was turned into the tree that weeps its fruit in spicy gum, the fruit of the wood: Adonis. For he, the future lover of Aphrodite, was born from the riven bark of the myrrh-tree.[1]

[1] C. Kerényi, *The Gods of the Greeks*, pp. 75–76.

ANNA AND MARY
Christian

Important to this story are the conception and birth of the heroine by a barren mother. The same theme occurs in many hero stories, that of John the Baptist being the best known.

She who was, from the beginning, the Virgin of virgins and the Immaculate Mother of the universe, appeared in due time as Mary, the daughter of Joachim and Anna. According to St. Jerome, Joachim was from the town of Nazareth in Galilee, and Anna from the City of David — Bethlehem; and the two were just *5* and godly folk who divided their wealth into three parts — one for the Temple, one for the poor, and one for their own needs. Anna, however, was barren and lived for twenty years with her husband without bearing him a child. But, moved to compassion by their holy lives, the Lord God at last sent his angel with the news that *10* there would be born to them a daughter. They were to give her the name Mary, and to dedicate her from infancy to the service of God, for, said the angel, "as she will be born to a barren mother, so will she herself, in a wondrous manner, bring forth the Son of the Most High, whose name shall be called Jesus, and through whom *15* will come salvation to all the nations."[1]

[1] Alan Watts, *Myth and Ritual in Christianity*, pp. 115–116.

MARY AND JESUS
Christian

The nativity is a fully developed hero-birth story in which is found the miraculous conception (the Holy Spirit is sometimes depicted in animal form, as a dove), the virgin birth, the purity of the mother, the maternal cave, and the hiding of the child from evil forces.

And in the sixth month the angel Gabriel was sent from God unto a city of Galilee, named Nazareth, to a virgin espoused to a man whose name was Joseph, of the house of David; and the virgin's name was Mary. And the angel came in unto her, and said, Hail, thou that art highly favored, the Lord is with thee: 5 blessed art thou among women. And when she saw him, she was troubled at his saying, and cast in her mind what manner of salutation this should be. And the angel said unto her, Fear not, Mary: for thou hast found favor with God. And, behold, thou shalt conceive in thy womb, and bring forth a son, and shalt call his name 10 JESUS. He shall be great, and shall be called the Son of the Highest; and the Lord God shall give unto him the throne of his father David: and he shall reign over the house of Jacob for ever; and of his kingdom there shall be no end. Then said Mary unto the angel, How shall this be, seeing I know not a man? And the angel 15 answered and said unto her, The Holy Ghost shall come upon thee, and the power of the Highest shall overshadow thee: therefore also that holy thing which shall be born of thee shall be called the Son of God. And, behold, thy cousin Elisabeth, she hath also conceived a son in her old age; and this is the sixth month 20 with her, who was called barren. For with God nothing shall be impossible. And Mary said, Behold the handmaid of the Lord; be it unto me according to thy word. And the angel departed from her.

And Mary arose in those days, and went into the hill country 25 with haste, into a city of Judah; and entered into the house of Zechariah, and saluted Elisabeth. And it came to pass, that, when Elisabeth heard the salutation of Mary, the babe leaped in her womb; and Elisabeth was filled with the Holy Ghost: and she spake out with a loud voice, and said, Blessed art thou among 30 women, and blessed is the fruit of thy womb. And whence is this to me, that the mother of my Lord should come to me? For, lo, as soon as the voice of thy salutation sounded in mine ears, the babe leaped in my womb for joy. And blessed is she that believed: for there shall be a performance of those things which were told her from the Lord. And Mary said, 5

> My soul doth magnify the Lord,
> and my spirit hath rejoiced in God my Saviour.
> For he hath regarded the low estate of his handmaiden:
> for, behold, from henceforth all generations shall call me
>   blessed. 10
> For he that is mighty hath done to me great things;
> and holy is his name.
> And his mercy is on them that fear him
> from generation to generation.
> He hath showed strength with his arm; 15
> he hath scattered the proud in the imagination of their
>   hearts.
> He hath put down the mighty from their seats,
> and exalted them of low degree.
> He hath filled the hungry with good things; 20
> and the rich he hath sent empty away.
> He hath holpen his servant Israel,
> in remembrance of his mercy;
> as he spake to our fathers,
> to Abraham, and to his seed for ever. 25

And Mary abode with her about three months, and returned to her own house.[1]

Now the birth of Jesus Christ was on this wise: When as his mother Mary was espoused to Joseph, before they came together, she was found with child of the Holy Ghost. Then Joseph her 30 husband, being a just man, and not willing to make her a public example, was minded to put her away privily. But while he thought on these things, behold, the angel of the Lord appeared unto him in a dream, saying, Joseph, thou son of David, fear not to take unto thee Mary thy wife: for that which is conceived in 35 her is of the Holy Ghost. And she shall bring forth a son, and thou shalt call his name JESUS: for he shall save his people from their

[1] Luke 1.

43

sins. Now all this was done, that it might be fulfilled which was
spoken of the Lord by the prophet, saying,

> Behold, a virgin shall be with child,
> and shall bring forth a son,
> and they shall call his name Immanuel,

which being interpreted is, God with us. Then Joseph being raised
from sleep did as the angel of the Lord had bidden him, and took
unto him his wife: and knew her not till she had brought forth
her firstborn son.[2]

And it came to pass in those days, that there went out a
decree from Caesar Augustus, that all the world should be taxed.
(And this taxing was first made when Cyrenius was governor of
Syria.) And all went to be taxed, every one into his own city. And
Joseph also went up from Galilee, out of the city of Nazareth, into
Judea, unto the city of David, which is called Bethlehem, (because he was of the house and lineage of David,) to be taxed with
Mary his espoused wife, being great with child. And so it was,
that, while they were there, the days were accomplished that she
should be delivered. And she brought forth her firstborn son, and
wrapped him in swaddling clothes, and laid him in a manger;
because there was no room for them in the inn.

And there were in the same country shepherds abiding in the
field, keeping watch over their flock by night. And, lo, the angel
of the Lord came upon them, and the glory of the Lord shone
round about them; and they were sore afraid. And the angel said
unto them, Fear not: for, behold, I bring you good tidings of great
joy, which shall be to all people. For unto you is born this day in
the city of David a Saviour, which is Christ the Lord. And this
shall be a sign unto you; Ye shall find the babe wrapped in swaddling clothes, lying in a manger. And suddenly there was with
the angel a multitude of the heavenly host praising God, and
saying,

> Glory to God in the highest,
> and on earth peace,
> good will toward men.

[2] Matthew 1.

44

And it came to pass, as the angels were gone away from them into heaven, the shepherds said one to another, Let us now go even unto Bethlehem, and see this thing which is come to pass, which the Lord hath made known unto us. And they came with haste, and found Mary and Joseph, and the babe lying in a manger. And when they had seen it, they made known abroad the saying which was told them concerning this child. And all they that heard it wondered at those things which were told them by the shepherds. But Mary kept all these things, and pondered them in her heart. And the shepherds returned, glorifying and praising God for all the things that they had heard and seen, as it was told unto them.[3]

Now when Jesus was born in Bethlehem of Judea in the days of Herod the king, behold, there came wise men from the east to Jerusalem, saying, Where is he that is born King of the Jews? for we have seen his star in the east, and are come to worship him. When Herod the king had heard these things, he was troubled, and all Jerusalem with him. And when he had gathered all the chief priests and scribes of the people together, he demanded of them where Christ should be born. And they said unto him, In Bethlehem of Judea: for thus it is written by the prophet,

And thou Bethlehem, in the land of Judah,
art not the least among the princes of Judah:
for out of thee shall come a Governor,
that shall rule my people Israel.

Then Herod, when he had privily called the wise men, inquired of them diligently what time the star appeared. And he sent them to Bethlehem, and said, Go and search diligently for the young child; and when ye have found him, bring me word again, that I may come and worship him also. When they had heard the king, they departed; and, lo, the star, which they saw in the east, went before them, till it came and stood over where the young child was. When they saw the star, they rejoiced with exceeding great joy. And when they were come into the house, they saw the young child with Mary his mother, and fell down, and worshipped him: and when they had opened their treasures, they

[3] Luke 2.

presented unto him gifts; gold, and frankincense, and myrrh. And being warned of God in a dream that they should not return to Herod, they departed into their own country another way.

And when they were departed, behold, the angel of the Lord appeareth to Joseph in a dream, saying, Arise, and take the young child and his mother, and flee into Egypt, and be thou there until I bring thee word: for Herod will seek the young child to destroy him. When he arose, he took the young child and his mother by night, and departed into Egypt: and was there until the death of Herod: that it might be fulfilled which was spoken of the Lord by the prophet, saying, Out of Egypt have I called my son.

Then Herod, when he saw that he was mocked of the wise men, was exceeding wroth, and sent forth, and slew all the children that were in Bethlehem, and in all the coasts thereof, from two years old and under, according to the time which he had diligently inquired of the wise men. Then was fulfilled that which was spoken by Jeremiah the prophet, saying,

In Ramah was there a voice heard,
lamentation, and weeping, and great mourning,
Rachel weeping for her children,
and would not be comforted,
because they are not.

But when Herod was dead, behold, an angel of the Lord appeareth in a dream to Joseph in Egypt, saying, Arise, and take the young child and his mother, and go into the land of Israel: for they are dead which sought the young child's life. And he arose, and took the young child and his mother, and came into the land of Israel. But when he heard that Archelaus did reign in Judea in the room of his father Herod, he was afraid to go thither: notwithstanding, being warned of God in a dream, he turned aside into the parts of Galilee: and he came and dwelt in a city called Nazareth: that it might be fulfilled which was spoken by the prophets, He shall be called a Nazarene.[4]

[4] Matthew 2.

46

THE WORLD CHILD:
Commentary on Part 1

Where there are heroes there are stories of the miraculous birth. King Sargon of Babylonia was born of a virgin, hidden in a basket, released into a river, and adopted by a menial. Heracles' mother-to-be was tricked by Zeus into a thirty-six-hour love bout appropriate to the conception of such a hero. John the Baptist was miraculously conceived by a barren mother. The Persian man-god Mithras was born on December 25 from a rock and was attended in some versions by lowly shepherds.

The birth myth to be found in the stories collected in the preceding pages is made up of several events, which are present in varying numbers in each tale. The most important component —one common to almost all of the stories—is the virgin birth, in which I include any kind of magic or divine conception whether by way of feather or pomegranate seed or white elephant. Sir James Frazer suggests that the virgin birth originated in primitive man's failure to connect sexual intercourse with pregnancy. For our early ancestors, he says, all birth was miraculous. Frazer's explanation, though perhaps historically questionable, makes a certain amount of psychological sense. Today we understand the scientific process of reproduction, but to the psyche, conception and birth, like the coming of spring, are miraculous events. All of us feel this; the religious man knows that we are all children of God or Fate. William Butler Yeats conveyed this aspect of the human psyche—this basic myth—in his poem of the conception of Helen of Troy, "Leda and the Swan," in which we feel the miraculous touch of the god's "dark webs," the "vague fingers," the "strange heart beating where it lies," and the "shudder in the loins."

There are times when the claim of divine or otherworldly conception is simply the only way out of an age-old dilemma. A London newspaper recently published an account of a woman who protested (apparently with some success) to her betrothed that her pregnancy was the result of the attentions of a space-helmeted, leather-clad man who had assured her that he was from Mars.

There are, of course, more important reasons for the virgin birth and for the emphasis so often placed on the virgin's early removal to heaven or on her immaculate state even after the birth. One of the primordial hopes is for a new beginning. Since the Adam figure, whatever his local form, man has sought a Messiah—a leader somehow untarnished by human failings. This is the longing for a second chance which we all have felt. The hero—the hope of the racial psyche and, metaphorically, of the individual psyche—must, like the first human, be born of the void.[1] Thus Jesus is born of a virgin; thus the Buddha is born "unsmeared by any impurity from his mother's womb"; and thus Mithras, Adonis, and Kutoyis are born of rock, tree, and clot of blood.

The association of the hero's birth with the unknown is further expressed in the theme of the hidden place where the child is born or placed soon after birth. These places—caves, stables, groves, rocks, and waterpots—are, of course, womb symbols, the womb being that of the universal great mother in her many forms. The great mother is impersonal; she is nobody's *own* mother. And, like nature, which in a sense she is, she is composed of good and evil—of the constructive and the destructive. The hero from the beginning is confronted by evil forces, be they Herods, jealous fathers, or demons. Man feels these forces because they are part of his innermost psyche. The hero of the new beginning is but one side of that psyche; he must struggle with the other. The struggle begins with the birth of the infant. Psychologically there is no such thing as total protection; evil must be accepted as a part of the natural arrangement of things. Thus the infant hero is so often exposed to nature—given back to the great mother to whom all of us really belong in spite of our protective parents. Most often he is released into the natural flow of the river. The river represents a purificatory rite of passage; in Christianity, for instance, it becomes Baptism. But most important, the river carries the hero—Moses, Sargon, Karna, or Siegfried—to an adopted parent, animal or ordinary human. The hero appears in the flow of life; he is reborn of the river, of the void, and he is adopted by all of us. No biological parent owns him; he must break away from local ties at the outset of his career.

The birth myth thus involves initiation, the search for origins, the hope of a fresh beginning, the acceptance of what we

---

[1] It should be pointed out here that creation stories are what might be called cosmological expressions of the birth myth and the psychological need it represents. See Appendix 2.

call evil as a permanent reality, and the adoption of the heroic principle by the human psyche. The birth myth is the beginning of the voyage to full individuation. The myth is revealed totally in all of the stories when viewed as one.

A major source book for the birth myth is Otto Rank's *The Myth of the Birth of the Hero,* in which the author tells the birth stories and presents a Freudian interpretation of the basic myth. A major difficulty with the Freudian approach is a tendency to equate myth and neurosis. Still, the brilliance of Rank's work is not to be denied. Another classic work on aspects of the subject is Jung and Kerényi's *Introduction to a Science of Mythology: The Myth of the Divine Child and the Mysteries of Eleusis,* a book which, along with Jung's *Symbols of Transformation,* speaks to the whole question of the hero's life. The same can be said of Joseph Campbell's *The Hero with a Thousand Faces* and, to a lesser extent, of Lord Raglan's *The Hero.*

2

CHILDHOOD, INITIATION, AND DIVINE SIGNS

The sense of wonder and of initiation into mysterious realities of form pervades this painting. The serpentlike arrow at the base speaks intrusively of the dangers implicit in the paradise of early awakening. [Paul Klee, *A Young Lady's Adventure* (1922), The Tate Gallery, London. Reproduced with permission. Copyright administered by S.P.A.D.E.M.]

KRISHNA
Indian

The hero is frequently called upon to prove his divine nature at an early age. Krishna kills a demoness and calms a storm while still a cradled infant.

. . . there were great rejoicings in Gokula for the birth of a son to Nand and Yasoda: the astrologers prophesied that the child would slay the demons and should be called Lord of the Herdgirls, the gopis, and his glory should be sung throughout the world. But Kans knew not where Shri Krishna had been born, and he sent out murderers to slay all children. Among his followers there was a rakshasi named Putana, who knew of the birth of Nand's son, and she went to Gokula for his destruction, taking the shape of a beautiful woman, but she had poison in her breasts. She went to Yasoda's house and made herself very friendly, and presently she took the boy on her lap and gave him her breast. But he held her tightly and drew hard, so that with the milk he took away her life. She fled away, but Krishna would not let her escape, and she fell dead, assuming her own hideous and huge form. Just then Nand returned from Mathura, where he had gone for paying tribute; he found the rakshasi lying dead, and all the folk of Braj standing about her. They told him what had taken place, and then they burnt and buried her enormous body. But her body gave out a most sweet fragrance when it was burnt, and the reason for that was that Shri Krishna had given her salvation when he drank her milk; blessed are all those whom Vishnu slays.

It was not long after this that a feast was held for rejoicings at the birth of Krishna; but he was forgotten in the general merrymaking, and lay by himself under a cart. Now another rakshasi, passing by, saw that he lay there sucking his toes, and to avenge Putana she sat on the cart as if to crush it; but Krishna gave a kick and broke the cart and killed the demoness. All the pots of milk and curds in the cart were broken, and the noise of the broken cart and flowing milk brought all the herd-boys and herd-girls to the spot, and they found Krishna safe and sound. When Shri Krishna was five months old another fiend came in the shape of a whirlwind to sweep him away from Yasoda's lap where he lay; but at once he grew so heavy that Yasoda had to lay him down. Then the storm became a cyclone, but no harm came to Krishna, for none could even lift him. But at last he allowed the whirlwind to take him up into the sky, and then, while the people of Braj were weeping and lamenting, Krishna dashed the rak- 5 shasa down and killed him, and the storm was over.[1]

---

[1] A. K. Coomaraswamy and Sister Nivedita, *Myths of the Hindus and Buddhists*, pp. 221–222.

HERACLES (HERCULES)
Greek

Heracles, like Krishna, proves himself in the cradle by defeating the evil serpents. Furthermore, he gains immortality by taking milk from the breast of Hera.

Alcmene, fearing Hera's jealousy, exposed her newly-born child in a field outside the walls of Thebes; and here, at Zeus's instigation, Athene took Hera for a casual stroll. 'Look, my dear! What a wonderfully robust child!' said Athene, pretending surprise as she stopped to pick him up. 'His mother must have 5 been out of her mind to abandon him in a stony field! Come, you have milk. Give the poor little creature suck!' Thoughtlessly Hera took him and bared her breast, at which Heracles drew with such force that she flung him down in pain, and a spurt of milk flew across the sky and became the Milky Way. 'The young monster!' 10 Hera cried. But Heracles was now immortal, and Athene returned him to Alcmene with a smile, telling her to guard and rear him well. The Thebans still show the place where this trick was played on Hera; it is called 'The Plain of Heracles.'

Some, however, say that Hermes carried the infant Heracles 15 to Olympus; that Zeus himself laid him at Hera's breast while she slept; and that the Milky Way was formed when she awoke and pushed him away, or when he greedily sucked more milk than his mouth would hold, and coughed it up. At all events, Hera was Heracles's foster-mother, if only for a short while; and 20 the Thebans therefore style him her son, and say that he had been Alcaeus before she gave him suck, but was renamed in her honour.

One evening, when Heracles had reached the age of eight or ten months or, as others say, one year, and was still unweaned, 25 Alcmene having washed and suckled her twins, laid them to rest under a lamb-fleece coverlet, on the broad brazen shield which Amphitryon had won from Pterelaus. At midnight, Hera sent two prodigious azure-scaled serpents to Amphitryon's house, with strict orders to destroy Heracles. The gates opened as they ap- 30 proached; they glided through, and over the marble floors to the nursery—their eyes shooting flames, and poison dripping from their fangs.

The twins awoke, to see the serpents writhed above them, with darting, forked tongues; for Zeus again divinely illumined the chamber. Iphicles screamed, kicked off the coverlet and, in an attempt to escape, rolled from the shield to the floor. His frightened cries, and the strange light shining under the nursery door, roused Alcmene. 'Up with you, Amphitryon!' she cried. Without waiting to put on his sandals, Amphitryon leaped from the cedarwood bed, seized his sword which hung close by on the wall, and drew it from its polished sheath. At that moment the light in the nursery went out. Shouting to his drowsy slaves for lamps and torches, Amphitryon rushed in; and Heracles, who had not uttered so much as a whimper, proudly displayed the serpents, which he was in the act of strangling, one in either hand. As they died, he laughed, bounced joyfully up and down, and threw them at Amphitryon's feet.

While Alcmene comforted the terror-stricken Iphicles, Amphitryon spread the coverlet over Heracles again, and returned to bed. At dawn, when the cock had crowed three times, Alcmene summoned the aged Teiresias and told him of the prodigy. Teiresias, after foretelling Heracles's future glories, advised her to strew a broad hearth with dry faggots of gorse, thorn and brambles, and burn the serpents upon them at midnight. In the morning, a maid-servant must collect their ashes, take them to the rock where the Sphinx had perched, scatter them to the winds, and run away without looking back. On her return, the palace must be purged with fumes of sulphur and salted spring water; and its roof crowned with wild olive. Finally, a boar must be sacrificed at Zeus's high altar. All this Alcmene did. But some hold that the serpents were harmless, and placed in the cradle by Amphitryon himself; he had wished to discover which of the twins was his son, and now he knew well.[1]

[1] Robert Graves, *The Greek Myths*, vol. 2, pp. 90–91.

ODYSSEUS
Greek

The initiatory task of the young Odysseus is a common one. He must perform his first kill in order to prove himself worthy.

Autolycus once visited Ithaca, to find his daughter just delivered of a son. Eurycleia brought in the baby and set it in his lap at the end of supper, saying, "Autolycus, invent a name for this your dear daughter's son—a child much prayed for," and Autolycus had answered, "Son-in-law and daughter, name him as I shall say. Forasmuch as I come here full of plaints against many dwellers upon earth, women as well as men, so call him Odysseus, for the odiousness: and when he is a man make him visit the palace of his mother's family at Parnassus, which is mine, and I will give him enough to send him joyfully home." And so it came about. Young Odysseus went for his gifts and Autolycus with his sons welcomed him in open-handed courtesy, while his grandmother Amphithea embraced him to kiss his face and two lovely eyes. Autolycus told his famous sons to order food. Hastily they produced a five-year-old bull which they flayed and flensed, before jointing its limbs to piece them cunningly small for the spits. After roasting them they served the portions round; and day-long till sunset all feasted, equally content. After sunset when the darkness came they stretched out and took the boon of sleep. At dawn they were for hunting, the sons of Autolycus with their hounds. Odysseus went too. Their way climbed steep Parnassus through the zone of trees till they attained its wind-swept upper folds just as the sun, newly risen from the calm and brimming river of Ocean, touched the plough-lands. Their beaters were entering a little glen when the hounds broke away forward, hot on a scent. After them ran the sons of Autolycus, with Odysseus pressing hard upon the pack, his poised spear trembling in his eager hand. A great boar was couching there in a thicket so dense and over-grown as to be proof against all dank-breathing winds; and proof, too, against the flashing sun-heat and the soaking rain; while its ground was deep in fallen leaves. About this rolled the thunder of their chase. When the tramp of men and dogs came close the boar sprang from his lair to meet them. With bristling spine and fire-red eyes he faced their charge. Odysseus in the van eagerly rushed in to stick him, brandishing the spear in his stout hand: but the boar struck first with a sideways lift of the head that drove in his tusk above the man's knee and gashed the flesh deeply, though not to the bone. Odysseus' return thrust took the beast on the right shoulder, the spear-point flashing right through and out. Down in the dust with a grunt dropped the boar, and its life fled. Then the sons of Autolycus turned to and skilfully bound up the wound of gallant god-like Odysseus. They staunched the dark blood with a chanted rune and made back at once to their dear father's house, and then Autolycus and the sons completed his cure, made him great gifts (delighting a delightful guest) and punctually returned him to his own land of Ithaca. Laertes and his lady mother, in welcoming him home, enquired of everything and especially of how he suffered that wound: and he recounted the whole story of the boar's gleaming tusk that ripped his leg while he hunted Parnassus with the sons of Autolycus.[1]

[1] Homer, *The Odyssey of Homer,* translated by T. E. Shaw, book XIX, pp. 266–267.

THESEUS
Greek

*The valor of Theseus, like that of his model, Heracles, is indi-
cated by his earliest deeds. His worth is further proven by his
removal of the sword and sandals from under the rock.*

One day Heracles, dining at Troezen with Pittheus, removed
his lion-skin and threw it over a stool. When the palace children
came in, they screamed and fled, all except seven-year-old
Theseus, who ran to snatch an axe from the woodpile, and returned boldly, prepared to attack a real lion.   5

At the age of sixteen years he visited Delphi, and offered his
first manly hair-clippings to Apollo. He shaved, however, only
the forepart of his head, like the Arabians and Mysians, or like
the war-like Abantes of Euboea, who thereby deny their enemies
any advantage in close combat. This kind of tonsure, and the   10
precinct where he performed the ceremony, are both still called
Thesean. He was now a strong, intelligent and prudent youth;
and Aethra, leading him to the rock underneath which Aegeus
had hidden the sword and sandals, told him the story of his birth.
He had no difficulty in moving the rock, since called the "Rock   15
of Theseus," and recovered the tokens. Yet, despite Pittheus's
warnings and his mother's entreaties, he would not visit Athens
by the safe sea route, but insisted on travelling overland; im-
pelled by a desire to emulate the feats of his cousin-german
Heracles, whom he greatly admired.[1]   20

---

[1] Robert Graves, *The Greek Myths*, vol. 1, p. 325.

KING ARTHUR
European

Arthur is a northern Theseus in his successful extraction of the sword from the rock. This feat is a motif in other heroic stories, such as the Ring saga revived by Wagner.

Arthur, though only fifteen years old at his father's death, was elected king at a general meeting of the nobles. It was not done without opposition, for there were many ambitious competitors; but Bishop Brice, a person of great sanctity, on Christmas eve addressed the assembly and represented that it would 5 well become them, at that solemn season, to put up their prayers for some token which should manifest the intentions of Providence respecting their future sovereign. This was done, and with such success, that the service was scarcely ended when a miraculous stone was discovered, before the church door, and in the 10 stone was firmly fixed a sword, with the following words engraven on its hilt:

I am hight Escalibore,
Unto a king fair tresore.

Bishop Brice, after exhorting the assembly to offer up their 15 thanksgivings for this signal miracle, proposed a law that, whoever should be able to draw out the sword from the stone, should be acknowledged as sovereign of the Britons; and his proposal was decreed by general acclamation. The tributary kings of Uther and the most famous knights successively put their strength to 20 the proof, but the miraculous sword resisted all their efforts. It stood till Candlemas; it stood till Easter, and till Pentecost, when the best knights in the kingdom usually assembled for the annual tournament. Arthur, who was at that time serving in the capacity of squire to his foster-brother, Sir Kay, attended his master to 25 the lists. Sir Kay fought with great valor and success, but had the misfortune to break his sword, and sent Arthur to his mother for a new one. Arthur hastened home, but did not find the lady; but having observed near the church a sword, sticking in a stone, he galloped to the place, drew out the sword with great ease, and 30 delivered it to his master. Sir Kay would willingly have assumed to himself the distinction conferred by the possession of the sword; but when, to confirm the doubters, the sword was replaced in the stone, he was utterly unable to withdraw it, and it would yield a second time to no hand but Arthur's. Thus decisively pointed out by Heaven as their king, Arthur was by general consent proclaimed as such, and an early day appointed for his solemn coronation.[1]

5

[1] Thomas Bulfinch, *Bulfinch's Mythology: The Age of Chivalry*, pp. 72–73.

CUCHULAINN
Irish

Like Theseus, Krishna, and Heracles, Cuchulainn is a boy-wonder. His early thirst for adventure foreshadows later deeds.

Before his fifth year, when already possessed of man's strength, he heard of the "boy corps" of his uncle Conchobar and went to test them, taking his club, ball, spear, and javelin, playing with these as he went. At Emain he joined the boys at play without permission; but this was an insult, and they set upon him, throwing at him clubs, spears, and balls, all of which he fended off, besides knocking down fifty of the boys, while his "contortion" seized him—the first reference to this curious phenomenon. Conchobar now interfered, but Cuchulainn would not desist until all the boys came under his protection and guarantee.

At Conchobar's court he performed extraordinary feats and expelled a band of invaders when the Ulstermen were in their yearly weakness. He was first known as Setanta, and was called Cuchulainn in the following way. Culann the smith had prepared a banquet for Conchobar, who, on his way to it, saw the youth holding the field at ball against three hundred and fifty others; and though he bade him follow, Setanta refused to come until the play was over. While the banquet was progressing, Culann let loose his great watch-dog, which had the strength of a hundred, and when Setanta reached the fort, the beast attacked him, whereupon he thrust his ball into its mouth, and seizing its hind legs, battered it against a rock. Culann complained that the safe-guard of his flocks and herds was destroyed, but the boy said that he would act as watch-dog until a whelp of its breed was ready; and Cathbad the Druid now gave him a name—Cu Chulainn, or "Culann's Dog." This adventure took place before he was seven years old. Baudis suggests that as Cuchulainn was not the hero's birth-name, a dog may have been his *manito*, his name being given him in some ceremonial way at puberty, a circumstance afterward explained by the mythical story of Culann's Hound.

One day Cuchulainn overheard Cathbad saying that whatever stripling assumed arms on that day would have a short life, but would be the greatest of warriors. He now demanded arms from Conchobar, but broke every set of weapons given him until he received Conchobar's own sword and shield; and he also destroyed seventeen chariots, so that nothing but Conchobar's own chariot sufficed him. Cuchulainn made the charioteer drive fast and far until they reached the *dun* of the sons of Nechtan, each of whom he fought and slew, cutting off their heads; while on his return he killed two huge stags and then captured twenty-four wild swans, fastening all these to the chariot. From afar Levarcham the prophetess saw the strange cavalcade approaching Emain and bade all be on their guard, else the warrior would slay them; but Conchobar alone knew who he was and recognized the danger from a youth whose appetite for slaughter had been whetted. A stratagem was adopted, based upon Cuchulainn's well-known modesty. A hundred and fifty women with uncovered breasts were sent to meet him, and while he averted his face, he was seized and plunged into vessels of cold water. The first burst asunder; the water of the second boiled with the heat from his body; that of the third became warm; and thus his rage was calmed.[1]

---

[1] Louis Gray, ed., *The Mythology of All Races*, vol. 3, *Celtic*, pp. 141–143.

SIEGFRIED
German and Norse

Siegfried resembles Cuchulainn in the uncontrolled quality of his youthful enthusiasm. He is also like the blundering Heracles of some stories. Even wicked deeds can be the sign of the hero.

One year passed on after another, till the prince grew almost to man's estate. But labour in the smithy was irksome to him, and when his comrades set him right, he beat them, threw them down, and, on one occasion, went so far as to drag the best smith among them—Wieland—by the hair to his master's feet. 5

"This will not do at all," said Mimer; "come here and forge yourself a good sword."

Siegfried was quite ready to do so. He asked for the best iron and the heaviest hammer, which was such a weight that it took both hands to wield it. Mimer drew the strongest bar of iron out 10 of the forge, glowing red, and laid it on the anvil. Siegfried swung the hammer with one hand, as though it had been a plaything; but when it came down upon the iron the blow was like a clap of thunder, the house shook to its foundation, the iron shivered into splinters, and the anvil sank a foot deep into the ground. 15

"This will never do," said the master as before; "we must try another plan, my boy, if you are to make yourself a suitable weapon! Go to the charcoal-burner in the pine wood, and fetch me as much of his charcoal as you can carry on your strong shoulders. Meanwhile I shall prepare the best iron to make you 20 a sword, such as never yet was possessed by any warrior."

Siegfried was so pleased to hear this, that picking up the largest axe he could find, he set out into the forest. It was a beautiful spring day. The birds were singing, and the grass was studded with violets and forget-me-nots. He plucked a bunch of 25 the flowers and stuck them in his leather cap, from a half-conscious feeling that they might perhaps bring him good luck. He went on further and further, till he reached the middle of a dark pine forest. Not a bird was to be seen; but the gloomy silence was broken by a gurgling, hissing, and roaring, that might 30 easily have affrighted a less daring spirit. He soon found the reason of the noise. A dismal swamp lay before him, in which

gigantic toads, snakes, and lind-worms were disporting themselves.

"I never saw so many horrible creatures in my life," said
Siegfried; "but I will soon stop their music."

So saying, he picked up dead trees and threw them into the 5
morass, till he had completely covered it. After which he hastened on to the charcoal-burner's house. Arrived there, he asked
the man to give him fire that he might burn the monsters.

"Poor boy," said the charcoal-burner, "I am very sorry for
you; but if you go back the way you came, the great dragon will 10
come out of his cave and make but a single mouthful of you.
Smith Mimer is a faithless man; he came here before you, and
told me that he had roused the worm against you, because you
were so unmanageable."

"Have no fear, good man," answered Siegfried; "I shall first 15
slay the worm, and then the smith. But now give me the fire, that
I may burn the poisonous brood."

The lad was soon back at the swamp. He set fire to the dry
wood with which he had covered it, and let it blaze. The wind
was favourable, and fanned the flames to a great fire, so that 20
the creatures were all burnt up in a short space of time. The lad
then went round the dismal swamp and found a small rivulet of
hot fat issuing from it. He dipped his finger in it, and found, on
withdrawing it, that it was covered with a horn-like skin. "Ah,"
he thought, "this would be useful in war." He therefore un- 25
dressed, and bathed his whole body in the liquid fat, so that he
was now covered with horn from head to foot, except in one
place, between his shoulders, where a leaf had stuck to his skin.
This he did not discover until later. He dressed himself again in
his leather garments, and walked on, his club resting on his 30
shoulder. Suddenly the dragon darted out upon him from its
hiding place; but three good blows of his club slew the monster.
He then went back to the smithy to take vengeance on the master
smith and his comrade. At sight of him, the men fled affrighted
into the forest, but the master awaited the youth's arrival. At 35
first Mimer tried the effect of flattering words; but finding they
were vain, he took to his sword. Siegfried then dealt him one
mighty blow, and had no need to strike again.

Having done this, the lad went into the smithy, and with
great patience and care forged himself a sword, whose blade he 40
hardened in the blood of the lind-worm. Then he set out for his

father's palace. The king sharply rebuked him for his evil deed in slaying the master smith, who was so good a subject, and so useful to the whole country. And the queen, in her turn, reproached him with many tears, for having stained his hands with innocent blood. Siegfried, sobered by his father's reproof, and softened by his mother's tears, did not try to excuse himself; but, falling at the queen's feet and hiding his face in his hands, he said the sight of her tears cut him to the heart, and for the future he vowed that his deeds should be those of a gentle knight. Then the hearts of the parents were comforted. 10

From that time forward Siegfried was changed. He listened to the advice of men of understanding, and strove to learn how to act wisely and well. Whenever he felt one of his old fits of passion coming over him, he thought of his mother's tears and his father's reproof, and conquered the evil spirit that threatened 15 to master him. The expectations of the people were great respecting him; they were sure that in him their nation had found a new hero. And then, he was so handsome and graceful, that the women admired him as much for his looks as the men did for his prowess.[1] 20

---

[1] W. Wägner, *Romances and Epics of Our Northern Ancestors,* "The Nibelung Story," pp. 148–152.

DAVID
Judaic

David's success over Goliath is in the nature of a divine sign.
The unknown youth becomes a hero by slaying a monster.

Now the Philistines gathered together their armies to battle, and were gathered together at Shochoh, which belongeth to Judah, and pitched between Shochoh and Azekah, in Ephes-dammim. And Saul and the men of Israel were gathered together, and pitched by the valley of Elah, and set the battle in array against the Philistines. And the Philistines stood on a mountain on the one side, and Israel stood on a mountain on the other side: and there was a valley between them. And there went out a champion out of the camp of the Philistines, named Goliath, of Gath, whose height was six cubits and a span. And he had a helmet of brass upon his head, and he was armed with a coat of mail; and the weight of the coat was five thousand shekels of brass. And he had greaves of brass upon his legs, and a target of brass between his shoulders. And the staff of his spear was like a weaver's beam; and his spear's head weighed six hundred shekels of iron: and one bearing a shield went before him. And he stood and cried unto the armies of Israel, and said unto them, Why are ye come out to set your battle in array? am not I a Philistine, and ye servants to Saul? choose you a man for you, and let him come down to me. If he be able to fight with me, and to kill me, then will we be your servants: but if I prevail against him, and kill him, then shall ye be our servants, and serve us. And the Philistine said, I defy the armies of Israel this day; give me a man, that we may fight together. When Saul and all Israel heard those words of the Philistine, they were dismayed, and greatly afraid.

Now David was the son of that Ephrathite of Bethlehem—Judah, whose name was Jesse; and he had eight sons: and the man went among men for an old man in the days of Saul. And the three eldest sons of Jesse went and followed Saul to the battle: and the names of his three sons that went to the battle were Eliab the firstborn, and next unto him Abinadab, and the third Shammah. And David was the youngest: and the three eldest followed Saul. But David went and returned from Saul to feed his father's sheep at Bethlehem. And the Philistine drew near morning and evening, and presented himself forty days.

And Jesse said unto David his son, Take now for thy brethren an ephah of this parched corn, and these ten loaves, and run to the camp to thy brethren; and carry these ten cheeses unto the captain of their thousand, and look how thy brethren fare, and 5 take their pledge.

Now Saul, and they, and all the men of Israel, were in the valley of Elah, fighting with the Philistines. And David rose up early in the morning, and left the sheep with a keeper, and took, and went, as Jesse had commanded him; and he came to the 10 trench, as the host was going forth to the fight, and shouted for the battle. For Israel and the Philistines had put the battle in array, army against army. And David left his carriage in the hand of the keeper of the carriage, and ran into the army, and came and saluted his brethren. And as he talked with them, behold, 15 there came up the champion, the Philistine of Gath, Goliath by name, out of the armies of the Philistines, and spake according to the same words: and David heard them.

And all the men of Israel, when they saw the man, fled from him, and were sore afraid. And the men of Israel said, Have ye 20 seen this man that is come up? surely to defy Israel is he come up: and it shall be, that the man who killeth him, the king will enrich him with great riches, and will give him his daughter, and make his father's house free in Israel. And David spake to the men that stood by him, saying, What shall be done to the man 25 that killeth this Philistine, and taketh away the reproach from Israel? for who is this uncircumcised Philistine, that he should defy the armies of the living God? And the people answered him after this manner, saying, So shall it be done to the man that killeth him. 30

And Eliab his eldest brother heard when he spake unto the men; and Eliab's anger was kindled against David, and he said, Why camest thou down hither? and with whom has thou left those few sheep in the wilderness? I know thy pride, and the naughtiness of thine heart; for thou art come down that thou 35 mightest see the battle. And David said, What have I now done? Is there not a cause? And he turned from him toward another, and spake after the same manner: and the people answered him again after the former manner.

And when the words were heard which David spake, they 40 rehearsed them before Saul: and he sent for him. And David said to Saul, Let no man's heart fail because of him; thy servant will go and fight with this Philistine. And Saul said to David, Thou art not able to go against this Philistine to fight with him: for thou art but a youth, and he a man of war from his youth. And David said unto Saul, Thy servant kept his father's sheep, 5 and there came a lion, and a bear, and took a lamb out of the flock: and I went out after him, and smote him, and delivered it out of his mouth: and when he arose against me, I caught him by his beard, and smote him, and slew him. Thy servant slew both the lion and the bear: and this uncircumcised Philistine 10 shall be as one of them, seeing he hath defied the armies of the living God. David said moreover, The Lord that delivered me out of the paw of the lion, and out of the paw of the bear, he will deliver me out of the hand of this Philistine. And Saul said unto David, Go, and the Lord be with thee. And Saul armed David 15 with his armor, and he put a helmet of brass upon his head; also he armed him with a coat of mail. And David girded his sword upon his armor, and he assayed to go; for he had not proved it. And David said unto Saul, I cannot go with these; for I have not proved them. And David put them off him. And he took his staff 20 in his hand, and chose him five smooth stones out of the brook, and put them in a shepherd's bag which he had, even in a scrip; and his sling was in his hand: and he drew near to the Philistine.

And the Philistine came on and drew near unto David; and the man that bare the shield went before him. And when the 25 Philistine looked about, and saw David, he disdained him: for he was but a youth, and ruddy, and of a fair countenance. And the Philistine said unto David, Am I a dog, that thou comest to me with staves? And the Philistine cursed David by his gods. And the Philistine said to David, Come to me, and I will give thy flesh 30 unto the fowls of the air, and to the beasts of the field. Then said David to the Philistine, Thou comest to me with a sword, and with a spear, and with a shield: but I come to thee in the name of the Lord of hosts, the God of the armies of Israel, whom thou hast defied. This day will the Lord deliver thee into mine hand; 35 and I will smite thee, and take thine head from thee; and I will give the carcasses of the host of the Philistines this day unto the fowls of the air, and to the wild beasts of the earth; that all the earth may know that there is a God in Israel. And all this assembly shall know that the Lord saveth not with sword and spear: 40 for the battle is the Lord's, and he will give you into our hands.

And it came to pass, when the Philistine arose, and came and drew nigh to meet David, that David hasted, and ran toward the army to meet the Philistine. And David put his hand in his bag, and took thence a stone, and slang it, and smote the Philistine in his forehead, that the stone sunk into his forehead; and he 5 fell upon his face to the earth.

So David prevailed over the Philistine with a sling and with a stone, and smote the Philistine, and slew him; but there was no sword in the hand of David. Therefore David ran, and stood upon the Philistine, and took his sword, and drew it out of the 10 sheath thereof, and slew him, and cut off his head therewith. And when the Philistines saw their champion was dead, they fled. And the men of Israel and of Judah arose, and shouted, and pursued the Philistines, until thou come to the valley, and to the gates of Ekron. And the wounded of the Philistines fell down by 15 the way to Shaaraim, even unto Gath, and unto Ekron. And the children of Israel returned from chasing after the Philistines, and they spoiled their tents. And David took the head of the Philistine, and brought it to Jerusalem; but he put his armor in his tent. 20

And when Saul saw David go forth against the Philistine, he said unto Abner, the captain of the host, Abner, whose son is this youth? And Abner said, As thy soul liveth, O king, I cannot tell. And the king said, Inquire thou whose son the stripling is. And as David returned from the slaughter of the Philistine, Abner 25 took him, and brought him before Saul with the head of the Philistine in his hand. And Saul said to him, Whose son art thou, thou young man? And David answered, I am the son of thy servant Jesse the Bethlehemite.[1]

---

[1] I Samuel 17.

BUGDHA
Indian

*It is significant that the Buddha should receive his divine sign
by way of gradual observation. Where the careers of Heracles,
Theseus, Cuchulainn, and most heroes involve violence and
war, the Buddha's greatness is achieved through contemplation.*

The young prince Gautama Sakyamuni, the Future Buddha,
had been protected by his father from all knowledge of age,
sickness, death, or monkhood, lest he should be moved to thoughts
of life renunciation; for it had been prophesied at his birth that
he was to become either a world emperor or a Buddha. The king — 5
prejudiced in favor of the royal vocation — provided his son with
three palaces and forty thousand dancing girls to keep his mind
attached to the world. But these only served to advance the inevitable; for while still relatively young, the youth exhausted
for himself the fields of fleshly joy and became ripe for the other 10
experience. The moment he was ready, the proper heralds auto-
matically appeared:

"Now on a certain day the Future Buddha wished to go to
the park, and told his charioteer to make ready the chariot.
Accordingly the man brought out a sumptuous and 'elegant 15
chariot, and, adorning it richly, he harnessed it to four state
horses of the Sindhava breed, as white as the petals of the white
lotus, and announced to the Future Buddha that everything was
ready. And the Future Buddha mounted the chariot, which was
like to a palace of the gods, and proceeded toward the park. 20

" 'The time for the enlightenment of the prince Siddhartha
draweth nigh,' thought the gods; 'we must show him a sign'; and
they changed one of their number into a decrepit old man,
broken-toothed, gray-haired, crooked and bent of body, leaning
on a staff, and trembling, and showed him to the Future Buddha, 25
but so that only he and the charioteer saw him.

"Then said the Future Buddha to the charioteer, 'Friend,
pray, who is this man? Even his hair is not like that of other men.'
And when he heard the answer, he said, 'Shame on birth, since to
every one that is born old age must come.' And agitated in heart, 30
he thereupon returned and ascended his palace.

" 'Why has my son returned so quickly?' asked the king.

" 'Sire, he has seen an old man,' was the reply; 'and because he has seen an old man, he is about to retire from the world.'

" 'Do you want to kill me, that you say such things? Quickly get ready some plays to be performed before my son. If we can but get him to enjoying pleasure, he will cease to think of retiring from the world.' Then the king extended the guard to half a league in each direction.

"Again on a certain day, as the Future Buddha was going to the park, he saw a diseased man whom the gods had fashioned; and having again made inquiry, he returned, agitated in heart, and ascended his palace.

"And the king made the same inquiry and gave the same order as before; and again extending the guard, placed them for three quarters of a league around.

"And again on a certain day, as the Future Buddha was going to the park, he saw a dead man whom the gods had fashioned; and having again made inquiry, he returned, agitated in heart, and ascended his palace.

"And the king made the same inquiry and gave the same orders as before; and again extending the guard placed them for a league around.

"And again on a certain day, as the Future Buddha was going to the park, he saw a monk, carefully and decently clad, whom the gods had fashioned; and he asked his charioteer, 'Pray, who is this man?' 'Sire, this is one who has retired from the world'; and the charioteer thereupon proceeded to sound the praises of retirement from the world. The thought of retiring from the world was a pleasing one to the Future Buddha."[1]

[1] Henry Clarke Warren, *Buddhism in Translations*, pp. 56-57.

MARY
Christian

The earthly form of Divine Wisdom, or Sophia, Mary is the chosen vessel for the Messiah and is appropriately marked by the divine sign.

When the child was three years old, her parents took her to the Temple at Jerusalem, and left her in the company of the Temple virgins, with whom she grew up until she was fourteen — constantly visited by the angels and enjoying always the mystical vision of God. Now that she had become a woman, it was the proper custom that she should be returned to her home and given in marriage. But Mary told the High Priest that it could not be so with her, since she had promised her virginity to God. Perplexed, and seeking guidance from the Most High, the High Priest entered into the sanctuary of the Temple, and, as he prayed, a Voice came forth from the inmost shrine of the Holy of Holies, commanding that all the marriageable men of the House of David should come to the Temple and each one lay a branch upon the altar. One of these branches, said the Voice, would burst into flower, and he to whom it belonged was to take the Virgin Mary as his wife. And so it came about that the branch which blossomed was that which belonged to Joseph, a carpenter from Bethlehem. This branch was no doubt that ancient cutting from the Tree of Eden, which, according to another legend, had been handed down among the patriarchs of Israel until it had at last found its way to Joseph; and now, as it blossomed upon the altar, the Holy Spirit appeared from heaven in the form of a dove, and rested upon it.[1]

[1] Alan Watts, *Myth and Ritual in Christianity*, p. 116.

JOAN OF ARC
French

Joan's visions are a sign of her saintly mission — of the power within that motivates her and is greater than her will or her body.

St Joan was in her fourteenth year when she experienced the earliest of those supernatural manifestations which were to lead her through the path of patriotism to death at the stake. At first it was a single voice addressing her apparently from near by, and accompanied by a blaze of light: afterwards, as the voices in- 5 creased in number, she was able to see her interlocutors whom she identified as St Michael, St Catherine, St Margaret and others. Only very gradually did they unfold her mission: it was a mission which might well appal her: she, a simple peasant girl, was to save France! She never spoke about these Voices in 10 Domrémy; she was too much afraid of her stern father. By May 1428 they had become insistent and explicit. She must present herself at once to Robert Baudricourt, who commanded the king's forces in the neighbouring town of Vaucouleurs. Joan succeeded in persuading an uncle who lived near Vaucouleurs to take her to 15 him, but Baudricourt only laughed and dismissed her, saying that her father ought to give her a good hiding.

At this time the military position was well-nigh desperate, for Orleans, the last remaining stronghold, had been invested by the English and was in danger of falling. After Joan's return to 20 Domrémy her Voices gave her no rest. When she protested that she was a poor girl who could neither ride nor fight, they replied; "It is God who commands it." Unable to resist such a call she secretly left home and went back to Vaucouleurs. Baudricourt's scepticism as to her mission was somewhat shaken when official 25 confirmation reached him of a serious defeat of the French which Joan had previously announced to him. He now not only consented to send her to the king but gave her an escort of three menat-arms. At her own request she travelled in male dress to protect herself. Although the little party reached Chinon, where the king 30 was residing, on March 6, 1429, it was not till two days later that Joan was admitted to his presence. Charles had purposely disguised himself, but she identified him at once and, by a secret sign communicated to her by her Voices and imparted by her to him alone, she obliged him to believe in the supernatural nature of her mission. She then asked for soldiers whom she might lead to the relief of Orleans. This request was opposed by La Trémouille, the king's favourite, and by a large section of the court, who regarded the girl as a crazy visionary or a scheming impostor. To settle the matter it was decided to send her to be examined by a learned body of theologians at Poitiers.

After a searching interrogatory extending over three weeks this council decided that they found nothing to disapprove of, and advised Charles to make prudent use of her services. Accordingly after her return to Chinon arrangements were pushed forward to equip her to lead an expeditionary force. A special standard was made for her bearing the words "Jesus: Maria," together with a representation of the Eternal Father to whom two kneeling angels were presenting a fleur-de-lis. On April 27 the army left Blois with Joan at its head clad in white armour, and in spite of some contretemps she entered Orleans on April 29. Her presence in the beleaguered city wrought marvels. By May 8, the English forts which surrounded Orleans had been captured and the siege raised, after she herself had been wounded in the breast by an arrow. All these events with their approximate dates she had prophesied before starting the campaign. She would fain have followed up these successes, for her Voices had told her that she would not last for long; but La Trémouille and the archbishop of Rheims were in favour of negotiating with the enemy. They persisted in regarding the relief of Orleans merely as a piece of good luck. However, the Maid was allowed to undertake a short campaign on the Loire with the Duc d'Alençon, one of her best friends. It was completely successful and ended with a victory at Patay in which the English forces under Sir John Fastolf suffered a crushing defeat. Joan now pressed for the immediate coronation of the Dauphin. The road to Rheims had practically been cleared and the last obstacle was removed by the unexpected surrender of Troyes.

But the French leaders dallied, and only very reluctantly did they consent to follow her to Rheims where, on July 17, 1429, Charles VII was solemnly crowned, Joan standing at his side with her standard. That event, which completed the mission originally entrusted to her by the Voices, marked also the close of her military successes.[1]

[1] *Butler's Lives of the Saints*, vol. 2, pp. 427–429.

JESUS
Christian

The child Jesus in the temple is, like the Buddha, wise before his years. His quest, too, will be one of peace. A second divine sign will come at the moment of his baptism by John.

And when eight days were accomplished for the circumcising of the child, his name was called JESUS, which was so named of the angel before he was conceived in the womb.

And when the days of her purification according to the law of Moses were accomplished, they brought him to Jerusalem, to 5 present him to the Lord;

(As it is written in the law of the Lord, Every male that openeth the womb shall be called holy to the Lord;)

And to offer a sacrifice according to that which is said in the law of the Lord, A pair of turtledoves, or two young pigeons. 10

And, behold, there was a man in Jerusalem, whose name was Simeon; and the same man was just and devout, waiting for the consolation of Israel: and the Holy Ghost was upon him.

And it was revealed unto him by the Holy Ghost, that he should not see death, before he had seen the Lord's Christ. 15

And he came by the Spirit into the temple: and when the parents brought in the child Jesus, to do for him after the custom of the law,

Then took he him up in his arms, and blessed God, and said,

Lord, now lettest thou thy servant depart in peace, according 20 to thy word:

For mine eyes have seen thy salvation,

Which thou hast prepared before the face of all people;

A light to lighten the Gentiles, and the glory of thy people Israel. 25

And Joseph and his mother marvelled at those things which were spoken of him.

And Simeon blessed them, and said unto Mary his mother, Behold, this child is set for the fall and rising again of many in Israel; and for a sign which shall be spoken against; 30

(Yea, a sword shall pierce through thy own soul also,) that the thoughts of many hearts may be revealed.

And there was one Anna, a prophetess, the daughter of Phanuel, of the tribe of Aser: she was of a great age, and had lived with an husband seven years from her virginity; 35

And she was a widow of about fourscore and four years, which departed not from the temple, but served God with fastings and prayers night and day.

And she coming in that instant gave thanks likewise unto the Lord, and spake of him to all them that looked for redemption in Jerusalem.

And when they had performed all things according to the law of the Lord, they returned into Galilee, to their own city Nazareth.

And the child grew, and waxed strong in spirit, filled with wisdom: and the grace of God was upon him.

Now his parents went to Jerusalem every year at the feast of the passover.

And when he was twelve years old, they went up to Jerusalem after the custom of the feast.

And when they had fulfilled the days, as they returned, the child Jesus tarried behind in Jerusalem; and Joseph and his mother knew not of it.

But they, supposing him to have been in the company, went a day's journey; and they sought him among their kinsfolk and acquaintance.

And when they found him not, they turned back again to Jerusalem, seeking him.

And it came to pass, that after three days they found him in the temple, sitting in the midst of the doctors, both hearing them, and asking them questions.

And all that heard him were astonished at his understanding and answers.

And when they saw him, they were amazed: and his mother said unto him, Son, why hast thou thus dealt with us? behold, thy father and I have sought thee sorrowing.

And he said unto them, How is it that ye sought me? wist ye not that I must be about my Father's business?

And they understood not the saying which he spake unto them.

And he went down with them, and came to Nazareth, and was subject unto them: but his mother kept all these sayings in her heart.

And Jesus increased in wisdom and stature, and in favour with God and man.[1]

[1] Luke 2.

MOSES
Judaic

*The burning bush is a divine sign for the young Moses. He alone
sees it, as he alone must lead the children of Israel.*

When Moses drew near to Mount Horeb, he was aware at
once that it was a holy place, for he noticed that passing birds
did not alight upon it. At his approach the mountain began to
move, as though to go forward and meet him, and it settled back
into quietude only when his foot rested upon it. The first thing
Moses noticed was the wonderful burning bush, the upper part
of which was a blazing flame, neither consuming the bush, nor
preventing it from bearing blossoms as it burnt, for the celestial
fire has three peculiar qualities: it produces blossoms, it does not
consume the object around which it plays, and it is black of color.
The fire that Moses saw in the bush was the appearance of the
angel Michael, who had descended as the forerunner of the
Shekinah herself to come down presently. It was the wish of
God to hold converse with Moses, who, however, was not inclined
to permit any interruption of the work under his charge. Therefore God startled him with the wonderful phenomenon of the
burning thorn-bush. That brought Moses to a stop, and then God
spoke with him.

There were good reasons for selecting the thorn-bush as the
vessel for a Divine vision. It was "clean," for the heathen could
not use it to make idols. God's choosing to dwell in the stunted
thorn-bush conveyed the knowledge to Moses that He suffers
along with Israel. Furthermore, Moses was taught that there is
nothing in nature, not even the insignificant thorn-bush, that
can exist without the presence of the Shekinah. Besides, the
thorn-bush may be taken as the symbol for Israel in several respects. As the thorn-bush is the lowliest of all species of trees,
so the condition of Israel in the exile is the lowliest as compared
with that of all the other nations, but as the thorn-bush releases
no bird that alights upon it without lacerating its wings, so the
nations that subjugate Israel will be punished. Also, as a garden
hedge is made of the thorn-bush, so Israel forms the hedge for
the world, the garden of God, for without Israel the world could
not endure. Furthermore, as the thorn-bush bears thorns and

roses alike, so Israel has pious and impious members, and as the thorn-bush requires ample water for its growth, so Israel can prosper only through the Torah, the celestial water. And the thorn-bush, the leaf of which consists of five leaflets, was to indicate to Moses that God had resolved to redeem Israel only for the sake of the merits of five pious men, Abraham, Isaac, Jacob, Aaron, and Moses. The numbers represented by the letters composing the Hebrew word for thorn-bush, Seneh, add up to one hundred and twenty, to convey that Moses would reach the age of one hundred and twenty years, and that the Shekinah would rest on Mount Horeb for one hundred and twenty days. Finally, in order to give Moses an illustration of His modesty, God descended from the exalted heavens and spake to him from a lowly thorn-bush instead of the summit of a lofty mountain or the top of a stately cedar tree.

The vision of the burning bush appeared to Moses alone; the other shepherds with him saw nothing of it. He took five steps in the direction of the bush, to view it at close range, and when God beheld the countenance of Moses distorted by grief and anxiety over Israel's suffering, He spake, "This one is worthy of the office of pasturing My people."

Moses was still a novice in prophecy, therefore God said to Himself, "If I reveal Myself to him in loud tones, I shall alarm him, but if I reveal Myself with a subdued voice, he will hold prophecy in low esteem," whereupon he addressed him in his father Amram's voice. Moses was overjoyed to hear his father speak, for it gave him the assurance that he was still alive. The voice called his name twice, and he answered, "Here am I! What is my father's wish?" God replied, saying, "I am not thy father. I but desired to refrain from terrifying thee, therefore I spoke with thy father's voice. I am the God of thy father, the God of Abraham, the God of Isaac, and the God of Jacob." These words rejoiced Moses greatly, for not only was his father Amram's name pronounced in the same breath with the names of the three Patriarchs, but it came before theirs, as though he ranked higher than they.

Moses said not a word. In silent reverence before the Divine vision he covered his face, and when God disclosed the mission with which He charged him, of bringing the Israelites forth from the land of Egypt, he answered with humility, "Who am I, that I should go unto Pharaoh, and bring forth the children of Israel out of Egypt?" Thereupon spake God, "Moses, thou art meek, and I will reward thee for thy modesty. I will deliver the whole land of Egypt into thine hand, and, besides, I will let thee ascend unto the throne of My glory, and look upon all the angels of the heavens."[1]

5

[1] Louis Ginzberg, *The Legends of the Jews*, vol. 2, pp. 303–305.

DIONYSOS (DIONYSUS)
Greek

The divine force here turns men into beasts and a ship into a vineyard. The world must know that this god embodies the miraculous metamorphic power which is fertility and life.

[After the child had been nursed] (or before, in some accounts), Zeus transformed him into a kid in order to hide him from the jealous Hera. Hermes then carried him to the nymphs of Nysa, a mountain that different writers have located in Thrace, Asia, and Africa. Some accounts identify these nymphs as the Hyades, formerly called the Dodonidae, and add that Dionysus later placed them in the stars out of gratitude. Whoever they were, the Nysaean nymphs reared the goat-child in a cave on the mountain. Later, when Dionysus had returned to human form, they became his followers, the maenads, and shared much of the persecution to which the god was subjected. When they grew old, Dionysus persuaded Medea to rejuvenate them, no doubt by boiling them with herbs in her ever-handy cauldron. Some say that Dionysus' principal nurse was the Euboean nymph Macris.

For some reason the "nurses" (as his female votaries seem to have been called) were not at hand on the day that Dionysus was kidnaped from the island of Icaria by piratical Tyrrhenian sailors. (This event, like many other trials of Dionysus, has been blamed on Hera.) Some say that the nurses were waiting for him on the island of Naxos, or that he had other reasons for wanting to go there. In any case, although he was a mere boy, he asked the sailors for passage to the island. They agreed and took him aboard, for they believed him to be the son of some wealthy family who would pay them well. Greed overcame them and they steered the ship off course, planning to hold the lad for ransom. Some add that he was so handsome that they also tried to rape him. The helmsman, Acoetes, did his best to save the passenger, for he sensed that he was more than an ordinary mortal, but the other sailors threatened or manhandled him for interfering.

Suddenly, in spite of a stiff breeze in its sails, the ship stood still. A sound of flutes was heard. Ivy and grapevines twined themselves about the oars and masts, or the oars turned to snakes.

81

The astonishment of the sailors turned to terror as wild beasts—panthers, lions, and bears—appeared on the deck. Some say that the captain was eaten by a lion, others that he ordered Acoetes to turn back to the proper course, but it was too late. In a frenzy of fear the sailors leaped into the sea, where they were changed into dolphins. Acoetes would have followed, but Dionysus restrained him, assuring him that he had won his favor by his attempts to save him. As for the dolphins, having once been human themselves, they ever afterward remained friendly to human beings. Dionysus placed one of them among the stars to commemorate his triumph and, no doubt, as a warning to pirates.

In a variant of this tale, Dionysus and some of his followers sailed together in the pirate ship. When he was bound by the sailors he told his friends to sing. They did so, and the sailors began a wild dance. It was so wild, in fact, that they danced off the boat into the sea, leaving the god and his company in full command.[1]

[1] Edward Tripp, ed., *Crowell's Handbook of Classical Mythology*, pp. 204–205.

ORIGINS AND INITIATION:
Commentary on Part 2

To deny the past which lives in us is to deny the source of psychic reality. The role of the child-hero is to lead us to that source. Without roots neither the hero nor the individual nor the race can be whole. The child-hero is more than human; he is a symbol of what Jung called "the pre-conscious childhood aspect of the collective psyche."[1] And he is the symbol of a natural drive which Jung describes as follows:

The "child" . . . is a personification of vital forces quite outside the limited range of our conscious mind. . . . It represents the strongest, the most ineluctable urge in every being, namely the urge to realize itself. It is, as it were, an incarnation of *the inability to do otherwise, equipped with all the powers of nature and instinct,* whereas the conscious mind is always getting tied up in its supposed ability to do otherwise. The urge and compulsion to self-realization is a *law of nature* and thus of invincible power. . . . The power is revealed in the miraculous doings of the child-hero. . . .[2]

Early in the process of self-realization or individuation the individual, represented here by the child-hero, must confront and control the fantasies and demons of his inner self—the demons and fantasies remaining from the personal and racial childhood, in which all adults are giants, all animals and fears monsters, and about which all memories are exaggerated. The childhood myth is a second birth, for as a child or youth the preordained hero must be initiated into his role as saviour or quester. This is the first of his rebirths, in this case from childhood into manhood. It is rebirth expressed in such rituals as adolescent circumcision and confirmation, ceremonies which are meant to dramatically deliver the child from the world of the nursery to that of adult responsibility.

In the myth the child proves himself by confronting a physical force or by receiving a divine blessing. He kills the giant—the irrational authority of the adult who would suppress him. He kills the monster or wild animal—the monstrous and wild de-

[1] Carl Gustav Jung and C. Kerényi, *Introduction to a Science of Mythology,* p. 111.
[2] Ibid., pp. 123–124. The italics are Jung's.

sires and instincts within us all. He draws the sword from the rock, proving that he is the equal of his father, who put it there. Or he performs a miracle, which indicates that God is within him. The chords struck by these events are rooted in our personal experience. Each of us has felt the frustration in childhood of being constantly thwarted by adults, of being treated as a child when we knew we were no longer one. We have all felt the need to prove in some way—in athletics, in sexual "conquests"—that we were no longer to be denied. Most of all, we have all felt the need to identify ourselves—in part by establishing our origins. Thus, as we grow older and more concerned with who we are, memories of childhood tend to take on more importance and often become increasingly idealized; the monsters grow, and the idyllic becomes more idyllic than ever.[3] The same applies to mankind as a species. As his knowledge of himself in the present —his biological and sociological self—develops, so does his thirst for history, archaeology, anthropology, and, it must be added, mythology. Man searches in these disciplines for his primitive stage—for his racial childhood and origins. Man, like the individual, cannot know who he is until he knows who he *was*. This is the source for the myth of the child-hero and his initiation—a myth which emerges from the stories collected in this section.

The student of mythology who wishes to explore the child motif more thoroughly should read the appropriate sections in Campbell's *The Hero with a Thousand Faces* and, above all, in Jung and Kerényi's *Introduction to a Science of Mythology*.

[3] Paradise myths might be seen as an expression of this longing for an idyllic past.

3

PREPARATION, MEDITATION, WITHDRAWAL, AND REFUSAL

In this modern "Angelus" the contemplative in isolation, like the hero of old in his stage of withdrawal to cave or mountain, is faced with a vision of the essence of her own inner reality. [Salvador Dali, *Portrait of Gala with the "Angelus" of Millet* (1935), oil on wood, 12¾ x 10½ in., Collection, The Museum of Modern Art, New York. Gift of Abby Aldrich Rockefeller. Reproduced with permission.]

BUDDHA
Indian

The withdrawal for contemplation under the Bo Tree is the central event in the Buddha's life. The hero overcomes the temptations of the "world" and sheds the "illusion" of material reality.

Now during the time that Gautama had been dwelling in the forest near by Uruvela, the daughter of the village headman, by name Sujata, had been accustomed to make a daily offering of food to eight hundred Brahmans, making the prayer—"May the Bodhisatta at length, receive an offering of food from me, attain enlightenment, and become a Buddha!" And now that the time had come when he desired to receive nourishing food, a Deva appeared in the night to Sujata and announced that the Bodhisatta had put aside his austerities and desired to partake of good and nourishing food, "and now shall your prayer be accomplished." Then Sujata with all speed arose early and went to her father's herd. Now for a long time she had been accustomed to take the milk of a thousand cows and to feed therewith five hundred, and again with their milk to feed two hundred and fifty, and so on until eight only were fed with the milk of the rest, and this she called "working the milk in and in." It was the full-moon day of the month of May when she received the message of the gods, and rose early, and milked the eight cows, and took the milk and boiled it in new pans, and prepared milk-rice. At the same time she sent her maid Punna to the foot of the great tree where she had been wont to lay her daily offerings. Now the Bodhisatta knowing that he would that day attain Supreme Enlightenment, was sitting at the foot of the tree, awaiting the hour for going forth to beg his food; and such was his glory that all the region of the East was lit up. The girl thought that it was the spirit of the tree who would deign to receive the offering with his own hands. When she returned to Sujata and reported this, Sujata embraced her and bestowed on her the jewels of a daughter, and exclaimed, "Henceforth thou shalt be to me in the place of an elder daughter!" And sending for a golden vessel she put the well-cooked food therein, and covered it with a pure white cloth, and bore it with dignity to the foot of the great Nigrodha-tree; and there she too saw the Bodhisatta, and believed him to be the spirit of the tree. Sujata approached him, and placed the vessel in his hand, and she met his gaze and said: "My lord, accept what I have offered thee," and she added "May there arise to thee as much of joy as has come to me!" and so she departed.

The Bodhisatta took the golden bowl, and went down to the bank of the river and bathed, and then dressing himself in the garb of an Arahat, he again took his seat, with his face towards the East. He divided the rice into forty-nine portions, and this food sufficed for his nourishment during the forty-nine days following the Enlightenment. When he had finished eating the milk rice, he took the golden vessel and cast it into the stream, saying, "If I am able to attain Enlightenment to-day, let this pot go up stream, but if not, may it go down stream." And he threw it into the water, and it went swiftly up the river until it reached the whirlpool of the Black Snake King, and there it sank.

The Bodhisatta spent the heat of the day in a grove of Sal-trees beside the stream. But in the evening he made his way to the foot of the tree of wisdom, and there, making the resolution: "Though my skin, my nerves and my bones should waste away and my life-blood dry, I will not leave this seat until I have attained Supreme Enlightenment," he took his seat with his face towards the East.

At this moment Mara the Fiend became aware that the Bodhisatta had taken his seat with a view to attaining Perfect Enlightenment; and thereupon, summoning the hosts of the demons, and mounting his elephant of war, he advanced towards the Tree of Wisdom. And there stood Maha Brahma holding above the Bodhisatta a white canopy of state, and Sakka, blowing the great trumpet, and with them were all the companies of gods and angels. But so terrible was the array of Mara that there was not one of all this host of the Devas that dared to remain to face him. The Great Being was left alone.

First of all, however, Mara assumed the form of a messenger, with disordered garments, and panting in haste, bearing a letter from the Sakya princes. And in the letter it was written that Devadatta had usurped the kingdom of Kapilavatthu and entered the Bodhisatta's palace, taken his goods and his wife, and cast Suddhodana into prison and they prayed him to return to restore peace and order. But the Bodhisatta reflected lust it was that had caused Devadatta thus to misuse the women, malice had made him imprison Suddhodana, while the Sakyas neutralized by cowardice failed to defend their King: and so reflecting on the folly and weakness of the natural heart, his own resolve to attain a higher and better state was strengthened and confirmed.[1]

Failing in this device, Mara now advanced to the assault with all his hosts, striving to overcome the Bodhisatta first by a terrible whirlwind, then by a storm of rain, causing a mighty flood: but the hem of the Bodhisatta's robe was not stirred, nor did a single drop of water reach him. Then Mara cast down upon him showers of rocks, and a storm of deadly and poisoned weapons, burning ashes and coals, and a storm of scorching sand and flaming mud; but all these missiles only fell at the Bodhisatta's feet as a rain of heavenly flowers, or hung in the air like a canopy above his head. Nor could he be moved by an onset of thick and fourfold darkness. Then finding all these means to fail, he addressed the Bodhisatta and said: "Arise, Siddhattha, from that seat, for it is not thine, but mine!" The Bodhisatta replied, "Mara! thou hast not accomplished the Ten Perfections, nor even the minor virtues. Thou hast not sought for knowledge, nor for the salvation of the world. The seat is mine." Then Mara was enraged, and cast at the Bodhisatta his Sceptre-javelin, which cleaves asunder a pillar of solid rock like a tender shoot of cane: and all the demon hosts hurled masses of rock. But the javelin hung in the air like a canopy, and the masses of rock fell down as garlands of flowers.

Then the Great Being said to Mara: "Mara, who is the witness that thou hast given alms?" Mara stretched forth his hand, and a shout arose from the demon hosts, of a thousand voices crying: "I am his witness!" Then the Fiend addressed the Bodhisatta, and enquired: "Siddhattha! who is the witness that thou has given alms?" and the Great Being answered: "Mara thou hast many and living witnesses that thou hast given alms, and no such witnesses have I. But apart from the alms I have given in other births, I call upon this solid earth to witness to my supernatural generosity when I was born as Vessantara." And drawing his right hand from his robe, he stretched it forth to touch the earth, and said: "Do you or do you not witness to my supernatural generosity when I was born as Vessantara?" And the great Earth replied with a voice of thunder: "I am witness of that." And

---

[1] "The sages of old first got Tao for themselves, and then got it for others. Before you possess this yourself, what leisure have you to attend to the doings of wicked men?" — Chuang Tzu [Coomaraswamy's note].

thereat the great elephant of Mara bowed down in adoration, and the demon hosts fled far away in dread.

Then Mara was abashed. But he did not withdraw, for he hoped to accomplish by another means what he could not effect by force: he summoned his three daughters, Tanha, Rati, and Raga, and they danced before the Bodhisatta like the swaying branches of a young leafy tree, using all the arts of seduction known to beautiful women. Again they offered him the lordship of the earth, and the companionship of beautiful girls: they appealed to him with songs of the season of spring, and exhibited their supernatural beauty and grace. But the Bodhisatta's heart was not in the least moved, and he answered:

Pleasure is brief as a flash of lightning
Or like an Autumn shower, only for a moment . . .
Why should I then covet the pleasures you speak of?
I see your bodies are full of all impurity:
Birth and death, sickness and age are yours.
I seek the highest prize, hard to attain by men —
The true and constant wisdom of the wise.

And when they could not shake the Bodhisatta's calm, they were filled with shame, and abashed: and they made a prayer to the Bodhisatta, wishing him the fruition of his labour:

That which your heart desires, may you attain,
And finding for yourself deliverance, deliver all![2]

And now the hosts of heaven, seeing the army of Mara defeated, and the wiles of the daughters of Mara vain, assembled to honour the Conqueror, they came to the foot of the Tree of Wisdom and cried for joy:

The Blessed Buddha — he hath prevailed!
And the Tempter is overthrown!

The victory was achieved while the sun was yet above the horizon. The Bodhisatta sank into ever deeper and deeper thought. In

[2] According to other books the temptation by the daughters of Mara is subsequent to the Supreme Enlightenment. In Plate A the Temptation by the Daughters of Mara takes place in the fifth week of the Forty-nine Days [Coomaraswamy's note].

the first watch of the night he reached the Knowledge of Former States of being, in the middle watch he obtained the heavenly eye of Omniscient Vision, and in the third watch he grasped the perfect understanding of the Chain of Causation which is the Origin of Evil, and thus at break of day he attained to Perfect Enlightenment. Therewith there broke from his lips the song of triumph:

Through many divers births I passed
Seeking in vain the builder of the house.[3]

But O framer of houses, thou art found—
Never again shalt thou fashion a house for me!
Broken are all thy beams,
The king-post shattered!
My mind has passed into the stillness of Nibbana
The ending of desire has been attained at last!

Innumerable wonders were manifest at this supreme hour. The earth quaked six times, and the whole universe was illuminated by the supernatural splendour of the sixfold rays that proceeded from the body of the seated Buddha. Resentment faded from the hearts of all men, all lack was supplied, the sick were healed, the chains of hell were loosed, and every creature of whatsoever sort found peace and rest.

Gautama, who was now Buddha, the Enlightened, remained seated and motionless for seven days, realizing the bliss of Nibbana; and thereafter rising, he remained standing for seven days more, steadfastly regarding the spot where had been won the fruit of countless deeds of heroic virtue performed in past births: then for seven days more he paced to and fro along a cloistered path from West to East, extending from the throne beneath the Wisdom Tree to the place of the Steadfast Gazing; and again for seven days he remained seated in a god-wrought pavilion near to the same place, and there reviewed in detail, book by book, all that is taught in the *Abhidhamma Pitaka*, as well as the whole doctrine of causality; then for seven days more he sat beneath the Nigrodha tree of Sujata's offering, meditating

[3] The house is, of course, the house—or rather the prison—of individual existence: the builder of the house is desire (*tankā*)—the will to enjoy and possess [Coomaraswamy's note].

on the doctrine and the sweetness of Nibbana—and according to some books it was at this time the temptation by the daughters of Mara took place; and then for seven days more while a terrible storm was raging, the snake king Mucalinda sheltered him with his sevenfold hood; and for seven days more he sat beneath a Rajayatana tree, still enjoying the sweetness of liberation.

And so passed away seven weeks, during which the Buddha experienced no bodily wants, but fed on the joy of contemplation, the joy of the Eightfold Path, and the joy of its fruit, Nibbana.

Only upon the last day of the seven weeks he desired to bathe and eat, and receiving water and a tooth-stick from the god Sakka, the Buddha bathed his face and seated himself at the foot of a tree. Now at that time two Brahman merchants were travelling with a caravan from Orissa to the middle country, and a Deva, who had been a blood relation of the merchants' in a former life, stopped the carts, and moved their hearts to make an offering of rice and honey cakes to the Lord. They went up to him accordingly, saying: "O Blessed One, have mercy upon us, and accept this food." Now the Buddha no longer possessed a bowl, and as the Buddhas never receive an offering in their hands, he reflected how he should take it. Immediately the Four Great Kings, the Regents of the Quarters appeared before him, each of them with a bowl; and in order that none of them should be disappointed, the Buddha received the four bowls, and placing them one above the other made them to be one, showing only the four lines round the mouth, and in this bowl the Blessed One received the food, and ate it, and gave thanks. The two merchants took refuge in the Buddha, the Norm, and the Order, and became professed disciples. Then the Buddha rose up and returned again to the tree of Sujata's offering and there took his seat. And there, reflecting upon the depth of truth which he had found, a doubt arose in his mind whether it would be possible to make it known to others: and this doubt is experienced by every Buddha when be becomes aware of the Truth. But Maha Brahma exclaiming: "Alas! the world will be altogether lost!" came thither in haste, with all the Deva hosts, and besought the Master to proclaim the Truth; and he granted their prayer.[4, 5]

---

[4] "Great truths do not take hold of the hearts of the masses. . . . And now, as all the world is in error, I, though I know the true path—how shall I, how shall I guide? If I know that I cannot succeed and yet try to force success, this would be but another source of error. Better, then, to desist and strive no more. But if I

MILAREPA
Tibetian

Milarepa is a follower of Buddha, and his withdrawal, too, is a quest for freedom from the material and for total knowledge of the "unknown."

1
When named I am the man apart;
I am the sage of Tibet;
I am Milarepa.
I hear little but counsel much;   5
I reflect little but persevere much;
I sleep little but endure in meditation much.
My narrow bed gives me ease to stretch & bend;
my thin clothing makes my body warm;
my scanty fare satisfies my belly.   10
Knowing one thing I have experience of all things;
knowing all things I comprehend them to be one.
I am the goal of every great meditator;
I am the meeting place of the faithful;
I am the coil of birth & death & decay.   15
I have no preference for any country;
I have no home in any place;
I have no store of provisions for my livelihood.
I have no fondness for material things;
I make no distinction between clean & unclean in food;   20
I have little torment of suffering.
I have little desire for self-esteem;
I have little attachment or bias;
I have found the freedom of Nirvana.
I am the comforter of the aged;   25
I am the madman who counts death happiness;
I am the playmate of children.

strive not, who will?" – Chuang Tzu. It is highly characteristic of the psychology of genius that when this doubt assails the Buddha he nevertheless immediately responds to a definite request for guidance; the moment the pupil puts the right questions, the teacher's doubts are resolved [Coomaraswamy's note].
  [5] Ananda Coomaraswamy, *Buddha and the Gospel of Buddhism*, pp. 30–38.

2

When the tiger-year was ending
& the hare-year beginning
on the sixth day of the month of the barking of the fox,
I grew weary of the things of this world;   5
& in my yearning for solitude
I came to the sanctuary wilderness, Mount Everest.
Then heaven & earth took counsel together
& sent forth the whirlwind as messenger.
The elements of wind & water seethed   10
& the dark clouds of the south rolled up in concert;
the sun & the moon were made prisoner
& the twenty-eight constellations of the moon were fastened
    together;
the eight planets in their courses were cast into chains   15
& the faint milky way was delivered into bondage;
the little stars were altogether shrouded in mist
& when all things were covered in the complexion of mist
for nine days & nine nights the snow fell,
steadily throughout the eighteen times of day & night it fell.   20
When it fell heavily the flakes were as big as the flock of wool,
& fell floating like feathered birds.
When the snow fell lightly the flakes were small as spindles,
& fell circling like bees.
Again, they were as small as peas or mustard-seed,   25
& fell turning like distaffs.
Moreover the snow surpassed measure in depth,
the peak of white snow above reached to the heavens
& the trees of the forest below were bowed down.
The dark hills were clad in white,   30
ice formed upon the billowing lakes
& the blue Tsangpo was constrained in its depths.
The earth became like a plain without hill or valley,
& in natural consequence of such a great fall
the lay folk were mewed up;   35
famine overtook the four-footed cattle,
& the small deer especially found no food;
the feathered birds above lacked nourishment,
& the marmots & field-mice below hid in their burrows;
the jaws of beasts of prey were stiffened together.   40

94

In such fearsome circumstances
this strange fate befell me, Milarepa.
There were these three: the snowstorm driving down from on
    high,
the icy blast of mid-winter,   5
& the cotton cloth which I, the sage Mila, wore;
& between them rose a contest on that white snow peak.
The falling snow melted into goodly water;
the wind, though rushing mightily, abated of itself,
& the cotton cloth blazed like fire.   10
Life & death wrestled there after the fashion of champions,
& swords crossed victorious blades.
That I won there the heroic fight
will be an example to all the faithful
& a true example to all great contemplatives;   15
more especially will it prove the greater excellence
of the single cotton cloth & the inner heat.

3
That the white ice-peak of Tise, great in fame,
is just a mountain covered with snow,   20
proves the whiteness of Buddha's teaching.
That the turquoise lake of Mapang, great in fame,
is water through which water flows,
proves the dissolution of all created things.
That I, Milarepa, great in fame,   25
am an old & naked man,
proves that I have forsaken & set at nought self-interest.
That I am a singer of little songs,
proves that I have learned to read the world as a book.[1]

[1] Jerome Rothenberg, ed., *Technicians of the Sacred*, pp. 251–254.

JESUS
Christian

Jesus, in keeping with the Oriental tradition, withdraws for a period of fasting and self-examination. Like the Buddha, he is tempted by the illusory values of the world. His inner strength prevails.

In those days came John the Baptist, preaching in the wilderness of Judea, and saying, Repent ye: for the kingdom of heaven is at hand. For this is he that was spoken of by the prophet Isaiah, saying,

The voice of one crying in the wilderness, 5
Prepare ye the way of the Lord,
make his paths straight.

And the same John had his raiment of camel's hair, and a leathern girdle about his loins, and his meat was locusts and wild honey. Then went out to him Jerusalem, and all Judea, and all 10 the region round about Jordan, and were baptized of him in Jordan, confessing their sins.

But when he saw many of the Pharisees and Sadducees come to his baptism, he said unto them, O generation of vipers, who hath warned you to flee from the wrath to come? Bring forth 15 therefore fruits meet for repentance: and think not to say within yourselves, We have Abraham to our father: for I say unto you, that God is able of these stones to raise up children unto Abraham. And now also the axe is laid unto the root of the trees: therefore every tree which bringeth not forth good fruit is hewn 20 down, and cast into the fire.

I indeed baptize you with water unto repentance: but he that cometh after me is mightier than I, whose shoes I am not worthy to bear: he shall baptize you with the Holy Ghost, and with fire: whose fan is in his hand, and he will thoroughly purge his floor, 25 and gather his wheat into the garner; but he will burn up the chaff with unquenchable fire.

Then cometh Jesus from Galilee to Jordan unto John, to be baptized of him. But John forbade him, saying, I have need to be baptized of thee, and comest thou to me? And Jesus answering 30 said unto him, Suffer it to be so now: for thus it becometh us to fulfil all righteousness. Then he suffered him. And Jesus, when he was baptized, went up straightway out of the water: and, lo, the heavens were opened unto him, and he saw the Spirit of God descending like a dove, and lighting upon him: and lo a voice from heaven, saying, This is my beloved Son, in whom I am well pleased. 5

Then was Jesus led up of the Spirit into the wilderness to be tempted of the devil. And when he had fasted forty days and forty nights, he was afterward ahungered. And when the tempter came to him, he said, If thou be the Son of God, command that these stones be made bread. But he answered and said, It is 10 written,

Man shall not live by bread alone,

but by every word that proceedeth out of the mouth of God. Then the devil taketh him up into the holy city, and setteth him on a pinnacle of the temple, and saith unto him, If thou be the 15 Son of God, cast thyself down: for it is written,

He shall give his angels charge concerning thee:

and in their hands they shall bear thee up,

lest at any time thou dash thy foot against a stone.

Jesus said unto him, It is written again, Thou shalt not tempt the 20 Lord thy God. Again, the devil taketh him up into an exceeding high mountain, and showeth him all the kingdoms of the world, and the glory of them; and saith unto him, All these things will I give thee, if thou wilt fall down and worship me. Then saith Jesus unto him, Get thee hence, Satan: for it is written, 25

Thou shalt worship the Lord thy God,

and him only shalt thou serve.

Then the devil leaveth him, and, behold, angels came and ministered unto him.[1]

[1] Matthew 3, 4.

MOSES
Judaic

Moses is called for the traditional forty days and nights to a place of seclusion where God can properly reveal his laws. Only prophets, such as Moses, are granted the vision of true reality, which is God.

And he said unto Moses, Come up unto the LORD, thou, and Aaron, Nadab, and Abihu, and seventy of the elders of Israel; and worship ye afar off.

And Moses alone shall come near the LORD: but they shall not come nigh; neither shall the people go up with him.   5

And Moses came and told the people all the words of the LORD, and all the judgments: and all the people answered with one voice, and said, All the words which the LORD hath said will we do.

And Moses wrote all the words of the LORD, and rose up early 10 in the morning, and builded an altar under the hill, and twelve pillars, according to the twelve tribes of Israel.

And he sent young men of the children of Israel, which offered burnt offerings, and sacrificed peace offerings of oxen unto the LORD.   15

And Moses took half of the blood, and put it in basins: and half of the blood he sprinkled on the altar.

And he took the book of the covenant, and read in the audience of the people: and they said, All that the LORD hath said will we do, and be obedient.   20

And Moses took the blood, and sprinkled it on the people, and said, Behold the blood of the covenant which the LORD hath made with you concerning all these words.

Then went up Moses, and Aaron, Nadab, and Abihu, and seventy of the elders of Israel: 25

And they saw the God of Israel: and there was under his feet as it were a paved work of a sapphire stone, and as it were the body of heaven in his clearness.

And upon the nobles of the children of Israel he laid not his hand: also they saw God, and did eat and drink.   30

And the LORD said unto Moses, Come up to me into the mount, and be there: and I will give thee tables of stone, and a law, and commandments which I have written; that thou mayest teach them.

And Moses rose up, and his minister Joshua: and Moses went up into the mount of God.

And he said unto the elders, Tarry ye here for us, until we come again unto you: and, behold, Aaron and Hur are with you: if any man have any matters to do, let him come unto them.

And Moses went up into the mount, and a cloud covered the mount.

And the glory of the LORD abode upon mount Sinai, and the cloud covered it six days: and the seventh day he called unto Moses out of the midst of the cloud.

And the sight of the glory of the LORD was like devouring fire on the top of the mount in the eyes of the children of Israel.

And Moses went into the midst of the cloud, and gat him up into the mount: and Moses was in the mount forty days and forty nights.[1]

_____

[1] Exodus 24.

ISAAC TENS
Gitksan Indian

In many "primitive" societies the shaman or medicine man fills the role of the prophet-seer-hero. Only he experiences fully the terror and ecstasy of communion with the unknown.

Thirty years after my birth was the time.

I went up into the hills to get firewood. While I was cutting up the wood into lengths, it grew dark towards the evening. Before I had finished my last stack of wood, a loud noise broke out over me, chu------, & a large owl appeared to me. The owl took hold of me, caught my face, & tried to lift me up. I lost consciousness. As soon as I came back to my senses I realized that I had fallen into the snow. My head was coated with ice, & some blood was running out of my mouth.

I stood up & went down the trail, walking very fast, with some wood packed on my back. On my way, the trees seemed to shake & to lean over me; tall trees were crawling after me, as if they had been snakes. I could see them.

At my father's home . . . I fell into a sort of trance. It seems that two shamans were working over me to bring me back to health. . . . When I woke up & opened my eyes, I thought that flies covered my face completely. I looked down, & instead of being on firm ground, I felt that I was drifting in a huge whirlpool. My heart was thumping fast.

Another time, I went to my hunting grounds on the other side of the river. . . . I caught two fishers in my traps, took their pelts, & threw the flesh & bones away. Farther along I looked for a bear's den amid the tall trees. As I glanced upwards, I saw an owl, at the top of a high cedar. I shot it, & it fell down in the bushes close to me. When I went to pick it up, it had disappeared. Not a feather was left; this seemed very strange. I walked down to the river, crossed over the ice, & returned to the village at Gitenmaks. Upon arriving at my fishing station on the point, I heard the noise of a crowd of people around the smoke-house, as if I were being chased away, pursued. I dared not look behind to find out what all this was about, but I hurried straight ahead. The voices followed in my tracks & came very close behind me. Then I wheeled around & looked back. There was no one in sight, only

trees. A trance came over me once more, & I fell down, unconscious. When I came to, my head was buried in a snowbank.

I got up & walked on the ice up the river to the village. There
I met my father who had just come out to look for me, for he had
missed me. We went back together to my house. Then my heart   5
started to beat fast, & I began to tremble, just as had happened
before, when the shamans were trying to fix me up. My flesh
seemed to be boiling, & I could hear s^u———. My body was quivering.
*While I remained in this state, I began to sing. A chant was
coming out of me without my being able to do anything to stop*   10
it. Many things appeared to me presently: huge birds & other
animals. . . . These were visible only to me, not to the others in
my house. Such visions happen when a man is about to become
a shaman; they occur of their own accord. The songs force
themselves out complete without any attempt to compose   15
them. But I learned & memorized those songs by repeating
them.

First Song
Death of the salmon,
my death   20

but the city
finds life in it

the salmon floats
in the canyon

ghosts in the city   25
below me

the robin cries over
my head &

this robin, the
woman I fly with   30

Second Song
where the dead sing, where
the grizzly

hides in the sky
& I watch him circle   35

101

the door to my house
swing shut   fires

are burning
beneath it   hard

vision, their faces
of faces in a crowd

Third Song
in mud to my knees,
a lake

where the shellfish
hold me, is

cutting my ankles,
in death

Fourth Song
a boat, a stranger's
boat, a canoe

& myself inside it, a
stranger inside it

it floats past trees,
past water

runs among
whirlpools

Fifth Song
& vision: beehives
were stinging my body

or the ghosts of bees,
giants

& the old woman
working me

until I grew   listened
in dreams, in her head[1]

---

[1] Jerome Rothenberg, ed., *Technicians of the Sacred*, pp. 50–53.

WUNZH

Ojibwa Indian

Wunzh's withdrawal is the prototype for the vigil of Hiawatha in Longfellow's poem and for the initiatory ceremony which all Indian youths underwent. The gift of corn—Mondawmin—is the symbol of all that is to be gained by communion with the Great Spirit.

In times past, a poor Indian was living with his wife and children in a beautiful part of the country. He was not only poor, but inexpert in procuring food for his family, and his children were all too young to give him assistance. Although poor, he was a man of a kind and contented disposition. He was always thank- 5
ful to the Great Spirit for everything he received. The same disposition was inherited by his eldest son, who had now arrived at the proper age to undertake the ceremony of the Keiguishimowin, or fast, to see what kind of a spirit would be his guide and guardian through life. Wunzh, for this was his name, had been an 10
obedient boy from his infancy, and was of a pensive, thoughtful, and mild disposition, so that he was beloved by the whole family. As soon as the first indications of spring appeared, they built him the customary little lodge at a retired spot, some distance from their own, where he would not be disturbed during this solemn 15
rite. In the mean time he prepared himself, and immediately went into it, and commenced his fast. The first few days, he amused himself, in the mornings, by walking in the woods and over the mountains, examining the early plants and flowers, and in this way prepared himself to enjoy his sleep, and, at the same 20
time, stored his mind with pleasant ideas for his dreams. While he rambled through the woods, he felt a strong desire to know how the plants, herbs, and berries grew, without any aid from man, and why it was that some species were good to eat, and others possessed medicinal or poisonous juices. He recalled these 25
thoughts to mind after he became too languid to walk about, and had confined himself strictly to the lodge; he wished he could dream of something that would prove a benefit to his father and family, and to all others. "True!" he thought, "the Great Spirit made all things, and it is to him that we owe our lives. But could 30
he not make it easier for us to get our food, than by hunting ani-

mals and taking fish? I must try to find out this in my visions."

On the third day he became weak and faint, and kept his bed. He fancied, while thus lying, that he saw a handsome young man coming down from the sky and advancing towards him. He was richly and gayly dressed, having on a great many garments of green and yellow colors, but differing in their deeper or lighter shades. He had a plume of waving feathers on his head, and all his motions were graceful.

"I am sent to you, my friend," said the celestial visitor, "by that Great Spirit who made all things in the sky and on the earth. He has seen and knows your motives in fasting. He sees that it is from a kind and benevolent wish to do good to your people, and to procure a benefit for them, and that you do not seek for strength in war or the praise of warriors. I am sent to instruct you, and show you how you can do your kindred good." He then told the young man to arise, and prepare to wrestle with him, as it was only by this means that he could hope to succeed in his wishes. Wunzh knew he was weak from fasting, but he felt his courage rising in his heart, and immediately got up, determined to die rather than fail. He commenced the trial, and after a protracted effort, was almost exhausted, when the beautiful stranger said, "My friend, it is enough for once; I will come again to try you;" and, smiling on him, he ascended in the air in the same direction from which he came. The next day the celestial visitor reappeared at the same hour and renewed the trial. Wunzh felt that his strength was even less than the day before, but the courage of his mind seemed to increase in proportion as his body became weaker. Seeing this, the stranger again spoke to him in the same words he used before, adding, "Tomorrow will be your last trial. Be strong, my friend, for this is the only way you can overcome me, and obtain the boon you seek." On the third day he again appeared at the same time and renewed the struggle. The poor youth was very faint in body, but grew stronger in mind at every contest, and was determined to prevail or perish in the attempt. He exerted his utmost powers, and after the contest had been continued the usual time, the stranger ceased his efforts and declared himself conquered. For the first time he entered the lodge, and sitting down beside the youth, he began to deliver his instructions to him, telling him in what manner he should proceed to take advantage of his victory.

"You have won your desires of the Great Spirit," said the

stranger. "You have wrestled manfully. To-morrow will be the seventh day of your fasting. Your father will give you food to strengthen you, and as it is the last day of trial, you will prevail. I know this, and now tell you what you must do to benefit your family and your tribe. To-morrow," he repeated, "I shall meet you and wrestle with you for the last time; and, as soon as you have prevailed against me, you will strip off my garments and throw me down, clean the earth of roots and weeds, make it soft, and bury me in the spot. When you have done this, leave my body in the earth, and do not disturb it, but come occasionally to visit the place, to see whether I have come to life, and be careful never to let the grass or weeds grow on my grave. Once a month cover me with fresh earth. If you follow my instructions, you will accomplish your object of doing good to your fellow-creatures by teaching them the knowledge I now teach you." He then shook him by the hand and disappeared.

In the morning the youth's father came with some slight refreshments, saying, "My son, you have fasted long enough. If the Great Spirit will favor you, he will do it now. It is seven days since you have tasted food, and you must not sacrifice your life. The Master of Life does not require that." "My father," replied the youth, "wait till the sun goes down. I have a particular reason for extending my fast to that hour." "Very well," said the old man, "I shall wait till the hour arrives, and you feel inclined to eat."

At the usual hour of the day the sky-visitor returned, and the trial of strength was renewed. Although the youth had not availed himself of his father's offer of food, he felt that new strength had been given to him, and that exertion had renewed his strength and fortified his courage. He grasped his angelic antagonist with supernatural strength, threw him down, took from him his beautiful garments and plume, and finding him dead, immediately buried him on the spot, taking all the precautions he had been told of, and being very confident, at the same time, that his friend would again come to life. He then returned to his father's lodge, and partook sparingly of the meal that had been prepared for him. But he never for a moment forgot the grave of his friend. He carefully visited it throughout the spring, and weeded out the grass, and kept the ground in a soft and pliant state. Very soon he saw the tops of the green plumes coming through the ground; and the more careful he was to obey his instructions in keeping the ground in order, the faster they grew. He was, however, careful to conceal the exploit from his father. Days and weeks had passed in this way. The summer was now drawing towards a close, when one day, after a long absence in hunting, Wunzh invited his father to follow him to the quiet and lonesome spot of his former fast. The lodge had been removed, and the weeds kept 5 from growing on the circle where it stood, but in its place stood a tall and graceful plant, with bright-colored silken hair, surmounted with nodding plumes and stately leaves, and golden clusters on each side. "It is my friend," shouted the lad; "it is the friend of all mankind. It is *Mondawmin*.[1] We need no longer 10 rely on hunting alone; for, as long as this gift is cherished and taken care of, the ground itself will give us a living." He then pulled an ear. "See, my father," said he, "this is what I fasted for. The great Spirit has listened to my voice, and sent us something new,[2] and henceforth our people will not alone depend upon the 15 chase or upon the waters."

He then communicated to his father the instructions given him by the stranger. He told him that the broad husks must be torn away, as he had pulled off the garments in his wrestling; and having done this, directed him how the ear must be held before 20 the fire till the outer skin became brown, while all the milk was retained in the grain. The whole family then united in a feast on the newly-grown ears, expressing gratitude to the Merciful Spirit who gave it. So corn came into the world.[3]

[1] The Algic name for corn. The word is manifestly a trinary compound from *monedo*, spirit; *min*, a grain or berry; and *iaw*, the verb substantive [Schoolcraft's note].

[2] The Zea mays, it will be recollected, is indigenous to America, and was unknown in Europe before 1495 [Schoolcraft's note].

[3] H. R. Schoolcraft, *The Myth of Hiawatha and Other Oral Legends Mythologic and Allegoric of the North American Indians*, pp. 99–104.

PLEIADES
Australian Aboriginal

The maidens of this tale, like Wunzh, practice withdrawal from the comforts of life in return for a greater boon. Their story is also a quest myth and an apotheosis.

In various parts of the world and among different races there are traditions that the lustre of the Pleiades is associated with acts in which women were concerned. There is an Australian legend on the subject. According to this story, it was the girls who had reached the age of adolescence who perceived the necessity 5 for bringing the body under subjection to the mind in order to restrain physical appetite and control the effects of pain and fear. They saw that without such control there could be no real racial advancement. Accordingly, they presented themselves to the elders of the tribe in order to undergo the trial by ordeal. The 10 elders explained to the girls that the test that they would have to submit to was a severe one. The girls, however, were firm in their resolve to undergo it. So every morning for three years, in a place apart from their brothers and sisters, the elders, to teach them moderation, gave them a small portion of the usual food, consist- 15 ing perhaps of a piece of fish or flesh of the emu, kangaroo, or wombat. This they received twice a day, at the hour of sunrise and at the hour of sunset. At the end of the third year they were taken for a long journey through the dense bush, where the thorns scratched their flesh, and across the plains and rivers, 20 travelling during the heat of the day, often almost fainting from fatigue, but ever pressing onward. After a week of such journeying had passed the elders called the girls before them and inquired whether they thought they were better able to control the appetite. To this the girls replied, "Our minds are made up. We 25 will control the appetite." The elders then said, "You are asked to fast for three days, and during this fasting time we will all travel."

So the girls set out with the elders on the journey. The way was long and difficult, and they were weak from lack of food. The 30 blazing sun seemed to them more ruthless and the way more rough and thorny than usual, but they were determined to conquer, and so they kept on their way undaunted. On the evening of the third day they arrived at the appointed camping-ground. The elders prepared the food for them for the following day. On the fourth morning they were given a flint knife, and were instructed to cut from the kangaroo or emu the amount of food they required. How tempting was the smell of the roasted flesh to the girls, who had travelled unceasingly for three days without breaking their fast! The temptation to cut a generous portion and satisfy the craving for food was very great. But each cut for herself only an ordinary portion. The elders praised the girls for their restraint. They said, "You have acquitted yourselves well so far; and now there are other appetites, and it is for you to control them as you have controlled your hunger." They replied, "We are ready to undergo any tests you please. Our minds are made up to subdue appetite and to conquer inclination." They then submitted themselves to various tests in order to learn to control other appetites, each test being more difficult than the former. In every case they were successful.

When the elders told them that it was necessary to overcome pain they again submitted themselves to their guidance, and the elders decided the particular form of discipline that the girls should undergo. In the presence of the other girls and boys they took the girls away to a selected spot, where all sacred ceremonies were performed. They ordered them to lie upon the ground. Then they took a stone axe and a pointed stick about eight or nine inches long. They told the girls one by one to open their mouths. The elders placed the point of a stick against a front tooth of each, then raised an axe and brought it down upon the stick, breaking the tooth off, and leaving the nerves exposed and quivering. The girls then rose from the ground, and sat awaiting the further commands of the elders. They were asked whether they felt the pain, to which they replied, "Yes, we felt the pain." Then the elders said, "Are you willing to have another tooth knocked out?" And the girls replied, "Yes, our minds are made up. We are going to control pain." And again the elders asked at the conclusion of this test, "Are you willing to undergo more severe testing?" The girls replied as before, "Yes, our minds are made up. We will control pain." They were then led to another camping-ground and commanded to stand in a row. An elder of the tribe approached with a flint knife. He stood before each of the girls for a while, and then drew the knife silently across her breast, and the blood flowed. This he did to each girl in succession. Another elder took the ashes of a particular kind of wood, and rubbed them into the wound. The effect of this was twofold; it intensified the pain, and helped to heal the wound.

A day or two was given to allow the wounds to heal, and then the elders called the girls before them and inquired if they were still willing to submit themselves to further testing. They replied, "Yes, we are willing to go through any tests. Our minds are made up." The elders then went alone through the bush and selected another camping-ground for the girls. At bed-time they were led to the spot, and told, "It is time to retire to rest. This is your camping-ground." The girls, weary and eager for rest, threw their opposum rugs on the ground. The night was dark and moonless and very warm. They lay there for a little while, and presently they felt things crawling over their bodies. They were afraid, but they refused to give way to fear. It may have been that each girl was afraid of what the others would think of her if she failed, and that thus each helped the others to be brave. By and by they discovered they were lying on a bed of ants. All through the night they lay there with the ants swarming over them. The time seemed very long. These girls had journeyed far, fasting, and their poor bodies were still tender with half-healed wounds. In the morning they presented themselves to the elders, smiling and showing no signs of the terrible night that they had passed.

Still their journey continued, and they underwent further tests, such as the piercing of the nose and the wearing of a stick through it to keep the wound open. Further, they were bidden to lie on a bed of hot cinders. Before each fresh trial they were asked if they were willing to undergo the tests. Their reply, which never varied, was, "Yes, we have made up our minds to conquer pain."

Now the elders were very pleased with the girls, and very proud of the powers of endurance that they showed, but they realized that it was necessary for them to overcome fear as well as the appetites and pain, so they called them together and said, "Girls! You have done very well, and have proved that you possess wonderful courage and endurance. The next stage is the control of fear. Do you wish to continue on the way?" The girls stood there in all their youth, and with glowing eyes; and they repeated the old phrase, "Yes, our minds are made up. We will conquer fear."

On a fresh camping-ground in the dark night, with the camp-fires gleaming on the trees, and casting dark, gloomy shadows, the elders told them tales about the *bunyip* and the *muldarpe.* This latter is a spirit which assumes many shapes. It may come as a kangaroo, or a wombat, or a lizard. The girls were told fearful stories of these dreadful beings, and of ghosts, to which they listened tremblingly. The more highly strung among them could scarcely refrain from crying out. They found themselves looking over their shoulders, and imagining that the dark shadows were the *bunyip* or the *muldarpe* or other spirits For hours they listened, until it was time to go to bed. After the elders had made the sign of good-night they told them that the place where they were camping was the burial-place of their great-grandfathers. They lay down to sleep, resolved not to be afraid of any ghosts or spirits.

Then the elders crept round the camp, making weird noises, so that the hair of the girls rose and their blood ran cold. Besides these sounds there were the usual bush-noises, such as the howl of the dingo, the shriek of the owl, and the falling of the decayed branches. But the girls were not to be turned from their purpose, and they lay there until the break of day. Then they rose and presented themselves to the elders, showing no signs of their disturbed night, their faces placid and their eyes clear and shining. The elders knew that the girls had conquered fear, and they rejoiced with pride. They sent out invitations to the adjoining tribes, and they made great rejoicing, and held many corrobberies in honour of the girls.

But the girls were not content with having conquered the appetites and pain and fear. They desired that their sisters should do the same. So the leader of the girls stepped out from the group, and said to the girls of the assembled tribes, "We have passed through the testing that our elders prescribed, and we have endured much pain. Now it is the desire of the Great Spirit that you should go through the same course of testing. You must know that the selfish person is not happy. This is because he thinks only of himself. Happiness comes through thinking of others and forgetting self. Greed and pain and fear are caused by thinking too much of self, and so it is necessary to vanquish self. Will you not go and do as we have done?" The girls of the other tribes eagerly assented, so proud were they of the victory of their sisters.

Then the Great Spirit was so pleased with them that he sent a great star spirit to convey the girls to the heavens without death or further suffering, in order that they might shine there as a pat-

110

tern and a symbol to their race. And on clear nights ever since that time the aboriginals look into the sky and revere this wonderful constellation, the Seven Sisters, and remember what the girls did, and always think of the story of how there came to be given to them a place in the heavens.[1]

5

[1] W. Ramsay Smith, *Myths and Legends of the Australian Aboriginals*, pp. 345–350.

PERCIVAL
European

As Wunzh is given corn, Percival in the Castle of Gurnemann receives the gift of true knighthood. Only after this preparation can he return to the world as a hero.

After Percival had ridden a long way he came to the castle of Gurnemann, an elderly man and a brave warrior. The old chief asked the youth to come in and spend the night under his roof, and Percival accepted the invitation with pleasure. He was so taken with his host's kindly manner, that before the evening was over he felt drawn to tell him of his mother and all his adventures since he had left her. Gurnemann persuaded the lad to remain with him for some time, and began to teach him how to become a true knight and hero.

"Do not always have your mother's name upon your lips," he would say, "for it sounds childish. Preserve her teaching faithfully in your heart, and you will please her more than by talking of her continually. A knight should be modest, love one maiden only, not play at love with many women. He should help the oppressed, and show kindness to all. When he has conquered an enemy he should show mercy; and when he is conquered he should not beg for life. To face death boldly is a hero's glory, and such death is better than a dishonoured life."

With these and other words of wisdom the old man strove to fit the youth for knighthood. At the same time he gave him fitting clothes, telling him it was no disrespect to his mother to cease to wear the curious garments with which she had provided him. Time passed on, and Percival proved such an apt pupil that Gurnemann grew as proud of him as if he had been his own son.

At last he told the youth that the time had come for him to go out into the world and draw his sword in defense of innocence and right, for Queen Konduiramur was hard pressed in her capital, Belripar, by the wild chief Klamide and his seneschal Kingram. Percival was nothing loath, and at once prepared to go and help the queen.[1]

---

[1] W. Wägner, *Romances and Epics of Our Northern Ancestors*, pp. 300–301.

MOHAMMED (MOHAMMAD)
Arabic

*The cave is a womblike place of preparation for a second birth.
Mohammed withdraws there to achieve security in the face of
his enemies and to feel the real presence of Allah. He emerges
with a new sense of unity with the unknown.*

Mohammad was now approaching his fortieth year. Always
pensive, he had of late become even more thoughtful and retiring. Contemplation and reflection engaged his mind. The debase-
ment of his people pressed heavily on him; the dim and imperfect
shadows of Judaism and Christianity excited doubts without sat- 5
isfying them; and his soul was perplexed with uncertainty as to
what was the true religion. Thus burdened, he frequently retired
to seek relief in meditation amongst the solitary valleys and rocks
near Mecca. His favourite spot was a cave in the declivities at the
foot of mount Hira, a lofty conical hill two or three miles north 10
of Mecca. Thither he would retire for days at a time; and his
faithful wife sometimes accompanied him. The continued solitude, instead of stilling his anxiety, magnified into sterner and
more impressive shapes the solemn realities which agitated his
soul. Close by was the grave of the aged Zeid, who, after spending 15
a lifetime in the same inquiries, had now passed into the state of
certainty; — might he himself not reach the same assurance
without crossing the gate of death?
All around was bleak and rugged. To the east and south, the
vision from the cave of Hira is bounded by lofty mountain ranges, 20
but to the north and west the weary prospect is thus described by
Burckhardt: — 'The country before us had a dreary aspect, not a
single green spot being visible; barren, black, and grey hills, and
white sandy valleys, were the only objects in sight.' There was
harmony here between external nature, and the troubled world 25
within. By degrees the impulsive and susceptible mind of Mohammad was wrought up to the highest pitch of excitement; and
he would give vent to his agitation in wild rhapsodical language,
enforced often with incoherent oaths, the counterpart of inward
struggling after truth. The following fragments [from the Koran] 30
belong probably to this period: —

By the declining day I swear!
Verily, man is in the way of ruin;
Excepting such as possess faith,
And do the things which are right,
And stir up one another unto truth and steadfastness.   5

And again —

By the rushing panting steeds!
Striking fire with flashing hoof,
That scour the land at early morn!
And, darkening it with dust,   10
Cleave thereby the Enemy!
Verily Man is to his Lord ungrateful,
And he himself is witness of it.
Verily he is keen after this world's good.
Ah! witteth he not that when what is in the graves shall be brought forth, 15
And that which is in men's breasts laid bare; —
Verily in that day shall the Lord be well informed of them.

Nor was he wanting in prayer for guidance to the great Being
who, he felt, alone could give it. The following petitions (though
probably adapted subsequently to public worship) contain per-   20
haps the germ of frequent prayer at this early period.

Praise be to God, the Lord of creation,
The most merciful, the most compassionate!
Ruler of the day of Reckoning!
Thee we worship, and invoke for help.   25
Lead us in the straight path; —
The path of those towards whom Thou hast been gracious;
Not of those against whom Thy wrath is kindled, or that walk in error.

. . .

Several years after, Mohammad thus alludes in the Koran to
the position of himself and his friend [Abu Bekr] in the cave of   30
mount Thaur: —

If ye will not assist the Prophet, verily GOD assisted him aforetime
when the Unbelievers cast him forth, in the company of a Second only;
when they two were in the cave alone, when the Prophet said unto his
companion, *Be not cast down, for verily God is with us.* And God caused 35
to descend tranquillity upon him, and strengthened him with hosts
which ye saw not, and made the word of the Unbelievers to be abased;
and the word of the Lord, that is exalted, for GOD is mighty and wise.

114

The 'sole companion,' or in Arabic phraseology *The Second of the Two*, became one of Abu Bekr's most honoured titles. Hassan, the contemporary poet of Medina, thus sings of him: —

And the Second of the two in the glorious Cave, while the foes were
    searching around, and they two had ascended the mountain;   5
And the Prophet of the Lord, they well knew, loved him, — more than all
    the world; he held no one equal unto him.

Legends cluster around the cave. A spider wove its web across the entrance. Branches sprouted, covering it in on every side. Wild pigeons settled on the trees to divert attention, and so 10 forth. Whatever may have been the real peril, Mohammad and his companion felt it, no doubt, to be a time of jeopardy. Glancing upwards at a crevice through which the morning light began to break, Abu Bekr whispered: 'What if one were to look through the chink, and see us underneath his very feet.' *Think not thus, Abu Bekr!*' said the Prophet; 'WE ARE TWO, BUT GOD IS IN THE 15 MIDST A THIRD.'[1]

[1] Sir William Muir, *The Life of Mohammad*, pp. 37–38, 138–139.

PENELOPE
Greek

Penelope's withdrawal is a preparation for union with her natural complement, Odysseus. The wily wife of the wily hero weaves her own "cave" of protection

. . . Penélopê replied:

        "Stranger, my looks,
my face, my carriage, were soon lost or faded
when the Akhaians crossed the sea to Troy,
Odysseus my lord among the rest.   5
If he returned, if he were here to care for me,
I might be happily renowned!
But grief instead heaven sent me—years of pain.
Sons of the noblest families on the islands,
Doulikhion, Samê, wooded Zakýnthos,   10
with native Ithakans, are here to court me,
against my wish; and they consume this house.
Can I give proper heed to guest or suppliant
or herald on the realm's affairs?

           How could I? 15

wasted with longing for Odysseus, while here
they press for marriage.

        Ruses served my turn
to draw the time out—first a close-grained web
I had the happy thought to set up weaving   20
on my big loom in hall. I said, that day:
'Young men—my suitors, now my lord is dead,
let me finish my weaving before I marry,
or else my thread will have been spun in vain.
It is a shroud I weave for Lord Laërtès   25
when cold Death comes to lay him on his bier.
The country wives would hold me in dishonor
if he, with all his fortune, lay unshrouded.'
I reached their hearts that way, and they agreed.
So every day I wove on the great loom,   30
but every night by torchlight I unwove it;
and so for three years I deceived the Akhaians.
But when the seasons brought a fourth year on,

as long months waned, and the long days were spent,
through impudent folly in the slinking maids
they caught me — clamored up to me at night;
I had no choice then but to finish it.
And now, as matters stand at last,   5
I have no strength left to evade a marriage,
cannot find any further way; my parents
urge it upon me, and my son
will not stand by while they eat up his property.
He comprehends it, being a man full grown,   10
able to oversee the kind of house
Zeus would endow with honor.[1]

---

[1] Robert Fitzgerald translation, *The Odyssey of Homer*, pp. 357–358.

ENDYMION
Greek

In the Endymion story the hero remains permanently in the security of the womb-cave and is, thus, eternally young.

Endymion was the handsome son of Zeus and the Nymph Calyce, an Aeolian by race though Carian by origin, and ousted Clymenus from the kingdom of Elis. His wife, known by many different names, such as Iphianassa, Hyperippe, Chromia, and Neis, bore him four sons; he also fathered fifty daughters on Selene, who had fallen desperately in love with him.

Endymion was lying asleep in a cave on Carian Mount Latmus one still night when Selene first saw him, lay down by his side, and gently kissed his closed eyes. Afterwards, some say, he returned to the same cave and fell into a dreamless sleep. This sleep, from which he has never yet awakened, came upon him either at his own request, because he hated the approach of old age; or because Zeus suspected him of an intrigue with Hera; or because Selene found that she preferred gently kissing him to being the object of his too fertile passion. In any case, he has never grown a day older, and preserves the bloom of youth on his cheeks. But others say that he lies buried at Olympia, where his four sons ran a race for the vacant throne, which Epeius won.[1]

[1] Robert Graves, *The Greek Myths*, vol. 1, p. 210.

THE SEVEN SLEEPERS
Christian

The motifs of eternal youth, of withdrawal for protection, and of rebirth are all present in this Christian cave legend of the Seven Sleepers.

The Seven Sleepers were natives of the city of Ephesus. The Emperor Decius, the persecutor of the Christians, came to Ephesus, and built temples in the centre of the city, that all might take part with him in the worship of the idols. And when he ordered all the Christians to be sought out, bound, and forced either to sacrifice or to die, so great was the fear of his punishments that friend disowned friend, father betrayed son, and son denied father. And there were seven Christians in Ephesus, named Maximian, Malchus, Martianus, Dionysius, John, Serapion and Constantine, who were sore afflicted at seeing all these things. And although they were among the first men of the palace, they disdained to offer sacrifice, and remained hidden in their houses, fasting and praying. They were accused and haled before Decius, and avowed that they were Christians; but he gave them the time until his return in which to renounce their faith. But they distributed their goods to the poor, and by common accord went to take refuge on Mount Celion, concealing themselves there. And each morning one of them, assuming the guise and seeming of a beggar, went into the city for provisions.

When Decius came back to Ephesus, and commanded that they be sought out and made to offer sacrifice, Malchus, who had gone into the town that day, returned in terror, to report the emperor's fury to his companions. And as they were overcome with fear, Malchus laid before them the bread which he had brought, that they might be strengthened by the food and made stronger for the combat. And while they sat at table and conversed with tears and sighs, the will of God caused all seven to fall into a deep sleep.

The following morning, when they were sought for and could not be found, and Decius was grieving at the loss of such youths, word was brought to him that they were in hiding on Mount Celion, and that they had distributed all their goods to the poor. Decius thereupon summoned their parents, and threatened them with death if they did not tell him all they knew. And the parents confirmed the accusations, and complained that their sons had given away their patrimony. And thinking what he should do in their regard, at the inspiration of God he commanded the mouth of the cave to be walled up with stones, that they might perish 5 of hunger and need. This was done, and two Christians, Theodore and Rufinus, wrote down an account of their martyrdom and placed it secretly among the stones.

After three hundred and seventy-two years, when Decius and his whole generation had passed away, in the thirtieth year of 10 the reign of Theodosius, there spread abroad the heresy of those who denied the resurrection of the dead. And the most Christian Emperor Theodosius was greatly aggrieved thereby, because he saw the faith of his subjects much disturbed; and he went into the inner chambers, put on a hair shirt, and knelt weeping day 15 after day. Seeing this, God in His mercy willed to comfort those who mourned and to confirm their hope of the resurrection of the dead; and opening the treasures of His loving-kindness, He raised up the Seven Sleepers. He inspired a certain man of Ephesus to build sheds for his shepherds on Mount Celion. And 20 when the stonemasons opened the cave, the Seven Sleepers awoke and greeted each other as though they had but passed the night in sleep; and then, recalling the anxiety of the day before, they asked Malchus, who had waited upon them, what Decius had decreed in their regard. But he answered, as he had said the 25 day before: 'We were sought for, that we might offer sacrifice. That is what the emperor plans for us!' And Maximian replied: 'God knows that we will not sacrifice!' And when he had rallied his companions, he ordered Malchus to go down to the city to buy bread, and to come back with more loaves than on the pre- 30 vious day, and report what the emperor had commanded.

Malchus therefore took five coins and set out; and coming out of the cave, and seeing the stones piled up, he wondered, but thought little of it. Timidly he came to the city gate, and was surprised to see the cross above it; and he went from gate to gate, 35 and his astonishment waxed the greater at seeing the cross over each, and the city changed. Signing himself, and thinking that he was dreaming, he came back to the first gate. Then he took courage, and covering his face, entered the city and came to the bread-sellers; and in the market-place he heard the people talking 40 of Christ, and his wonder knew no bounds. And he said to himself: 'How is it that yesterday no one dared to utter the name of Christ, and today all confess him? I would think that this was not the city of the Ephesians, for it is otherwise built, but I know of no other such like city!' And when he asked, he was told that this was Ephesus; and he thought that he must be wandering in mind, and was about to turn back to rejoin his companions. But he went to the venders of bread; and when he offered his coins in payment, the venders looked with wonderment, and said to each other that this youth must have discovered an ancient treasure. And when Malchus saw them talking to each other, he thought that they were about to drag him to the emperor: and terrified, he besought them to let him go free, and to keep the loaves and the coins for themselves. But they laid hold on him, and said: 'Whence art thou? Surely thou hast found a treasure of the old emperors! Show us therefore where it is, and we shall share it with thee and shall conceal thee; for otherwise thou canst not remain hid!'

So great was Malchus' fear that he found naught to reply to them; and when he remained silent, they put a rope about his neck and dragged him through the streets to the centre of the city, and the rumour went abroad that some youth had discovered a treasure. And when the whole populace came together and looked upon him wondering, he sought to convince them that he had found nothing; but looking about, he saw no one that knew him, and seeking some of his kin, whom he in sooth thought to be alive, he found none; so that he stood like one demented in the midst of the townsfolk. And when Saint Martin the bishop and the proconsul Antipater had heard of all this, they ordered the citizens to bring him to them warily, with his coins. And when their servitors led him toward the church, he thought that he was being led to the emperor. Then the bishop and the proconsul, surprised at the sight of the coins, asked him where he had unearthed the unknown treasure. But he answered that he had found nothing, but had had these coins from his parents' purse. And when he was asked from what city he came, he replied: 'Well I know that I am of this city, if indeed this be Ephesus!' And the proconsul said: 'Summon hither thy kinsmen, that they may bear witness for thee!' But when he gave their names, and no one recognized them, all thought that he was making false pretense, in order to escape. And the proconsul said: 'How shall we believe thee, that this is thy parents' money, when its inscription is more than three hundred and seventy-seven years old, and it comes from the first days of the Emperor Decius, and is in no wise like to our coinage? And if thy parents are of a time so long past, how canst thou seek to deceive the ancients and the wise men of Ephesus? Therefore shall I order thee to be handed over to the law, until thou confess what thou hast found!'

Then Malchus fell down before them, and said: 'In God's name, my lords, tell me what I ask, and I shall tell you what is in my heart! Where is the Emperor Decius now, who yesterday was in this city?' And the bishop replied: 'My son, in the whole earth there is now no emperor called Decius. Only in olden times was there such a one!' And Malchus said: 'Herein, my lord, am I sore bewildered, and no one believes me. But follow me and I shall show you my companions who are on Mount Celion, and believe ye them! For this do I know, that we fled from the face of the Emperor Decius, and yestereve I saw Decius enter this city, if forsooth this be Ephesus!' Then the bishop, thinking within himself, said to the proconsul: 'There is some vision, which God wills to make manifest in this youth!' They therefore set out with him, and a great multitude of the people followed.

And first Malchus went in to his companions; and then the bishop, going in after him, found the scroll among the stones, sealed with two silver seals. And calling all the people together he read the writing to them, and all who heard were filled with awe. Then they saw the saints of God sitting in the cave, their faces like roses in bloom; and falling down they glorified God. And straightway the bishop and the proconsul sent to the Emperor Theodosius, asking him to come with all haste, and witness this new miracle of God. And he, rising at once from the ground where he lay mourning, came from Constantinople to Ephesus, glorifying God; and all went out to meet him, and together they went up to the cave. And as soon as the saints saw the emperor, their faces shone like the sun. And the emperor went in and threw himself before them, and gave glory to God; and rising he embraced them and wept over each, and said: 'Seeing you, it is as if I saw our Lord raising Lazarus to life!' Then Saint Maximian said to him: 'Believe us, that for thy sake God has raised us up before the day of the great resurrection, that thou mayest have unwavering faith in the resurrection of the dead! For we indeed have risen and are alive, and as an infant is in the womb of his mother and lives and feels no ill, so were we alive, lying asleep and feeling naught.'

When he had said these things, the saints bowed their heads to the earth, in the sight of all, and fell asleep, and surrendered their souls according to the will of God. And the emperor arose 5 and fell upon them, weeping and kissing them; and he ordered that golden coffins be made for them. But that very night they appeared to him, and said that as they had hitherto lain in the earth and had risen therefrom, so he should return them to the earth, until the Lord should raise them up again. The emperor 10 therefore commanded that the cave be adorned with gilded stones. And he proclaimed that all the bishops who had professed the resurrection of the dead should receive indulgence.

The saints are said to have slept for three hundred and seventy-seven years; but this may be doubted, because they rose 15 from the dead in the year 448, and Decius only reigned for one year and three months, namely in the year 252. Thus they slept for only one hundred and ninety-six years.[1]

---

[1] Jacobus De Voragine, *The Golden Legend*, pp. 382–386.

ODYSSEUS AND ACHILLES
Greek

The withdrawal is sometimes more a refusal of the call to heroism than a stage of meditation or preparation. Heroism makes demands that something in us necessarily resists. More "serious" refusals are contained even in the stories of such religious heroes as Moses and Jesus.

Now, Odysseus had been warned by an oracle: 'If you go to Troy, you will not return until the twentieth year, and then alone and destitute.' He therefore feigned madness, and Agamemnon, Menelaus, and Palamedes found him wearing a peasant's felt cap shaped like a half-egg, ploughing with an ass and an ox yoked together, and flinging salt over his shoulder as he went. When he pretended not to recognize his distinguished guests, Palamedes snatched the infant Telemachus from Penelope's arms and set him on the ground before the advancing team. Odysseus hastily reined them in to avoid killing his only son and, his sanity having thus been established, was obliged to join the expedition. . . .

Now, Thetis knew that her son Achilles would never return from Troy if he joined the expedition, since he was fated either to gain glory there and die early, or to live a long but inglorious life at home. She disguised him as a girl, and entrusted him to Lycomedes, king of Scyros, in whose palace he lived under the name of Cercysera, Aissa, or Pyrrha; and had an intrigue with Lycomedes's daughter Deidameia, by whom he became the father of Pyrrhus, later called Neoptolemus. But some say that Neoptolemus was the son of Achilles and Iphigeneia.

Odysseus, Nestor, and Ajax were sent to fetch Achilles from Scyros, where he was rumoured to be hidden. Lycomedes let them search the palace, and they might never have detected Achilles, had not Odysseus laid a pile of gifts—for the most part jewels, girdles, embroidered dresses and such—in the hall, and asked the court-ladies to take their choice. Then Odysseus ordered a sudden trumpet-blast and clash of arms to sound outside the palace and, sure enough, one of the girls stripped herself to the waist and seized the shield and spear which he had included among the gifts. It was Achilles, who now promised to lead his Myrmidons to Troy.[1]

---

[1] Robert Graves, *The Greek Myths*, vol. 2, pp. 279–281.

THE UNKNOWN WITHIN THE SELF:
Commentary on Part 3

In the myth contained in the preceding stories the hero withdraws from the "world," usually to meditate in preparation for later deeds. It will be suggested by some that this myth lacks the universality of the birth myth or the initiation myth—that it is confined for the most part to the mystical religions, that it is relatively foreign to the Egyptians, the Greeks, and the Nordic peoples, for instance. To some extent this is true. The meditation theme is most prevalent in the religions of the Far East—especially Buddhism and Hinduism—and in Christianity. Nearly all of the saints or hero figures of these religions experience a stage of withdrawal and ascetic discipline. Indeed, the hermitic act might be called the central one for the Eastern religions and for certain movements within Christianity. In the latter case such figures as Saint Anthony, Saint Francis, and John the Baptist come to mind, not to speak of Dante, whose *Vita Nuova* can be seen as a meditative preparation for the trials of the *Divine Comedy*. And the emphasis placed on secluded religious orders in both Buddhism and Christianity is significant.

Withdrawal is not absolutely unknown, however, to the ancient cults and religions of the Near East. The descent to the underworld so important to these religions and so much less important to the mystical religions is a withdrawal from the world in preparation for resurrection. But this subject will be treated in Part 6.

The meditative withdrawal seems least important in the Greek religion. But even here there are traces of it, as in the Endymion story, where we find the important cave motif. And there is the related formula in which the hero withdraws from action or refuses the call to action. Both of these cases apply to the great Achilles, who sulks in his tent during the Trojan War, and who, as a boy, had been dressed in women's clothes in order that the ambassadors of Agamemnon might not recognize him during the "draft call" for the same war. Odysseus, too, attempts to avoid the war by trickery. But this ancient draft-dodging is more closely related to the motif which Joseph Campbell calls the "refusal of the call," in which the hero chooses not to take on the task demanded of him.[1] There are traces of it in Moses' first reactions to God's call. It is a motif common to many heroes.

[1] Joseph Campbell, *The Hero with a Thousand Faces*, pp. 59–68.

The withdrawal act of the great hermits—of the Buddha and Jesus and their followers—is a positive act. It is a spiritual rite of passage—a rebirth of the self. When the hero withdraws into the wilderness or to the mountain or cave (the last of these is reminiscent of the womb-cave of the birth myth), he literally withdraws into himself to emerge later with the divinity he has found there; he emerges as a shaman, who has had direct experience of the unknown in himself. As is the case with all of the major rites of passage, this is a losing of the self to find the self, and it involves physical and mental suffering; the god within is not so easily born. The hero is frequently tempted by demons of the sensual and material world, who represent those forces which deter most of us, finally, from an honest experience of the inner self—an experience so necessary to the process of self-realization and individuation.

The mystical religions, which are the ones most conscious of this process, are understandably most concerned with withdrawal. It is the savior—the Buddha or the Christ—in these religions who is able to do the impossible by putting aside his potential for worldly power in exchange for the joys of the spirit. Coomaraswamy says of the Hindu Dance of Shiva, which expresses these joys, that it represents "the release of . . . souls of men from the snare of illusion," and that the "place of the dance, the center of the universe, is within the heart."[2] For Christ the withdrawal reaches its fullest expression not in the forty days in the wilderness but in the crucifixion itself. And for the Buddhist the Bo Tree story holds the same central position that the crucifixion does for the Christian. The two stories are analogous as the greatest acts of the two heroes. And they are analogous in their common use of the tree as a center or symbolic world heart.

The withdrawal theme is related also to the quest myth, which we will consider next. The quest often has as a goal eternal youth or immortality, and it will be noticed that in the Endymion story as well as in the Seven Sleepers story this is a dominant theme. There is much of this in the apotheosis myth as well, since the hero there is man's hope for a definitive break in the cycle of birth, life, and death.

In summary, the myth of the hero's meditative withdrawal

[2] Ananda Coomaraswamy, *The Dance of Shiva*, p. 76.

is the myth of the preparation of the shaman—the great teacher-savior—who, having faced the unknown in himself, can now convey and apply his experience to us.

Some of the relevant works for the study of this myth are Coomaraswamy's *The Dance of Shiva* as well as his other books on Hinduism and Buddhism, Erich Neumann's *Mystical Man*, Jung's *Answer to Job,* and Evelyn Underhill's *Mysticism: A Study in the Nature and Development of Man's Spiritual Consciousness.*

4

TRIAL AND QUEST

Perhaps the best known of modern paintings, Picasso's *Guernica* conveys as forcefully as the stories of the labors of Hercules or the trials of the Buddha the heroic agon and adventure that is the search for wholeness in a world threatened by chaos. [Pablo Picasso, *Guernica* (1937), oil on canvas, 11 ft., 5½ in. x 25 ft., 5¾ in. Collection, The Museum of Modern Art, New York. On extended loan to the Museum of Modern Art, New York, from the artist's estate. Reproduced with permission.]

HERACLES (HERCULES)
Greek

The story of the twelve labors of Heracles is one of the world's most famous symbolic records of the trials and glories of adult life. Here the hero travels to all corners of the earth in search of the tasks which will "make his name."

Before he was eighteen he had done many famous deeds in the country of Thebes, and Creon, the king, gave him his daughter in marriage. But he could not long escape the anger of Juno, who afflicted him with a sudden madness, so that he did not know what he was doing and in a fit of frenzy killed both his wife and his children. When he came to his senses, in horror and shame at what he had done, he visited the great cliffs of Delphi, where the eagles circle all day and where Apollo's oracle is. There he asked how he could be purified of his sin and he was told by the oracle that he must go to Mycenae and for twelve years obey all the commands of the cowardly king Eurystheus, his kinsman. It seemed a hard and cruel sentence, but the oracle told him also, that at the end of many labours he would be received among the gods.

Hercules therefore departed to the rocky citadel of Mycenae that looks down upon the blue water of the bay of Argos. He was skilled in the use of every weapon, having been educated, like Jason was, by the wise centaur Chiron. He was tall and immensely powerful. When Eurystheus saw him he was both terrified of him and jealous of his great powers. He began to devise labours that would seem impossible, yet Hercules accomplished them all.

First he was ordered to destroy and to bring back to Mycenae the lion of Nemea which for long had ravaged all the countryside to the north. Hercules took his bow and arrows, and, in the forest of Nemea, cut himself a great club, so heavy that a man nowadays could hardly lift it. This club he carried ever afterwards as his chief weapon.

He found that his arrows had no effect on the tough skin of the lion, but, as the beast sprang at him, he half-stunned it with his club, then closing in with it, he seized it by the throat and killed it with his bare hands. They say that when he carried back on his shoulders to Mycenae the body of the huge beast, Eurys-theus fled in terror and ordered Hercules never again to enter the gates of the city, but to wait outside until he was told to come in. Eurystheus also built for himself a special strong room of brass into which he would retire if he was ever again frightened by the power and valiance of Hercules. Hercules himself took the skin of the lion and made it into a cloak which he wore ever afterwards, sometimes with the lion's head covering his own head like a cap, sometimes with it slung backwards over his shoulders.

The next task given to Hercules by Eurystheus was to destroy a huge water snake, called the Hydra, which lived in the marshes of Argos, was filled with poison and had fifty venomous heads. Hercules, with his friend and companion, the young Iolaus, set out from Mycenae and came to the great cavern, sacred to Pan, which is a holy place in the hills near Argos. Below this cavern a river gushes out of the rock. Willows and plane-trees surround the source and the brilliant green of grass. It is the freshest and most delightful place. But, as the river flows downwards to the sea, it becomes wide and shallow, extending into pestilential marshes, the home of stinging flies and mosquitoes. In these marshes they found the Hydra, and Hercules, with his great club, began to crush the beast's heads, afterwards cutting them off with his sword. Yet the more he laboured, the more difficult his task became. From the stump of each head that he cut off two other heads, with forked and hissing tongues, immediately sprang. Faced with an endless and increasing effort, Hercules was at a loss what to do. It seemed to him that heat might prove more powerful than cold steel, and he commanded Iolaus to burn the root of each head with a red-hot iron immediately it was severed from the neck. This plan was successful. The heads no longer sprouted up again, and soon the dangerous and destructive ani-mal lay dead, though still writhing in the black marsh water among the reeds. Hercules cut its body open and dipped his arrows in the blood. Henceforward these arrows would bring certain death, even if they only grazed the skin, so powerful was the Hydra's poison.

Eurystheus next ordered Hercules to capture and bring back alive a stag, sacred to Diana and famous for its great fleetness of foot, which lived in the waste mountains and forests, and never yet had been approached in the chase. For a whole year

Hercules pursued this animal, resting for the hours of darkness and pressing on next day in its tracks. For many months he was wholly outdistanced; valleys and forests divided him from his prey. But at the end of the year the stag, weary of the long hunt, could run no longer. Hercules seized it in his strong hands, tied first its forelegs and then its hind legs together, put the body of the beast, with its drooping antlered head, over his neck, and proceeded to return to the palace of King Eurystheus. However, as he was on his way through the woods, he was suddenly aware of a bright light in front of him, and in the middle of the light he saw standing a tall woman or, as he immediately recognized, a goddess, grasping in her hands a bow and staring at him angrily with her shining eyes. He knew at once that this was the archer goddess Diana, she who had once turned Actaeon into a stag and who now was enraged at the loss of this other stag which was sacred to her. Hercules put his prey on the ground and knelt before the goddess. "It was through no desire of my own," he said, "that I have captured this noble animal. What I do is done at the command of my father Jupiter and of the oracle of your brother Apollo at Delphi." The goddess listened to his explanation, smiled kindly on him and allowed him to go on his way, when he had promised that, once the stag had been carried to Eurystheus, it would be set free again in the forests that it loved. So Hercules accomplished this third labour.

He was not, however, to be allowed to rest. Eurystheus now commanded him to go out to the mountains of Erymanthus and bring back the great wild boar that for long had terrorized all the neighbourhood. So Hercules set out once more and on his way he passed the country where the centaurs had settled after they had been driven down from the north in the battle that had taken place with the Lapiths at the wedding of Pirithous. In this battle they had already had experience of the hero's strength, but still their manners were rude and rough. When the centaur Pholus offered Hercules some of the best wine to drink, the other centaurs became jealous. Angry words led to blows, and soon Hercules was forced to defend himself with his club and with his arrows, the poison of which not only caused death, but also the most extreme pain. Soon he scattered his enemies in all directions, driving them over the plains and rocks. Some he dashed to the ground with his club; others, wounded by the poisoned arrows, lay writhing in agony, or kicking their hooves in the air.

Some took refuge in the house of the famous centaur Chiron, who had been schoolmaster to Hercules and who, alone among the centaurs, was immortal. As he pursued his enemies to this good centaur's house, shooting arrows at them as he went, Hercules, by an unhappy accident, wounded Chiron himself. Whether it was because of grief that his old pupil had so injured him, or whether it was because of the great pain of the wound, Chiron prayed to Jupiter that his immortality should be taken away from him. Jupiter granted his prayer. The good centaur died, but he was set in Heaven in a constellation of stars which is still called either Sagittarius or else The Centaur.

Hercules mourned the sad death of his old master. Then he went on to Erymanthus. It was winter and he chased the great boar up to the deep snow in the passes of the mountains. The animal's short legs soon grew weary of ploughing through the stiff snow and Hercules caught it up when it was exhausted and panting in a snowdrift. He bound it firmly and slung the great body over his back. They say that when he brought it to Mycenae, Eurystheus was so frightened at the sight of the huge tusks and flashing eyes that he hid for two days in the brass hiding place that he had had built for him.

The next task that Hercules was ordered to do would have seemed to anyone impossible. There was a king of Elis called Augeas, very rich in herds of goats and cattle. His stables, they say, held three thousand oxen and for ten years these stables had never been cleaned. The dung and muck stood higher than a house, hardened and caked together. The smell was such that even the herdsmen, who were used to it, could scarcely bear to go near. Hercules was now ordered to clean these stables, and, going to Elis, he first asked the king to promise him the tenth part of his herds if he was successful in his task. The king readily agreed, and Hercules made the great river Alpheus change his course and come foaming and roaring through the filthy stables. In less than a day all the dirt was cleared and rolled away to the sea. The river then went back to its former course and, for the first time in ten years, the stone floors and walls of the enormous stables shone white and clean.

Hercules then asked for his reward, but King Augeas, claiming that he had performed the task not with his own hands, but by a trick, refused to give it to him. He even banished his own son who took the side of Hercules and reproached his father for not keeping his promise. Hercules then made war on the kingdom of Elis, drove King Augeas out and put his son on the throne. Then, with his rich reward, he returned to Mycenae, ready to undertake whatever new task was given him by Eurystheus.

Again he was ordered to destroy creatures that were harmful 5
to men. This time they were great birds, like cranes or storks, but much more powerful, which devoured human flesh and lived around the black waters of the Stymphalian lake. In the reeds and rocky crags they lived in huge numbers and Hercules was at a loss how to draw them from their hiding places. It was the 10
goddess Minerva who helped him by giving him a great rattle of brass. The noise of this rattle drove the great birds into the air in throngs. Hercules pursued them with his arrows, which rang upon their horny beaks and legs but stuck firm in the bodies that tumbled one after the other into the lake. The whole brood of 15
these monsters was entirely destroyed and now only ducks and harmless water-fowl nest along the reedy shores.

Hercules had now accomplished six of his labours. Six more remained. After the killing of the Stymphalian birds he was commanded to go to Crete and bring back from there alive a 20
huge bull which was laying the whole island waste. Bare-handed and alone he grappled with this bull, and, once again, when he brought the animal back into the streets of Mycenae, Eurystheus fled in terror at the sight both of the hero and of the great beast which he had captured. 25

From the southern sea Hercules was sent to the north to Thrace, over which ruled King Diomedes, a strong and warlike prince who savagely fed his famous mares on human flesh. Hercules conquered the king in battle and gave his body to the very mares which had so often fed upon the bodies of the king's 30
enemies. He brought the mares back to King Eurystheus, who again was terrified at the sight of such fierce and spirited animals. He ordered them to be taken to the heights of Mount Olympus and there be consecrated to Jupiter. But Jupiter had no love for these unnatural creatures, and, on the rocky hill- 35
sides, they were devoured by lions, wolves, and bears.

Next Hercules was commanded to go to the country of the Amazons, the fierce warrior women, and bring back the girdle of their queen Hippolyte. Seas and mountains had to be crossed, battles to be fought; but Hercules in the end accomplished the 40
long journey and the dangerous task. Later, as is well known,

135

Hippolyte became the wife of Theseus of Athens and bore him an ill-fated son, Hippolytus.

Hercules had now travelled in the south, the north and the east. His tenth labour was to be in the far west, beyond the country of Spain, in an island called Erythia. Here lived the giant Geryon, a great monster with three bodies and three heads. With his herdsman, and his two-headed dog, called Orthrus, he looked after huge flocks of oxen, and, at the command of Eurystheus, Hercules came into his land to lift the cattle and to destroy the giant. On his way, at the very entrance to the Atlantic he set up two great marks, ever afterwards to be known by sailors and called the Pillars of Hercules. Later, as he wandered through rocks and over desert land, he turned his anger against the Sun itself, shooting his arrows at the great god Phoebus Apollo. But Phoebus pitied him in his thirst and weariness. He sent him a golden boat, and in this boat Hercules crossed over to the island of Erythia. Here he easily destroyed both watchdog and herdsman, but fought for long with the great three-bodied giant before he slew him, body after body. Then he began to drive the cattle over rivers and mountains and deserts from Spain to Greece. As he was passing through Italy he came near the cave where Cacus, a son of Vulcan, who breathed fire out of his mouth, lived solitary and cruel, since he killed all strangers and nailed their heads, dripping with blood, to the posts at the entrance of his rocky dwelling. While Hercules was resting, with the herds all round him, Cacus came out of his cave and stole eight of the best animals of the whole herd. He dragged them backwards by their tails, so that Hercules should not be able to track them down.

When Hercules awoke from his rest, he searched far and wide for the missing animals, but, since they had been driven into the deep recesses of Cacus's cave, he was unable to find them. In the end he began to go on his way with the rest of the herd, and, as the stolen animals heard the lowing of the other cattle, they too began to low and bellow in their rocky prison. Hercules stopped still, and soon out of the cave came the fire-breathing giant, prepared to defend the fruits of his robbery and anxious to hang the head of Hercules among his other disgusting trophies. This, however, was not to be. The huge limbs and terrible breath of Cacus were of no avail against the hero's strength and fortitude. Soon, with a tremendous blow of his club, he stretched out Cacus dead on the ground. Then he drove the great herd on over mountains and plains, through forests and rivers to Mycenae.

Hercules' next labour again took him to the far west. He was commanded by Eurystheus to fetch him some of the golden apples of the Hesperides. These apples grew in a garden west even of the land of Atlas. Here the sun shines continually, but always cool well-watered trees of every kind give shade. All flowers and fruits that grow on earth grow here, and fruit and flowers are always on the boughs together. In the centre of the garden is the orchard where golden apples gleam among the shining green leaves and the flushed blossom. Three nymphs, the Hesperides, look after this orchard, which was given by Jupiter to Juno as a wedding present. It is guarded also by a great dragon that never sleeps, and coils its huge folds around the trees. No one except the gods knows exactly where this beautiful and remote garden is, and it was to this unknown place that Hercules was sent.

He was helped by Minerva and by the nymphs of the broad river Po in Italy. These nymphs told Hercules where to find Nereus, the ancient god of the sea, who knew the past, the present and the future. "Wait for him," they said, "until you find him asleep on the rocky shore, surrounded by his fifty daughters. Seize hold of him tightly and do not let go until he answers your question. He will, in trying to escape you, put on all kinds of shapes. He will turn to fire, to water, to a wild beast or to a serpent. You must not lose your courage, but hold him all the tighter, and, in the end, he will come back to his own shape and will tell you what you want to know."

Hercules followed their advice. As he watched along the sea god's shore he saw, lying on the sand, half in and half out of the sea, with seaweed trailing round his limbs, the old god himself. Around him were his daughters, the Nereids, some riding on the backs of dolphins, some dancing on the shore, some swimming and diving in the deeper water. As Hercules approached, they cried out shrilly at the sight of a man. Those on land leaped back into the sea; those in the sea swam further from the shore. But their cries did not awake their father till Hercules was close to him and able to grip him firmly in his strong hands. Immediately the old god felt the hands upon him, his body seemed to disappear into a running stream of water; but Hercules felt the body that he could not see, and did not relax his grasp. Next it seemed that his hands were buried in a great pillar of fire; but the fire did not scorch the skin and Hercules could still feel the aged limbs through the fire. Then it was a great lion with wide-open jaws that appeared to be lying and raging on the sands; then a bear, then a dragon. Still Hercules clung firmly to his prisoner, and in the end he saw again the bearded face and seaweed-dripping limbs of old Nereus. The god knew for what purpose Hercules had seized him, and he told him the way to the garden of the Hesperides.

It was a long and difficult journey, but at the end of it Hercules was rewarded. The guardian nymphs (since this was the will of Jupiter) allowed him to pick from the pliant boughs two or three of the golden fruit. The great dragon bowed its head to the ground at their command and left Hercules unmolested. He brought back the apples to Eurystheus, but soon they began to lose that beautiful sheen of gold that had been theirs in the western garden. So Minerva carried them back again to the place from which they came, and then once more they glowed with their own gold among the other golden apples that hung upon the trees.[1]

[1] Rex Warner, *The Stories of the Greeks*, pp. 94–101. For the twelfth and final labor see Part 6.

PROMETHEUS
Greek

The labors and quest of Prometheus involve a struggle with godhead itself. The hero is symbolic of man's pride in the divinity within himself.

There are many different stories told as to how men themselves came into being. Some say that they appeared lying on the ground under the ash trees and so were, in some sense, the children of the nymphs who are the guardian spirits of those trees. According to others they were formed inside the earth by the gods out of earth and fire and all the elements that can be mixed with them. It is said too that they were actually created by Prometheus himself. However this may be, it is agreed that in the beginning man was a weak, ignorant and defenceless creature.

But Prometheus, for some reason of his own, loved this weak and pitiful race. He saw them living like animals in caves, adapting themselves as best they could to each day that came, and he it was who taught them how to distinguish the seasons, one from another, how to follow the risings and the settings of the stars, the beginning of civilisation. He taught them how to use numbers and how to form letters to serve as signs for the sounds they made in speech and so finally to become the means by which knowledge could be recorded and the beauty and strength of thought and feeling be made to last for ever. He told them the way to tame wild animals, cattle and horses and dogs, so that they might relieve man's burden and help him in his work. He showed the sailors how to build boats that could float upon the waters and be carried forward on wings of sails. He taught them the meaning of the behaviour of birds and of their flight, so that by observing them they might know the future. In a word, it was Prometheus who gave men every art and every science; and finally he gave them the gift of fire. According to one story Prometheus stole the fire from the island of Lemnos where stood the forge and workshop of Hephaestus, the master craftsman among the gods; according to other stories he took the fire from the very hearth of Zeus himself on Olympus and brought it to man concealed in the hollow stem of a plant.

Now Zeus was a jealous god. He grudged men all the gifts that Prometheus had given them and he was angry with Prometheus for granting to these wretched creatures of an hour the ability to shape their lives into something better and to raise their thoughts up to the heaven itself. And so when he found that Prometheus had given to man this final gift of fire, he burst out into uncontrollable rage. He ordered his two invincible servants, Power and Violence, to seize Prometheus and to carry him to the highest peak of the dreadful Caucasus. There among the crawling glaciers, beneath the lashing hail and winds of storm, or, in the summer time, shelterless against the scorching heat of the sun, Prometheus was to be bound fast with unbreakable chains. The task of making these massive chains and of fastening them upon the victim's body was given to Hephaestus, and, though Hephaestus shrank from the dreadful deed of so torturing a brother god, he feared the power of Zeus and did not dare to disobey. Indeed he hated the skill of his hand, but he was forced to use it, and so he flung the hard chains around the immortal body of Prometheus and, with great blows of his hammer, nailed and fastened him to the towering rocks. He groaned as he did this work, for he pitied the good Titan; but the servants of Zeus, Power and Violence, merely mocked him for his weak spirit and hurled their insults at Prometheus himself. "You did good to men," they said, "against the will of Zeus. Now see if there is any help to be found in men." And they taunted him with his name, which means "Forethought." "You will need more forethought than you have," they said, "if you are ever to break out again into freedom from these eternal chains."

But neither to them nor to Hephaestus did Prometheus speak a word, and so they left him nailed against the mountain side, a god tortured at the hands of gods. And as for Prometheus, though his body was chained to the rocks, his mind remained stubborn and unconquered. Zeus had the power to control his body in unbreakable fetters, but not Zeus himself could alter or subdue his fixed and steady mind and persuade him that there was anything in this punishment but black ingratitude and base injustice. Zeus owed the very power he wielded to the help given him by Prometheus; nor had Prometheus ever rebelled against the power of Zeus; his only crime had been to help mortal men to escape from savagery and to raise themselves, by knowledge, higher than the beasts.

Now there were many of the gods who pitied Prometheus and among these was the Titan, Father Oceanus, who surrounds the world with his life-giving stream. He left the self-made caves of rock in which he lived and came up to earth to give Prometheus the best advice he could, urging him to make his submission to Zeus. "For Zeus," he said, "has absolute power, and it is useless to fight against it. Whether you are right or wrong, it will make no difference. Surely it is better to relax your anger and to speak humbly to one who is more powerful than you are. And, if only you will do this, I myself will go to Zeus and will beg him to forgive you and the other gods will join me in their prayers."

But Prometheus would have none of this intervention, which seemed to him both disgraceful and useless. Zeus, he considered, was behaving like some dictator, whose lust for power was forcing him beyond the limits. Zeus had already destroyed many of the older gods and for these now Prometheus began to feel pity. There was his own brother, Atlas, who, by the will of Zeus, stood in the regions of the west and carried on his vast shoulders the whole weight of the heavens, a difficult burden which he could never shake off. And there was the great hundred-headed monster Typhon, the child of Heaven and Earth, who had been blasted to ruin by the thunderbolt of Zeus and now lay, a useless frame, beneath the roots of Etna, though still his anger boiled and the hot heaving of his breath would, from time to time, force fire and molten rock into the air and devastate all the fields of smiling Sicily. And so Prometheus told Oceanus to beware lest, if he took the side of one of the older gods, some such a fate as this might fall upon him too. As for himself, he said, no power and no pain would ever make him bow the knee to the tyrant of the gods. For century after century Zeus might hurl fresh pain upon him but would never conquer his unyielding spirit. Nor was Zeus himself secure for ever in his power. For, just as Ouranos had given way to Cronos and Cronos himself had been overmastered by Zeus, so, said Prometheus, there was a moment fixed in the hidden and distant future when Zeus, if he made a certain marriage, would become the father of a son mightier than himself, one who would laugh at lightning and thunderbolts, since he would possess a weapon far greater than these, and who with a motion of the hand would brush aside the great trident of Poseidon, the earth-shaker. Prometheus, who was wise with the wisdom of his mother Earth, knew the secret of this wedding and who it was, if ever she became the bride of Zeus, that was destined to bear a child more powerful than the present supreme ruler of gods and men. But, said Prometheus, he would never reveal this secret—never, until he was released from these chains and restored to the honours he had before. Nor could any exercise of supreme power make him in any manner of way alter his mind.

So Oceanus returned to the deep sea caves where he lives remote from the quarrels of gods in heaven and of men on earth. He might have wished that Prometheus could have been less unbending in his spirit, but he feared for himself if he were to do more in the matter.

But Zeus, who hears everything, had heard the words spoken by Prometheus and knew that in the possession of this chained and helpless captive was a secret which, if it were not told, might at some time or other, near or far, mean the end of his own power and an ignominious fall. He could not bear to think that anyone could hold, or could be allowed to remain holding, an advantage over him, and so he sent down from Olympus his messenger, the god Hermes, to that crag in the Caucasus where Prometheus stood chained. Hermes came and delivered his message, which was that Prometheus must tell at once that secret of which he had been boasting; if he did not, punishment far more fearful than any he had yet known would come down upon him.

But Prometheus treated both the message and the messenger with contempt. "I hate and despise," he said, "your master Zeus, and I would rather be the slave for ever to this bitter barren rock than his trusted servant. I know the power of Zeus and, though I may feel it, I do not fear it. Let him let loose upon me all the fires of his lightning, all the blows of thunder from above and beneath the earth. Let him mix earth and heaven together over my head. Never, till I am released from these bonds, shall I reveal to him the thing he wishes to know and the thing which will, in the end, plunge him downward from his dictatorship."

Nor did any words that Hermes could speak have any effect upon the Titan's unbending pride. "Try," Hermes begged him, "to make your thought follow the meaning of your position. Be humble, since there is no help. For, if you persist in refusing to speak, Father Zeus will convulse this whole mountain with thunder and lightning. You will be buried in the depths of the earth and you will groan as the weight of the earth bears down upon you. And then, shattered and broken, you will be brought up to the light of day; and now, every day, the winged hound of Zeus, his great eagle, will fly to you and every day will tear the flesh of your body into rags, feasting upon your liver and gnawing it black; and every night the flesh will grow again to be destroyed and torn to fragments as the next day comes. There will be no end ever to these fearful pains, nor am I threatening anything that will not be done; for Zeus will bring every word I have spoken to actual fact."

But no threat and no certain knowledge could turn the mind of Prometheus. "You have told me," he said, "nothing that I did not know already. The hound of Zeus may tear my body into shreds; my frame may be broken and shattered beneath earthquakes and falling skies; my mind remains immortal and unsubdued."

So Hermes departed hurriedly, lest he might find himself involved in that terrible convulsion of nature that he knew was now to fall upon the mountain where still Prometheus stood to challenge a superior power. And soon indeed came the crashing and reverberation of thunder, the roar and howling of winds, the quaking of the earth and the loose-flung torches and solid sheets of burning and corroding lightning. Yet in this shattering storm and conflagration of nature Prometheus, flung from wave to wave of terror, pierced by the jagged rocks and overloaded by the pressing weight of mountain ranges, never altered for one moment the fixed resolution of a mind determined to resist. Nor, later, when his mangled body was restored to the upper air, did he weaken beneath the pain as every day the eagle of Zeus came to feed upon his flesh. Every night the flesh was renewed and every day there was reiterated pain. Yet still Prometheus kept his secret and still, in the face of unending persecution, defied the supreme power.

How could this story end except in the fulfillment of the threat which Prometheus had made, or else in some alteration in the character of either Zeus or Prometheus or both? It seems that it was this latter thing that happened. It seems, though this is a hard thing to say of gods, that Zeus, as he grew older in power, grew wiser and more merciful; and it may be too that Prometheus himself, though he lost nothing of his resolution, may have relaxed something of his pride. What is certain is that some form of persuasion was found to intervene between these mighty antagonists. Prometheus was freed and freed by the son of Zeus, Hercules, who climbed the high Caucasus and, after shooting down the eagle with his arrows, released the great Titan from his chains. And Prometheus revealed the secret which he had kept so long and through such sufferings. It was that if Zeus, as he was minded to do, were to marry the sea-goddess, silver-footed Thetis, then she would bear a son stronger than the father. And so Zeus and the other blessed gods betrothed Thetis to a mortal, fearing the event if she were to marry one of them. They chose for her husband the great king of Thessaly, Peleus, and by him, as is well known, she became the mother of the greatest warrior of all men who lived upon the earth, though he died very young, the fleet-footed Achilles.

As for Zeus and for Prometheus, their quarrel was over. Each had, in a manner, submitted to the other, and, though differences still arose among the blessed gods, never again was there to be any struggle in heaven for supreme power.[1]

[1] Rex Warner, *The Stories of the Greeks,* pp. 316–321.

THESEUS AND ARIADNE
Greek

Theseus's quest leads to the very depths, represented by the lab-
yrinth and the monster who lurks there. It is a quest that takes
on more meaning in the context of the myth of the descent to
the underworld with the help of a woman.

It is a matter of dispute whether Medea persuaded Aegeus
to send Theseus against Poseidon's ferocious white bull, or
whether it was after her expulsion from Athens that he under-
took the destruction of this fire-breathing monster, hoping
thereby to ingratiate himself further with the Athenians. Brought 5
by Heracles from Crete, let loose on the plain of Argos, and driven
thence across the Isthmus to Marathon, the bull had killed men
by the hundred between the cities of Probalinthus and Tricoryn-
thus, including (some say) Minos's son Androgeus. Yet Theseus
boldly seized those murderous horns and dragged the bull in 10
triumph through the streets of Athens, and up the steep slope of
the Acropolis, where he sacrificed it to Athene, or to Apollo. . . .

In requital for the death of Androgeus, Minos gave orders
that the Athenians should send seven youths and seven maidens
every ninth year—namely at the close of every Great Year—to 15
the Cretan Labyrinth, where the Minotaur waited to devour them.
This Minotaur, whose name was Asterius, or Asterion, was the
bull-headed monster which Pasiphae had borne to the white bull.
Soon after Theseus's arrival at Athens the tribute fell due for the
third time, and he so deeply pitied those parents whose children 20
were liable to be chosen by lot, that he offered himself as one of
the victims, despite Aegeus's earnest attempts at dissuasion. . . .

On the two previous occasions, the ship which conveyed the
fourteen victims had carried black sails, but Theseus was confident that the gods were on his side, and Aegeus therefore gave 25
him a white sail to hoist on return, in signal of success; though
some say that it was a red sail, dyed in juice of the kerm-oak
berry.

When the lots had been cast at the Law Courts, Theseus led
his companions to the Dolphin Temple where, on their behalf, 30
he offered Apollo a branch of consecrated olive, bound with
white wool. The fourteen mothers brought provisions for the

voyage, and told their children fables and heroic tales to hearten them. Theseus, however, replaced two of the maiden victims with a pair of effeminate youths, possessed of unusual courage and presence of mind. These he commanded to take warm baths, avoid the rays of the sun, perfume their hair and bodies with unguent oils, and practise how to talk, gesture, and walk like women. He was thus able to deceive Minos by passing them off as maidens. . . .

The Delphic Oracle had advised Theseus to take Aphrodite for his guide and companion on the voyage. He therefore sacrificed to her on the strand; and lo! the victim, a she-goat, became a he-goat in its death-throes. This prodigy won Aphrodite her title of Epitragia.

Theseus sailed on the sixth day of Munychion [April]. . . .

When the ship reached Crete some days afterwards, Minos rode down to the harbour to count the victims. Falling in love with one of the Athenian maidens—whether it was Periboea (who became the mother of Ajax) or Eriboea, or Phereboea, is not agreed, for these three bore confusingly similar names—he would have ravished her then and there, had Theseus not protested that it was his duty as Poseidon's son to defend virgins against outrage by tyrants. Minos, laughing lewdly, replied that Poseidon had never been known to show delicate respect for any virgins who took his fancy.

'Ha!' he cried, 'prove yourself a son of Poseidon, by retrieving this bauble for me!' So saying, he flung his golden signet ring into the sea.

'First prove that you are a son of Zeus!' retorted Theseus.

This Minos did. His prayer: 'Father Zeus, hear me!' was at once answered by lightning and a clap of thunder. Without more ado, Theseus dived into the sea, where a large school of dolphins escorted him honourably down to the palace of the Nereids. Some say that Thetis the Nereid then gave him the jewelled crown, her wedding gift from Aphrodite, which Ariadne afterwards wore; others, that Amphitrite the Sea-goddess did so herself, and that she sent the Nereids swimming in every direction to find the golden ring. At all events, when Theseus emerged from the sea, he was carrying both the ring and the crown. . . .

Aphrodite had indeed accompanied Theseus: for not only did both Periboea and Phereboea invite the chivalrous Theseus to their couches, and were not spurned, but Minos's own daughter

Ariadne fell in love with him at first sight. 'I will help you to kill my half-brother, the Minotaur,' she secretly promised him, 'if I may return to Athens with you as your wife.' This offer Theseus gladly accepted, and swore to marry her. Now, before Daedalus left Crete, he had given Ariadne a magic ball of thread, and instructed her how to enter and leave the Labyrinth. She must open the entrance door and tie the loose end of the thread to the lintel; the ball would then roll along, diminishing as it went and making, with devious turns and twists, for the innermost recess where the Minotaur was lodged. This ball Ariadne gave to Theseus, and instructed him to follow it until he reached the sleeping monster, whom he must seize by the hair and sacrifice to Poseidon. He could then find his way back by rolling up the thread into a ball again.

That same night Theseus did as he was told; but whether he killed the Minotaur with a sword given him by Ariadne, or with his bare hands, or with his celebrated club, is much disputed. . . .

When Theseus emerged from the Labyrinth, spotted with blood, Ariadne embraced him passionately, and guided the whole Athenian party to the harbour. For, in the meantime, the two effeminate-looking youths had killed the guards of the women's quarters, and released the maiden victims. They all stole aboard their ship . . . and rowed hastily away. But although Theseus had first stove in the hulls of several Cretan ships, to prevent pursuit, the alarm sounded and he was forced to fight a sea-battle in the harbour, before escaping, fortunately without loss, under cover of darkness.

Some days later, after disembarking on the island then named Dia, but now known as Naxos, Theseus left Ariadne asleep on the shore, and sailed away. Why he did so must remain a mystery. Some say that he deserted her in favour of a new mistress, Aegle, daughter of Panopeus; others that, while windbound on Dia, he reflected on the scandal which Ariadne's arrival at Athens would cause. Others again, that Dionysus, appearing to Theseus in a dream, threateningly demanded Ariadne for himself, and that, when Theseus awoke to see Dionysus's fleet bearing down on Dia, he weighed anchor in sudden terror; Dionysus having cast a spell which made him forget his promise to Ariadne and even her very existence.

Whatever the truth of the matter may be, Dionysus's priests at Athens affirm that when Ariadne found herself alone on the

147

deserted shore, she broke into bitter laments, remembering how she had trembled while Theseus set out to kill her monstrous half-brother; how she had offered silent vows for his success; and how, through love of him, she had deserted her parents and motherland. She now invoked the whole universe for vengeance, and Father Zeus nodded assent. Then, gently and sweetly, Dionysus with his merry train of satyrs and maenads came to Ariadne's rescue. He married her without delay, setting Thetis's crown upon her head, and she bore him many children. . . .

Ariadne was soon revenged on Theseus. Whether in grief for her loss, or in joy at the sight of the Attic coast, from which he had been kept by prolonged winds, he forgot his promise to hoist the white sail, Aegeus, who stood watching for him on the Acropolis, where the Temple of the Wingless Victory now stands, sighted the black sail, swooned, and fell headlong to his death into the valley below. But some say that he deliberately cast himself into the sea, which was thenceforth named the Aegean.[1]

[1] Robert Graves, *The Greek Myths*, vol. 1, pp. 336–343.

KUTOYIS
Blackfoot Indian

The hero's quest always involves the thirst for absolute knowledge. Kutoyis wants to see "all the people."

After Kutoyis had looked about the inside of the lodge, he looked out through a hole in the lodge covering, and then, turning round, he said to the old people: "How is it there is nothing to eat in this lodge? I see plenty of food over by the other lodge." "Hush up," said the old woman, "you will be heard. That is our son-in- 5 law. He does not give us anything at all to eat." "Well," said Kutoyis, "where is your piskun?" The old woman said, "It is down by the river. We pound on it and the buffalo come out."

Then the old man told him how his son-in-law abused him. "He has taken my weapons from me, and even my dogs; and for 10 many days we have had nothing to eat, except now and then a small piece of meat our daughter steals for us."

"Father," said Kutoyis, "have you no arrows?" "No, my son," he replied; "but I have yet four stone points."

"Go out then and get some wood," said Kutoyis. "We will 15 make a bow and arrows. In the morning we will go down and kill something to eat."

Early in the morning Kutoyis woke the old man, and said, "Come, we will go down now and kill when the buffalo come out." When they had reached the river, the old man said: "Here is the 20 place to stand and shoot. I will go down and drive them out." As he pounded on the jam, a fat cow ran out, and Kutoyis killed it.

Meantime the son-in-law had gone out, and as usual knocked on the old man's lodge, and called to him to get up and go down to help him kill. The old woman called to him that her husband 25 had already gone down. This made the son-in-law very angry. He said: "I have a good mind to kill you right now, old woman. I guess I will by and by."

The son-in-law went on down to the jam, and as he drew near, he saw the old man bending over, skinning a buffalo. "Old man," 30 said he, "stand up and look all around you. Look well, for it will be your last look." Now when he had seen the son-in-law coming, Kutoyis had lain down and hidden himself behind the buffalo's carcass. He told the old man to say to his son-in-law, "You had

better take your last look, for I am going to kill you, right now."
The old man said this. "Ah!" said the son-in-law, "you make me
angrier still, by talking back to me." He put an arrow to his bow
and shot at the old man, but did not hit him. Kutoyis told the old
man to pick up the arrow and shoot it back at him, and he did so. 5
Now they shot at each other four times, and then the old man said
to Kutoyis: "I am afraid now. Get up and help me." So Kutoyis
got up on his feet and said: "Here, what are you doing? I think
you have been badly treating this old man for a long time."

Then the son-in-law smiled pleasantly, for he was afraid of 10
Kutoyis. "Oh, no," he said, "no one thinks more of this old man
than I do. I have always taken great pity on him."

Then Kutoyis said: "You lie. I am going to kill you now." He
shot him four times, and the man died. Then Kutoyis told the old
man to go and bring down the daughter who had acted badly 15
toward him. He did so, and Kutoyis killed her. Then he went up
to the lodges and said to the younger woman, "Perhaps you loved
your husband." "Yes," she said, "I love him." So he killed her,
too. Then he said to the old people: "Go over there now, and live
in that lodge. There is plenty there to eat, and when it is gone I 20
will kill more. As for myself, I will make a journey around about.
Where are there any people? In what direction?" "Well," said the
old man, "up above here on Badger Creek and Two Medicine,
where the piskun is, there are some people."

Kutoyis went up to where the piskun was, and saw there 25
many lodges of people. In the centre of the camp was a large
lodge, with a figure of a bear painted on it. He did not go into this
lodge, but went into a very small one near by, where two old
women lived; and when he went in, he asked them for something to eat. They set before him some lean dried meat and some 30
belly fat. "How is this?" he asked. "Here is a piskun with plenty
of fat meat and back fat. Why do you not give me some of that?"
"Hush," said the old women. "In the big lodge near by, lives a big
bear and his wives and children. He takes all those nice things
and leaves us nothing. He is the chief of this place." 35

Early in the morning, Kutoyis told the old women to get their
dog travois, and harness it, and go over to the piskun, and that he
was going to kill for them some fat meat. He reached there just
about the time the buffalo were being driven in, and shot a cow,
which looked very scabby, but was really very fat. Then he helped 40

150

the old women to butcher, and when they had taken the meat to camp, he said to them, "Now take all the choice fat pieces, and hang them up so that those who live in the bear lodge will notice them."

They did this, and pretty soon the old chief bear said to his children: "Go out now, and look around. The people have finished killing by this time. See where the nicest pieces are, and bring in some nice back fat." A young bear went out of the lodge, stood up and looked around, and when it saw this meat close by, at the old women's lodge, it went over and began to pull it down. "Hold on there," said Kutoyis. "What are you doing here, taking the old women's meat?" and he hit him over the head with a stick that he had. The young bear ran home crying, and said to his father, "A young man has hit me on the head." Then all the bears, the father and mother, and uncles and aunts, and all the relations, were very angry, and all rushed out toward the old women's lodge.

Kutoyis killed them all, except one little child bear, a female, which escaped. "Well," said Kutoyis, "you can go and breed bears, so there will be more."

Then said Kutoyis to the old women: "Now, grandmothers, where are there any more people? I want to travel around and see them." The old women said: "The nearest ones are at the point of rocks (on Sun River). There is a piskun there." So Kutoyis travelled off toward this place, and when he reached the camp, he entered an old woman's lodge.

The old woman set before him a plate of bad food. "How is this?" he asked. "Have you nothing better than this to set before a stranger? You have a piskun down there, and must get plenty of fat meat. Give me some pemmican." "We cannot do that," the old woman replied, "because there is a big snake here, who is chief of the camp. He not only takes the best pieces, but often he eats a handsome young woman, when he sees one." When Kutoyis heard this he was angry, and went over and entered the snake's lodge. The women were cooking up some sarvis berries. He picked up the dish, and ate the berries, and threw the dish out of the door. Then he went over to where the snake was lying asleep, pricked him with his knife, and said: "Here, get up. I have come to see you." This made the snake angry. He partly raised himself up and began to rattle, when Kutoyis cut him into pieces with his knife. Then he turned around and killed all his wives and children, except one little female snake, which escaped by crawling into a crack in the rocks. "Oh, well," said Kutoyis, "you can go and breed young snakes, so there will be more. The people will not be afraid of little snakes." Kutoyis said to the old woman, "Now you go into this snake's lodge and take it for yourself, and everything that is in it." . . .

Then he asked some of these people: "Where are there any other people? I want to visit all the people." They said to him: "There is a camp to the westward up the river, but you must not take the left-hand trail going up, because on the trail lives a woman, a handsome woman, who invites men to wrestle with her and then kills them. You must avoid her." This was what Kutoyis was looking for. This was his business in the world, to kill off all the bad things. So he asked the people just where this woman lived, and asked where it was best to go to avoid her. He did this, because he did not wish the people to know that he wanted to meet her.

He started on his way, and at length saw this woman standing by the trail. She called out to him, "Come here, young man, come here; I want to wrestle with you." "No," replied the young man, "I am in a hurry. I cannot stop." But the woman called again, "No, no, come now and wrestle once with me." When she had called him four times, Kutoyis went up to her. Now on the ground, where this woman wrestled with people, she had placed many broken and sharp flints, partly hiding them by the grass. They seized each other, and began to wrestle over these broken flints, but Kutoyis looked at the ground and did not step on them. He watched his chance, and suddenly gave the woman a wrench, and threw her down on a large sharp flint, which cut her in two; and the parts of her body fell asunder.

Then Kutoyis went on, and after a while came to where a woman kept a sliding place; and at the far end of it there was a rope, which would trip people up, and when they were tripped, they would fall over a high cliff into deep water, where a great fish would eat them. When this woman saw him coming, she cried out, "Come over here, young man, and slide with me." "No," he replied, "I am in a hurry." She kept calling him, and when she had called the fourth time, he went over to slide with her. "This sliding," said the woman, "is a very pleasant pastime." "Ah!"

said Kutoyis, "I will look at it." He looked at the place, and, looking carefully, he saw the hidden rope. So he started to slide, and took out his knife, and when he reached the rope, which the woman had raised, he cut it, and when it parted, the woman fell over backward into the water, and was eaten up by the big fish. . . .[1] 5

---

[1] George Bird Grinnell, *Blackfoot Lodge Tales*, pp. 32–37.

KYAZIMBA
Tanzanian

*A longing for immortality is implicitly or explicitly present in
the hero's quest. Kyazimba searches for the land where the sun
rises—for eternal prosperity.*

An East African tribe, for example, the Wachago of Tangan-
yika, tell of a very poor man named Kyazimba, who set out in
desperation for the land where the sun rises. And he had traveled
long and grown tired, and was simply standing, looking hopelessly in the direction of his search, when he heard someone ap- 5
proaching from behind. He turned and perceived a decrepit little
woman. She came up and wished to know his business. When he
had told her, she wrapped her garment around him, and, soaring
from the earth, transported him to the zenith, where the sun
pauses in the middle of the day. Then with a mighty din a great 10
company of men came from eastward to that place, and in the
midst of them was a brilliant chieftain, who, when he had arrived, slaughtered an ox and sat down to feast with his retainers.
The old woman asked his help for Kyazimba. The chieftain
blessed the man and sent him home. And it is recorded that he 15
lived in prosperity ever after.[1]

---

[1] Joseph Campbell, *The Hero with a Thousand Faces*, p. 69.

GAWAIN AND PERCIVAL
European

*The search for the Holy Grail, like the search for the rising sun
or the struggle in the labyrinth, is a search for life renewal.
This is further expressed here in the figure of the Fisher King,
whom Gawain revives.*

The Sangreal was the cup from which our Saviour drank at
his last supper. He was supposed to have given it to Joseph of
Arimathea, who carried it to Europe, together with the spear with
which the soldier pierced the Saviour's side. From generation to
generation, one of the descendants of Joseph of Arimathea had 5
been devoted to the guardianship of these precious relics; but on
the sole condition of leading a life of purity in thought, word, and
deed. For a long time the Sangreal was visible to all pilgrims, and
its presence conferred blessings upon the land in which it was
preserved. But, at length, one of those holy men to whom its 10
guardianship had descended so far forgot the obligation of his
sacred office as to look with unhallowed eye upon a young female
pilgrim whose robe was accidentally loosened as she knelt before
him. The sacred lance instantly punished his frailty, spontaneously
falling upon him and inflicting a deep wound. The marvellous 15
wound could by no means be healed, and the guardian of the
Sangreal was ever after called "Le Roi Pecheur"—the Sinner
King [the Fisher King]. The Sangreal withdrew its visible presence from the crowds who came to worship, and an iron age succeeded to the happiness which its presence had diffused among 20
the tribes of Britain.

...Merlin, ... that great prophet and enchanter, sent a message
to King Arthur by Sir Gawain, directing him to undertake the
recovery of the Sangreal, informing him at the same time that
the knight who should accomplish that sacred quest was al- 25
ready born, and of a suitable age to enter upon it. Sir Gawain
delivered his message, and the king was anxiously revolving
in his mind how best to achieve the enterprise when, at the
vigil of Pentecost, all the fellowship of the Round Table being
met together at Camelot, as they sat at meat, suddenly there 30
was heard a clap of thunder, and then a bright light burst forth,
and every knight, as he looked on his fellow, saw him, in seeming,

fairer than ever before. All the hall was filled with sweet odors, and every knight had such meat and drink as he best loved. Then there entered into the hall the Holy Grail, covered with white samite, so that none could see it, and it passed through the hall suddenly, and disappeared. During this time no one spoke a word, but when they had recovered breath to speak, King Arthur said, "Certainly we ought greatly to thank the Lord for what he hath showed us this day." Then Sir Gawain rose up and made a vow that for twelve months and a day he would seek the Sangreal, and not return till he had seen it, if so he might speed. When they of the Round Table heard Sir Gawain say so, they arose, the most part of them, and vowed the same. When King Arthur heard this, he was greatly displeased, for he knew well that they might not gainsay their vows. "Alas!" said he to Sir Gawain, "you have nigh slain me with the vow and promise that ye have made, for ye have bereft me of the fairest fellowship that ever were seen together in any realm of the world; for when they shall depart hence, I am sure that all shall never meet more in this world."[1]

One day [Percival] came to a great lake which he had never seen before. He saw a man seated in a boat, fishing. The man was richly dressed, but pale and sad. Percival asked if he could get food and shelter anywhere about for himself and his tired horse, and was told that if he went straight on, and did not lose his way, he would come to a castle, where he would be kindly received. He started in the direction indicated by the fisherman, and reached the castle at nightfall, after a long and toilsome search. There he met with so much kindness and consideration, garments even being provided for him "by Queen Repanse's orders," that he was filled with amazement. When freshly attired he was taken into the hall, which was brilliantly lighted. Four hundred knights were seated on softly-cushioned seats at small tables, each of which was laid for four. They all sat grave and silent, as though in expectation. When Percival entered, they rose and bowed, and a ray of joy passed over each woeful countenance.

The master of the house, who much resembled the fisherman Percival had seen on the lake, sat in an armchair near the fire, wrapped in sables, and was apparently suffering from some wasting disease.

[1] Thomas Bulfinch, *Bulfinch's Mythology: The Age of Chivalry*, pp. 157–159.

The deep silence that reigned in the hall was at length broken by the host, who invited Percival, in a low, weak voice, to sit down beside him, telling him that he had been long expected and, at the same time, giving him a sword of exquisite workmanship. The young knight was filled with astonishment. A servant now entered carrying the head of a lance stained with blood, with which he walked round the room in silence. Percival would much have liked to ask the meaning of this strange ceremony and also how his arrival had come to be expected, but he feared lest he should be deemed unwarrantably curious. While thus thinking, the door opened again and a number of beautiful blue-eyed maidens came in, two and two, with a velvet cushion embroidered with pearls, an ebony stand, and various other articles. Last of all came Queen Repanse bearing a costly vessel, whose radiance was more than the human eye could steadfastly gaze upon.

"The holy Grail," Percival heard whispered by one voice after another. He longed to question some one; but felt too much awed by the strangeness and solemnity of all he saw.

The maidens withdrew, and the squires and pages of the knights came forward. Then from the shining vessel streamed an endless supply of the costliest dishes and wines, which they set before their masters. The lord of the castle, however, only ate of one dish, and but a small quantity of that. Percival glanced round the great hall. What could this strange stillness and sadness mean?

When the meal was at an end, the lord of the castle dragged himself to his feet, leaning on two servants. He looked eagerly at his guest, and then retired with a deep sigh. Servants now came to conduct Percival to his sleeping apartment. Before leaving the hall they opened the door of a room in which a venerable old man slept on a low couch. His still handsome face was framed in a coronal of white curls. His sleep was uneasy, and his lips quivered as though he were trying to speak. The servants closed the door again, and led Percival to his chamber.

When he entered the room he looked about him, and at once became aware of a picture embroidered on the silken tapestry, that arrested his attention. It was the picture of a battle, in which the most prominent figure, a knight strangely like the lord of the castle in appearance, was sinking to the ground, wounded by a spear of the same kind as the broken weapon that had been carried round the hall. Much as he desired to know the meaning of

157

this, he determined to ask no questions till the following morning, though the servants told him that his coming had been long expected, and deliverance was looked for at his hands; and they went away, sighing deeply.

His sleep was disturbed by bad dreams, and he awoke next morning unrefreshed. He found his own clothes and armour beside his bed; but no one came to help him. He got up and dressed. All the doors in the castle were locked except those that led out to the ramparts, where his horse stood saddled and bridled at the drawbridge. No sooner had he crossed the bridge than it was drawn up behind him, and a voice called out from the battlements:

"Accursed of God, thou that wast chosen to do a great work, and hast not done it. Go, and return no more. Walk thy evil way till it leads thee down to hell."[2]

[Gawain is entertained at the castle of the Fisher King.]

At the last came in fair procession, as it were, four seneschals, and as the last passed the door was the palace filled — nor were it fitting that I say more. In the sight of all there paced into the hall two maidens fair and graceful, bearing two candlesticks; behind each maid there came a youth, and the twain held between them a sharp spear. After these came other two maidens, fair in form and richly clad, who bare a salver of gold and precious stones, upon a silken cloth; and behind them, treading soft and slow, paced the fairest being whom since the world began God had wrought in woman's wise, perfect was she in form and feature, and richly clad withal. Before her she held on a rich cloth of samite a jewel wrought of red gold, in form of a base, whereon there stood another, of gold and gems, fashioned even as a reliquary that standeth upon an altar. This maiden bare upon her head a crown of gold, and behind her came another, wondrous fair, who wept and made lament, but the others spake never a word, only drew nigh unto the host, and bowed them low before him.

Sir Gawain might scarce trust his senses, for of a truth he knew the crowned maiden well, and that 'twas she who aforetime had spoken to him of the Grail, and bade him as he ever saw her

[2] W. Wägner, *Romances and Epics of Our Northern Ancestors,* pp. 302–305.

158

again, with five maidens in her company, to fail not to ask what they did there—and thereof had he great desire.

As he mused thereon the four who bare spear and salver, the youths with the maidens, drew nigh and laid the spear upon the table, and the salver beneath it. Then before Sir Gawain's eyes there befell a great marvel, for the spear shed three great drops of blood into the salver that was beneath, and the old man, the host, took them straightway. Therewith came the maiden of whom I spake, and took the place of the other twain, and set the fair reliquary upon the table—that did Sir Gawain mark right well—he saw therein a bread, whereof the old man brake the third part, and ate.

With that might Sir Gawain no longer contain himself, but spake, saying, "Mine host, I pray ye for the sake of God, and by His Majesty, that ye tell me what meaneth this great company, and these marvels I behold?" And even as he spake all the folk, knights and ladies alike, who sat there, sprang from their seats with a great cry, and the sound as of great rejoicing. Straightway the host bade them again be seated as before, and make no sound until he bade, and this they did forthwith. . . .

"Sir Gawain, this marvel which is of God may not be known unto all, but shall be held secret, yet since ye have asked thereof, sweet kinsman and dear guest, I may not withhold the truth. 'Tis the Grail which ye now behold. Herein have ye won the world's praise, for manhood and courage alike have ye right well shown, in that ye have achieved this toilsome quest. Of the Grail may I say no more save that ye have seen it, and that great gladness hath come of this your question. For now are many set free from the sorrow they long had borne, and small hope had they of deliverance. Great confidence and trust had we all in Percival, that he would learn the secret things of the Grail, yet hence did he depart even as a coward who ventured naught, and asked naught. Thus did his quest miscarry, and he learned not that which of a surety he should have learned. So had he freed many a mother's son from sore travail, who live, and yet are dead. Through the strife of kinsmen did this woe befall, when one brother smote the other for his land: and for that treason was the wrath of God shown on him and on all his kin, that all were alike lost. . . ."[3]

[3] Jessie Weston, trans., *Sir Gawain at the Grail Castle*, pp. 40–43.

GILGAMESH
Sumerian–Babylonian

The voyage to the "island at the far ends of the earth" is explicitly a search for "the secret of eternal life." The Sumerian hero acts out man's most constant desire.

And even as he cried he saw that his companion no longer stirred nor opened his eyes; and when he felt Enkidu's heart it was beating no more.

Then Gilgamesh took a cloth and veiled the face of Enkidu, even as men veil a bride on the day of her espousal. And he paced 5 to and fro and cried aloud, and his voice was the voice of a lioness robbed of her whelps. And he stripped off his garments and tore his hair and gave himself up to mourning.

All night long he gazed upon the prostrate form of his companion and saw him grow stiff and wizened, and all the beauty 10 was departed from him. "Now," said Gilgamesh, "I have seen the face of death and am sore afraid. One day I too shall be like Enkidu."

When morning came he had made a bold resolve.

On an island at the far ends of the earth, so rumor had it, 15 lived the only mortal in the world who had ever escaped death — an old, old man, whose name was Utnapishtim. Gilgamesh decided to seek him out and to learn from him the secret of eternal life.

As soon as the sun was up he set out on his journey, and at 20 last, after traveling long and far, he came to the end of the world and saw before him a huge mountain whose twin peaks touched the sky and whose roots reached down to nethermost hell. In front of the mountain there was a massive gate, and the gate was guarded by fearsome and terrible creatures, half man and half 25 scorpion.

Gilgamesh flinched for a moment and screened his eyes from their hideous gaze. Then he recovered himself and strode boldly to meet them.

When the monsters saw that he was unafraid, and when they 30 looked on the beauty of his body, they knew at once that no ordinary mortal was before them. Nevertheless they challenged his passage and asked the purpose of his coming.

Gilgamesh told them that he was on his way to Utnapishtim, to learn the secret of eternal life.

"That," replied their captain, "is a thing which none has ever learned, nor was there ever a mortal who succeeded in reaching that ageless sage. For the path which we guard is the path of the sun, a gloomy tunnel twelve leagues long, a road where the foot of man may not tread."

"Be it never so long," rejoined the hero, "and never so dark, be the pains and the perils never so great, be the heat never so searing and the cold never so sharp, I am resolved to tread it!"

At the sound of these words the sentinels knew for certain that one who was more than a mortal was standing before them, and at once they threw open the gate.

Boldly and fearlessly Gilgamesh entered the tunnel, but with every step he took the path became darker and darker, until at last he could see neither before nor behind. Yet still he strode forward, and just when it seemed that the road would never end, a gust of wind fanned his face and a thin streak of light pierced the gloom.

When he came out into the sunlight a wondrous sight met his eyes, for he found himself in the midst of a faery garden, the trees of which were hung with jewels. And even as he stood rapt in wonder the voice of the sun-god came to him from heaven.

"Gilgamesh," it said, "go no farther. This is the garden of delights. Stay awhile and enjoy it. Never before have the gods granted such a boon to a mortal, and for more you must not hope. The eternal life which you seek you will never find."

But even these words could not divert the hero from his course and, leaving the earthly paradise behind him, he proceeded on his way.

Presently, footsore and weary, he saw before him a large house which had all the appearance of being a hospice. Trudging slowly toward it, he sought admission.

But the alewife, whose name was Siduri, had seen his approach from afar and, judging by his grimy appearance that he was simply a tramp, she had ordered the postern barred in his face.

Gilgamesh was at first outraged and threatened to break down the door, but when the lady called from the window and explained to him the cause of her alarm his anger cooled, and he reassured her, telling her who he was and the nature of his journey and the reason he was so disheveled. Thereupon she raised the latch and bade him welcome.

Later in the evening they fell to talking, and the alewife attempted to dissuade him from his quest. "Gilgamesh," she said, "that which you seek you will never find. For when the gods created man they gave him death for his portion; life they kept for themselves. Therefore enjoy your lot. Eat, drink, and be merry; for *that* were you born!"

But still the hero would not be swerved, and at once he proceeded to inquire of the alewife the way to Utnapishtim.

"He lives," she repiled, "on a faraway isle, and to reach it you must cross an ocean. But the ocean is the ocean of death, and no man living has sailed it. Howbeit, there is at present in this hospice a man named Urshanabi. He is the boatman of that aged sage, and he has come hither on an errand. Maybe you can persuade him to ferry you across."

So the alewife presented Gilgamesh to the boatman, and he agreed to ferry him across.

"But there is one condition," he said. "You must never allow your hands to touch the waters of death, and when once your pole has been dipped in them you must straightway discard it and use another, lest any of the drops fall upon your fingers. Therefore take your ax and hew down six-score poles; for it is a long voyage, and you will need them all."

Gilgamesh did as he was bidden, and in a short while they had boarded the boat and put out to sea.

But after they had sailed a number of days the poles gave out, and they had well nigh drifted and foundered, had not Gilgamesh torn off his shirt and held it aloft for a sail.

Meanwhile, there was Utnapishtim, sitting on the shore of the island, looking out upon the main, when suddenly his eyes descried the familiar craft bobbing precariously on the waters.

"Something is amiss," he murmured. "The gear seems to have been broken."

And as the ship drew closer he saw the bizarre figure of Gilgamesh holding up his shirt against the breeze.

"That is not my boatman," he muttered. "Something is surely amiss."

When they touched land Urshanabi at once brought his passenger into the presence of Utnapishtim, and Gilgamesh told him why he had come and what he sought.

"Young man," said the sage, "that which you seek you will never find. For there is nothing eternal on earth. When men draw up a contract they set a term. What they acquire today, tomorrow they must leave to others. Age-long feuds in time die out. Rivers which rise and swell, in the end subside. When the butterfly leaves the cocoon it lives but a day. Times and seasons are appointed for all."

"True," replied the hero. "But you yourself are a mortal, no whit different from me; yet you live forever. Tell me how you found the secret of life, to make yourself like the gods."

A faraway look came into the eyes of the old man. It seemed as though all the days of all the years were passing in procession before him. Then, after a long pause, he lifted his head and smiled.

"Gilgamesh," he said slowly, "I will tell you the secret—a secret high and holy, which no one knows save the gods and myself." And he told him the story of the great flood which the gods had sent upon the earth in the days of old, and how Ea, the kindly lord of wisdom, had sent him warning of it in the whistle of the wind which soughed through the wattles of his hut. At Ea's command he had built an ark, and sealed it with pitch and asphalt, and loaded his kin and his cattle within it, and sailed for seven days and seven nights while the waters rose and the storms raged and the lightnings flashed. And on the seventh day the ark had grounded on a mountain at the end of the world, and he had opened a window in the ark and sent out a dove, to see if the waters had subsided. But the dove had returned, for want of place to rest. Then he had sent out a swallow, and the swallow too had come back. And at last he had sent out a raven, and the raven had not returned. Then he had led forth his kinsmen and his cattle and offered thanksgiving to the gods. But suddenly the god of the winds had come down from heaven and led him back into the ark, along with his wife, and set it afloat upon the waters once more, until it came to the island on the far horizon, and there the gods had set him to dwell forever.*

When Gilgamesh heard the tale he knew at once that his quest had been vain, for now it was clear that the old man had no secret formula to give him. He had become immortal, as he now revealed, by special grace of the gods and not, as Gilgamesh had

* For similar flood myths see Appendix 3.

imagined, by possession of some hidden knowledge. The sun-god had been right, and the scorpion-men had been right, and the alewife had been right: that which he had sought he would never find—at least on this side of the grave.

When the old man had finished his story he looked steadily into the drawn face and tired eyes of the hero. "Gilgamesh," he said kindly, "you must rest awhile. Lie down and sleep for six days and seven nights." And no sooner had he said these words than, lo and behold, Gilgamesh was fast asleep.

Then Utnapishtim turned to his wife. "You see," said he, "this man who seeks to live forever cannot even go without sleep. When he awakes he will, of course, deny it—men were liars ever—so I want you to give him proof. Every day that he sleeps bake a loaf of bread and place it beside him. Day by day those loaves will grow staler and moldier, and after seven nights, as they lie in a row beside him; he will be able to see from the state of each how long he has slept."

So every morning Utnapishtim's wife baked a loaf, and she made a mark on the wall to show that another day had passed; and naturally, at the end of six days, the first loaf was dried out, and the second was like leather, and the third was soggy, and the fourth had white specks on it, and the fifth was filled with mold, and only the sixth looked fresh.

When Gilgamesh awoke, sure enough, he tried to pretend that he had never slept. "Why," said he to Utnapishtim, "the moment I take a nap you go jogging my elbow and waking me up!" But Utnapishtim showed him the loaves, and then Gilgamesh knew that he had indeed been sleeping for six days and seven nights.

Thereupon Utnapishtim ordered him to wash and cleanse himself and make ready for the journey home. But even as the hero stepped into his boat to depart Utnapishtim's wife drew near.

"Utnapishtim," said she, "you cannot send him away empty-handed. He has journeyed hither with great effort and pain, and you must give him a parting gift."

The old man raised his eyes and gazed earnestly at the hero. "Gilgamesh," he said, "I will tell you a secret. In the depths of the sea lies a plant. It looks like a buckthorn and pricks like a rose. If any man come into possession of it, he can, by tasting it, regain his youth!"

When Gilgamesh heard these words he tied heavy stones to

his feet and let himself down into the depths of the sea; and there, on the bed of the ocean, he espied the plant. Caring little that it pricked him, he grasped it between his fingers, cut the stones from his feet, and waited for the tide to wash him ashore.

Then he showed the plant to Urshanabi the boatman. "Look," he cried, "it's the famous plant called Graybeard-grow-young! Whoever tastes it, gets a new lease on life! I will carry it back to Erech and give it to the people to eat. So will I at least have some reward for my pains!"

After they had crossed the perilous waters and reached land, Gilgamesh and his companion began the long journey on foot to the city of Erech. When they had traveled fifty leagues the sun was already beginning to set, and they looked for a place to pass the night. Suddenly they came upon a cool spring.

"Here let us rest," said the hero, "and I will go bathe."

So he stripped off his clothes and placed the plant on the ground and went to bathe in the cool spring. But as soon as his back was turned a serpent came out of the waters and, sniffing the fragrance of the plant, carried it away. And no sooner had it tasted of it than at once it sloughed off its skin and regained its youth.

When Gilgamesh saw that the precious plant had now passed from his hands forever he sat down and wept. But soon he stood up and, resigned at last to the fate of all mankind, he returned to the city of Erech, back to the land whence he had come.[1]

---

[1] Theodor H. Gaster, *The Oldest Stories in the World*, pp. 35–42.

PELE, HIIAKA, AND LOHIAU
Polynesian

This complex triangle tale of the goddesses Pele and Hiiaka'
and their beloved Lohiau is a resurrection story as well as a
quest narrative.

At one time Pele fell in love with a mortal; and this is the
story of the fiery wooing. Pele, her brothers, and sisters one day, to
amuse themselves with a taste of mortal enjoyments, left their
lurid caves in the crater of Kilauea, and went down to the coast of
Puna to bathe, surf-ride, sport in the sands, and gather squid, 5
limpets, edible seaweed, and like delicacies. As they had assumed
human forms for the time, so for the time they experienced
human appetites.

While the others were amusing themselves in various ways
Pele, in the guise of an old woman, sought repose and sleep in the 10
shade of a *hala*-tree. Her favourite sister was Hiiaka', her full
name being Hiiaka-i-ka-pali-o-Pele. She was younger than Pele,
and they frequently occupied the same grotto under the burning
lake of Kilauea.

Hiiaka' accompanied her sister, and, sitting beside her, kept 15
her cool with a *kahili* (feather plume). Her eyelids growing heavy,
Pele settled herself to sleep, instructing Hiiaka' to allow her
under no circumstances to be disturbed, no matter how long she
might sleep, be it for hours or be it for days; she then fell into a
sound sleep. 20

Hardly was she lapped in the silence of forgetfulness when the
sound of a beaten drum fell on her ear; a distant beating, but regular as if to the impulse of music. Before leaving the crater she
had heard the same sound, but had paid little attention to it. Now
in her dreams, however, her curiosity was awakened, and assum- 25
ing her spiritual form she set off in the direction from which the
sound seemed to come. Leaving her slumbering body in the care
of Hiiaka', Pele followed the sound all over Hawaii; and always it
seemed just before her, but never there, so that she could not
overtake it. At Upolu it came to her from over the sea, and she 30
followed it to the island of Maui. It was still beyond, and she
followed to Molokai; still beyond, and she followed to Oahu; still
beyond, and she followed to Kauai. She stood on the peak of

Haupu, when she saw at last that the sound came from the beach at Kaena.

Hovering unseen over the place, she observed that the sound she had so long followed was that of the *pahu-hula*, or *hula* drum, beaten by Lohiau, the young and handsome Prince of Kauai, who was noted not only for the splendour of his *hula* entertainments, where danced the most beautiful women of the island, but also for his own personal graces as dancer and musician. The favourite deity of Lohiau was Laka-kane, the god of the *hula* and similar sport, and it was this god who, in a spirit of mischief, had conveyed the sound to Pele, awaking in her the curiosity that urged her on and on.

The beach was thronged with dancers, musicians, and spectators, all enjoying themselves under the shade of the *hala-* and coconut-trees, with the Prince as leader and the centre of attraction. Assuming the form of a beautiful woman, Pele suddenly appeared among them. Displaying every imaginable charm of form and feature, her presence was at once noted; and, a way being opened for her to the Prince, he received her graciously and invited her to a seat near him, where she could best witness the entertainment.

Glancing at the beautiful stranger from time to time in the midst of his performances, Lohiau at length became so fascinated that he failed to follow the music, when he yielded the instrument to another, and seated himself beside the enchantress. In answer to his inquiry she informed the Prince that she was a stranger in Kauai, and had come from the direction of the rising sun.

"You are most welcome," said Lohiau, adding, after a pause, "but I cannot rejoice that you have come."

"And why, since I do not come as your enemy?" asked Pele, increasing, with her glances, the turmoil within him.

"Because until now," answered the Prince "my thought has been that there are beautiful women in Kauai."

"I see you know how to shape your speech to suit the fancies of women," said Pele provocatively.

"Not better than I know how to love them," answered Lohiau. "Would you be convinced?"

"Lohiau is in his own kingdom, and has but to command," was her reply; and her play of modesty completed the enthralment of the Prince.

Thus Pele became the wife of Lohiau. He knew nothing of her but what delighted him, nor did he care to inquire about that which he could not discover without inquiry. He saw that she was beautiful above all women, and for a few days they lived so happily together that life seemed a dream to him, as it was a dream to her. But the time had to come when she must return to Hawaii; and, pledging him to remain true to her, she left him with protestations of affection and the promise of a speedy return; and on the wings of the wind she was wafted back to the shores of Puna, where her sister was still patiently watching and waiting in the shade of the *hala*.

Lohiau was inconsolable. As each day passed, he thought she would be with him the next, until more than a month went by, when he refused food, and died in grief at her absence. The strange death of the Prince caused much comment, for he was physically strong, and suffered from no malady. Some declared that he had been prayed to death by enemies; some that he had been poisoned; but an old *kaula* (prophet), who had seen Pele at Kaena and noted her actions, advised against further inquiry concerning the cause of death, offering as a reason the opinion that the strangely beautiful and unknown woman he had taken as wife was an immortal, who had become attached to her earthly husband and called his spirit to her.

The Prince was much loved by his people; and his body, wrapped in many folds of *tapa*, was kept in state for some time in the royal house. It was guarded by the high chiefs of the kingdom, and every night funeral hymns were chanted round it, and *mele* recited of the deeds of the dead prince and his ancestors.

Let us return now to Pele. Her body had been carefully watched by her brothers and sisters, who had not dared to disturb it; and her return was greeted with joy, for the fires of Kilauea had almost died out with neglect. Pele rose to her feet in the form of the old woman she had assumed when falling asleep in the care of Hiiaka'; and without referring to her adventures in Kauai, or to the cause of her long slumber, she returned with the others to Kilauea, and with a breath renewed the dying fires of the crater. Hiiaka' asked and received from Pele permission to remain for a few days at the beach with her loved friend Hopoe, a young woman of Puna, who had lost both her parents in an eruption of Kilaeua.

It is probable that Pele, on leaving Kauai, notwithstanding her fervent words to the contrary, never expected, or particularly desired, to see Lohiau again; but he had so endeared himself to her during their brief union that she found it difficult to forget him; and, after struggling against the feeling for some time, she resolved to send for him. But to whom could she entrust the important mission? She applied to her sisters at the crater one after another; but the way was beset with evil spirits, and one after another refused to go.

In this dilemma Pele sent her brother Lono-i-ka-onolii to bring Hiiaka' from the beach, well knowing that she would not refuse to undertake the journey, however hazardous. Hiiaka' accepted the mission, with the understanding that during her absence her friend Hopoe should remain in the guardianship of Pele.

Arrangements were made for her immediate departure. Pele conferred upon her some of her own powers, and for a companion servant gave her Pauo-palae, a woman of proved sagacity and prudence.

With a farewell from the relatives of Hiiaka' and many an admonition from Pele they took their departure; and, travelling as mortals, they were subject to the fatigues and perils of mortals. They met a woman, whose name was Omeo, and who was leading a hog to the volcano as a sacrifice to Pele. She desired to accompany them; and, they agreeing, she hastened to the crater with her offering, returned, and followed Hiiaka' and her companion. Proceeding through the forests toward the coast of Hilo, they were impeded by a hideous demon, who threw himself across their path in a narrow defile and attempted to destroy them; but Pele was aware of their danger, and ordered her brothers to protect them with a rain of fire and thunder, which drove the monster to his den and enabled them to escape.

The forests abounded in mischievous gnomes and fairies, nymphs and monsters guarded the streams; the air was peopled with spirits, for a thin veil only separated the living from the dead, the natural from the supernatural.

Again they had not gone far when they encountered a man of fierce appearance who was either insane or possessed of demons; but he lacked the power or the disposition to injure them, and they passed on unharmed. Coming to a small stream, they found the waters dammed by a huge *mo'o*, or lizard *(moko)*, lying in the bed. He was more than a hundred paces in length, with eyes the size of great calabashes. He glared viciously, and opened his mouth as if to devour the travellers; but Hiiaka' tossed a stone into his mouth which on touching his throat became red-hot, and with a roar of pain that made the trees tremble he disappeared down the stream.

After many adventures with monsters and evil spirits they reached the coast at Honoipo, where they found a number of men and women engaged in the sport of surf-riding. As they were about to start on another trial Hiiaka' in a spirit of mischief turned their surf-boards into stone, and they fled from the beach in terror, fearing that some sea-god was preparing to devour them.

Observing a fisherman drawing in a line, Hiiaka' caused a human head to be fastened to the submerged hook. The man raised it to the surface, stared at it in horror for a moment, then dropped the line and paddled swiftly away, to the great amusement of Hiiaka' and her companions.

Embarking in a canoe, the travellers reached Maui, crossed it with further adventures, then sailed with a fisherman for Oahu. They landed at Maka-puu, journeyed overland to Kou — now Honolulu — and from Haena made sail for Kauai. Arriving at Kaena, Hiiaka' saw the spirit hand of Lohiau beckoning to her from the mouth of a cave up in the cliffs. Turning to her companion she said, "We have failed; the lover of Pele is dead! I see his spirit beckoning from the *pali* [cliff] where it is held and hidden by the lizard-women Kilioa and Kalamainu."

Instructing her companions to proceed to the *puoa* where the body of Lohiau was lying in state, Hiiaka' started at once up the *pali*, to give battle to the demons and rescue the spirit of the dead prince. Ascending the cliff and entering the cave, she waved her *pau*, and with angry hisses the demons disappeared. She searched for the spirit of Lohiau, and at last found it in a niche of the rocks where it had been imprisoned by a moonbeam. Taking it tenderly in her hand, she folded it in her *pau* and in an invisible form floated down with it to the *puoa*.

Waiting until after nightfall, Hiiaka' entered the chamber of death unseen, and restored the spirit to the body of Lohiau. Recovering life and consciousness, the bewildered Prince looked about him. The guards were filled with fear when he raised his head, and would have fled in alarm had they not been prevented by Hiiaka', who that instant appeared before them in mortal form. Holding up her hand to command obedience, she said, "Fear nothing; say nothing of this to anyone living, and do nothing except as you may be ordered. The Prince has returned to life, and may recover if properly cared for. His body is weak and wasted. Let him at once be secretly removed to the seashore. The night is dark, and this may be done without observation."

Not doubting that these instructions were from the gods, the guards obeyed, and Lohiau was soon comfortably resting in a hut by the seashore, with Hiiaka' and her companion attending to his wants.

The return of the Prince to health and strength was rapid, and in a few days he reappeared among his friends, to their amazement and great joy. In answer to their inquiries he told them that he owed to the gods his restoration to life. This did not altogether satisfy them, but no other explanation was offered.[1]

[1] Johannes Andersen, *Myths and Legends of the Polynesians*, pp. 268–274.

SETH

Christian

Seth's voyage, like Gilgamesh's, has eternal life as its goal. He seeks the "oil of mercy" which he hopes will revive Adam. Although, again like Gilgamesh, he fails, he is given a vision which foreshadows the Christ who will revive Adam through his death and resurrection.

When Adam is about to die, he bids his son Seth go to Paradise for the oil of mercy. The path will be apparent, since, as Adam and Eve left Paradise, their footprints were burned upon the grass, and no vegetation has ever grown there. Seth is refused the oil of mercy, but is granted three glimpses of Paradise. ⁵ In the first he beholds a dry tree; in the second, an adder twined about the trunk; in the third, a newborn baby in the top. He is told that the dry tree and the serpent represent the sin of man and that the baby is Christ, who will be the oil of mercy. Seth receives three kernels of the tree of life and plants them in the ¹⁰ mouth of his dead father. From the kernels three trees grow — a cedar, a cypress, and a pine — and remain growing in the vale of Hebron until the time of Moses.

These three trees are uprooted by Moses and become the wands with which he sweetens the waters of Marah and brings ¹⁵ forth water from a rock.

David inherits the wands, which are now united to form a single staff. With it he changes the color and shape of some Ethiopians. The staff is replanted and grows into a tree.

Later Solomon attempts to use it in building his Temple, but ²⁰ in whatever way the tree is cut, it is always too long or too short. Perceiving its miraculous power, Solomon has the tree placed in the Temple.

One day a lady named Maximilla accidentally sits on the tree, and, when it bursts into flame, she is inspired to prophecy. The ²⁵ Jews, hearing that Christ will die upon this wood, put Maximilla to death and hurl the tree into a pit.

Miracles are performed until the tree is removed by the Jews and placed over a brook to serve as a bridge. The holy nature of the wood is announced by Sibyl, who refuses to walk on it and ³⁰ instead wades through the brook barefooted.

172

As the time of the Crucifixion approaches, a cross is made of the tree. The cross, however, cannot be lifted by any except Christ, since it was destined for him. By his dying on it he becomes the redeemer or the oil of mercy for mankind.[1]

[1] *Cursor mundi,* summarized in E. C. Quinn, *The Quest of Seth,* pp. 2–3.

QUETZALCOATL
Toltec and Aztec

The Aztec hero is tempted by the hope that he may return from his voyage "as a young boy." His, too, is thus a quest for immortality.

In Tollan dwelt Quetzalcoatl. And in Tollan all the arts and crafts that we know of were first practised, for Quetzalcoatl taught them to the people there. He taught them the smelting of silver and the clearing and setting of precious stones; he taught the craft of building with stones; he taught them how to make statues, and paint signs in books, and keep count of the moons and suns. All crafts except the craft of war Quetzalcoatl taught the people of Tollan. And they made sacrifice to him with bread, and flowers, and perfumes, and not as other peoples made sacrifice to the other gods—by tearing the hearts out of the opened breasts of men and women.

He lived in a house that was made of silver: four chambers that house had: the chamber to the east was of gold, the chamber to the west was set with stones of precious green—emeralds and turquoises and nephrite stones, the chamber to the south was set with coloured sea-shells, and the chamber to the north was set with jasper. The house was thatched with the feathers of bright-plumaged birds. All the birds of rich plumage and sweet song were gathered in that place. In the fields the maize grew so big that a man could not carry more than one stalk in his arms; pumpkins were great in their round as a man is high; cotton grew in the fields red and yellow, blue, and black, and white, and men did not have to dye it. All who lived where Quetzalcoatl was had everything to make them prosperous and happy.

There was a time when they did not have maize, when they lived upon roots and on what they gained in the chase. Maize there was, but it was hidden within a mountain, and no one could come to where it was. Different gods had tried to rend the mountain apart that they might come to where the maize was; but this could not be done. Then Quetzalcoatl took the form of a black ant; with a red ant to guide him he went within the mountain Tonacatepetl, and he came to where the maize was: he took the grain, and laboriously he bore it back to men. Then men planted fields with maize; they had crops for the first time; they built cities, and they lived settled lives, and Quetzalcoatl showed them all the crafts that they could learn from him. They honoured him who dwelt in the shining house. And Quetzalcoatl had many servants; some of them were dwarfs, and all were swift of foot.

Then it came to pass that Tezcatlipoca, he who can go into all places, he who wanders over the earth stirring up strife and war amongst men, descended upon Tollan by means of spider-webs. And from the mountain he came down on a blast of wind of such coldness that it killed all the flowers in Quetzalcoatl's bright garden. And Quetzalcoatl, feeling that coldness, said to his servants, "One has come who will drive me hence; perhaps it were better that I went before he drives me, and drank from a fountain in the Land of the Sun, whence I may return, young as a boy." So he said, and his servants saw him burn down his house of silver with its green precious stones and its thatch of bright plumage, and its door-posts of white and red shells. And they saw him call upon his birds of sweet song and rich plumage, and they heard him bidding them to fly into the land of Anahuac.

Then Tezcatlipoca, that god and that sorcerer, went to where Quetzalcoatl stood, and took him into the ball-court that the two might play a game together. All the people of the city stood round to watch that game. The ball had to be cast through a ring that was high upon the wall. Quetzalcoatl took up the ball to cast it. As he did Tezcatlipoca changed himself into a jaguar and sprang upon him. Then Quetzalcoatl fled. And Tezcatlipoca chased him, driving him through the streets of the city, and out into the high-ways of the country.

His dwarfs fled after him and joined themselves to him. With them he crossed the mountains and came to a hill on which a great tree grew. Under it he rested. As he rested he looked into a mirror and he said, "I am grown to be an old man." Then he threw the mirror down and took up stones and cast them at the tree.

He went on, and his dwarfs made music for him, playing on flutes as they went before him. Once again he became weary, and he rested on a stone by the wayside; there, looking back towards Tollan, he wept, and his tears pitted the stone on which he sat, and his hands left their imprints upon it where he grasped the stone. The stone is there to this day with the pits and the imprints upon it. He rose up, and once again he went on his way. And men from Tollan met him, and he instructed them in crafts that he had not shown them before.

But he did not give them the treasure of jewels that his dwarfs and humpbacked servants carried for him. He flung this treasure into the fountain Cozcaapan; there it stays to this day — Quetzalcoatl's treasure. On his way he passed over a Fire-mountain and over a mountain of snow. On the mountain of snow his dwarfs and humpbacked servants all died from the cold. Bitterly he bewailed them in a song he made in that place.

Then Quetzalcoatl went down the other side of the mountain, and he came to the sea-shore. He made a raft of snakes, and on that raft he sailed out on the sea. Or so some say, telling Quetzalcoatl's story. And those who tell this say that he came to the land of Tlappallan in the Country of the Sun, and there he drank of the Water of Immortality. They say that he will one day return from that land young as a boy. . . .[1]

[1] Padraic Colum, *Myths of the World*, pp. 298–300.

FAUST
German

Faust, like Adam and Eve, sinfully strives to achieve godhead.
His quest is theologically evil but humanistically heroic.

Faustus in his study.

Faustus. Settle thy studies Faustus, and begin
    To sound the depth of that thou wilt profess.
    Having commenced, be a divine in show—
    Yet level at the end of every art   5
    And live and die in Aristotle's works.
    Sweet *Analytics*, 'tis thou hast ravished me.
    Bene disserere est finis logices.
    Is to dispute well logic's chiefest end?
    Affords this art no greater miracle?   10
    Then read no more, thou has attained that end.
    A greater subject fitteth Faustus' wit:
    Bid *on kai me on* farewell, and Galen come:
    Be a physician Faustus, heap up gold,
    And be eternized for some wondrous cure.   15
    Summum bonum medicinae sanitas,
    The end of physic is our body's health.
    Why Faustus hast thou not attained that end?
    Are not thy bills hung up as monuments
    Whereby whole cities have escaped the plague   20
    And thousand desperate maladies been cured?
    Yet art thou still but Faustus and a man.
    Could'st thou make men to live eternally
    Or being dead raise them to life again,
    Then this profession were to be esteemed.   25
    Physic farewell! Where is Justinian?
    Si una eademque res legatur duobus, alter rem, alter
      valorem rei, et cetera.
    A petty case of paltry legacies.
    Exhereditare filium non potest pater, nisi—   30
    Such is the subject of the *Institute*
    And universal body of the law!
    This study fits a mercenary drudge

Who aims at nothing but external trash,
Too servile and illiberal for me.
When all is done, divinity is best.
Jerome's Bible, Faustus, view it well.
Stipendium peccati mors est. Ha! *Stipendium et cetera.*   5
> The reward of sin is death? That's hard: *Si peccasse
> negamus, fallimur, et nulla est in nobis veritas.* If we say
> that we have no sin, we deceive ourselves, and there is no
> truth in us. Why, then belike, we must sin, and so conse-
> quently die.   10

Ay, we must die an everlasting death.
What doctrine call you this? *Che sera, sera:*
What will be, shall be! Divinity, adieu!
These metaphysics of magicians
And negromantic books are heavenly;   15
Lines, circles, letters, characters—
Ay, these are those that Faustus most desires.
O, what a world of profit and delight,
Of power, of honor, and omnipotence
Is promised to the studious artisan!   20
All things that move between the quiet poles
Shall be at my command: emperors and kings
Are but obeyed in their several provinces
But his dominion that exceeds in this
Stretcheth as far as doth the mind of man: 25
A sound magician is a demi-god!
Here tire my brains to get a deity!

Enter Wagner.

Wagner, commend me to my dearest friends,
The German Valdes and Cornelius.   30
Request them earnestly to visit me.
Wagner. I will, sir.   *Exit.*
Faustus. Their conference will be a greater help to me
> Than all my labors, plod I ne'er so fast.

Enter the [Good] Angel and [the Evil] Spirit.   35

Good Angel. O Faustus, lay that damnèd book aside
> And gaze not on it lest it tempt thy soul

And heap God's heavy wrath upon thy head!
Read, read the Scriptures—that is blasphemy!
Bad Angel. Go forward Faustus, in that famous art
Wherein all nature's treasure is contained.
Be thou on earth as Jove is in the sky,   5
Lord and commander of these elements!

                              Exeunt Angels.

Faustus. How am I glutted with conceit of this!
Shall I make spirits fetch me what I please?
Resolve me of all ambiguities?   10
Perform what desperate enterprise I will?
I'll have them fly to India for gold,
Ransack the ocean for orient pearl,
And search all corners of the new-found world
For pleasant fruits and princely delicates;   15
I'll have them read me strange philosophy
And tell the secrets of all foreign kings;
I'll have them wall all Germany with brass
And make swift Rhine circle fair Wittenberg;
I'll have them fill the public schools with silk   20
Wherewith the students shall be bravely clad.
I'll levy soldiers with the coin they bring
And chase the Prince of Parma from our land
And reign sole king of all the provinces!
Yea, stranger engines for the brunt of war   25
Than was the fiery keel at Antwerp bridge
I'll make my servile spirits to invent.

            Enter Valdes and Cornelius.

Come German Valdes and Cornelius
And make me blest with your sage conference.   30
Valdes, sweet Valdes, and Cornelius,
Know that your words have won me at the last
To practice magic and concealèd arts.
Philosophy is odious and obscure,
Both law and physic are for petty wits,   35
Divinity is basest of the three—
Unpleasant, harsh, contemptible, and vile.
'Tis magic, magic, that hath ravished me!
Then, gentle friends, aid me in this attempt

And I, that have with subtle syllogisms
Graveled the pastors of the German church
And made the flow'ring pride of Wittenberg
Swarm to my problems as th' infernal spirits
On sweet Musaeus when he came to hell,   5
Will be as cunning as Agrippa was,
Whose shadows made all Europe honor him.
Valdes. Faustus, these books, thy wit, and our experience
    Shall make all nations to canonize us.
    As Indian Moors obey their Spanish lords,   10
    So shall the spirits of every element
    Be always serviceable to us three:
    Like lions shall they guard us when we please,
    Like Almain rutters with their horsemen's staves
    Or Lapland giants trotting by our sides;   15
    Sometimes like women or unwedded maids
    Shadowing more beauty in their airy brows
    Then has the white breasts of the queen of love;
    From Venice shall they drag huge argosies
    And from America the golden fleece   20
    That yearly stuffs old Philip's treasury,
    If learnèd Faustus will be resolute.
Faustus. Valdes, as resolute am I in this
    As thou to live; therefore object it not.
Cornelius. The miracles that magic will perform   25
    Will make thee vow to study nothing else.
    He that is grounded in astrology,
    Enriched with tongues, well seen in minerals,
    Hath all the principles magic doth require.
    Then doubt not Faustus but to be renowned   30
    And more frequented for this mystery
    Than heretofore the Delphian oracle.
    The spirits tell me they can dry the sea
    And fetch the treasure of all foreign wracks,
    Yea, all the wealth that our forefathers hid   35
    Within the massy entrails of the earth.
    Then tell me Faustus, what shall we three want?
Faustus. Nothing, Cornelius. O, this cheers my soul!
    Come, show me some demonstrations magical
    That I may conjure in some bushy grove   40
    And have these joys in full possession.

Valdes. Then haste thee to some solitary grove,
    And bear wise Bacon's and Albanus' works,
    The Hebrew Psalter, and New Testament;
    And whatsoever else is requisite
    We will inform thee ere our conference cease.   5
Cornelius. Valdes, first let him know the words of art,
    And then, all other ceremonies learned,
    Faustus may try his cunning by himself.
Valdes. First I'll instruct thee in the rudiments,
    And then wilt thou be perfecter than I.   10
Faustus. Then come and dine with me, and after meat
    We'll canvass every quiddity thereof,
    For ere I sleep I'll try what I can do:
    This night I'll conjure though I die therefor!

                           Exeunt omnes.[1] 15

---

[1] Christopher Marlowe, *Doctor Faustus*, I, i.

JESUS
Christian

Jesus shows the way to eternal life in the Kingdom of God. His whole life is a quest to teach spiritually dead man how to be reborn in God.

In that hour Jesus rejoiced in spirit, and said, I thank thee, O Father, Lord of heaven and earth, that thou hast hid these things from the wise and prudent, and hast revealed them unto babes: even so, Father; for so it seemed good in thy sight. All things are delivered to me of my Father: and no man knoweth 5 who the Son is, but the Father; and who the Father is, but the Son, and he to whom the Son will reveal him.

And he turned him unto his disciples, and said privately, Blessed are the eyes which see the things that ye see: for I tell you, that many prophets and kings have desired to see those 10 things which ye see, and have not seen them; and to hear those things which ye hear, and have not heard them.

And, behold, a certain lawyer stood up, and tempted him, saying. Master, what shall I do to inherit eternal life? He said unto him, What is written in the law? how readest thou? And he 15 answering said,

Thou shalt love the Lord thy God
with all thy heart, and with all thy soul,
and with all thy strength, and with all thy mind;
and thy neighbor as thyself. 20

And he said unto him, Thou hast answered right: this do, and thou shalt live.

But he, willing to justify himself, said unto Jesus, And who is my neighbor? And Jesus answering said, A certain man went down from Jerusalem to Jericho, and fell among thieves, which 25 stripped him of his raiment, and wounded him, and departed, leaving him half dead. And by chance there came down a certain priest that way; and when he saw him, he passed by on the other side. And likewise a Levite, when he was at the place, came and looked on him, and passed by on the other side. But a certain 30 Samaritan, as he journeyed, came where he was; and when he saw him, he had compassion on him, and went to him, and bound up his wounds, pouring in oil and wine, and set him on his own beast, and brought him to an inn, and took care of him. And on the morrow when he departed, he took out two pence, and gave them to the host, and said unto him, Take care of him: and whatsoever thou spendest more, when I come again, I will repay thee. Which now of these three, thinkest thou, was neighbor unto him that fell among the thieves? And he said, He that showed mercy on him. Then said Jesus unto him, Go, and do thou likewise.[1]

Now when Jesus had heard that John was cast into prison, he departed into Galilee; and leaving Nazareth, he came and dwelt in Capernaum, which is upon the seacoast, in the borders of Zebulun and Naphtali: that it might be fulfilled which was spoken by Isaiah the prophet, saying,

The land of Zebulun, and the land of Naphtali,
by the way of the sea, beyond Jordan,
Galilee of the Gentiles;
the people which sat in darkness saw great light;
and to them which sat in the region and shadow of death
light is sprung up.

From that time Jesus began to preach, and to say, Repent: for the kingdom of heaven is at hand.

And Jesus, walking by the sea of Galilee, saw two brethren, Simon called Peter, and Andrew his brother, casting a net into the sea: for they were fishers. And he saith unto them, Follow me, and I will make you fishers of men. And they straightway left their nets, and followed him. And going on from thence, he saw other two brethren, James the son of Zebedee, and John his brother, in a ship with Zebedee their father, mending their nets; and he called them. And they immediately left the ship and their father, and followed him.

And Jesus went about all Galilee, teaching in their synagogues, and preaching the gospel of the kingdom, and healing all manner of sickness and all manner of disease among the people. And his fame went throughout all Syria: and they brought unto him all sick people that were taken with divers diseases and torments, and those which were possessed with devils, and those which were lunatic, and those that had the palsy; and he healed them. And there followed him great multitudes of people from Galilee, and from Decapolis, and from Jerusalem, and from Judea, and from beyond Jordan.

[1] Luke 10.

And seeing the multitudes, he went up into a mountain: and when he was set, his disciples came unto him: and he opened his mouth, and taught them, saying,

Blessed are the poor in spirit: for theirs is the kingdom of heaven.

Blessed are they that mourn: for they shall be comforted.

Blessed are the meek: for they shall inherit the earth.

Blessed are they which do hunger and thirst after righteousness: for they shall be filled.

Blessed are the merciful: for they shall obtain mercy.

Blessed are the pure in heart: for they shall see God.

Blessed are the peacemakers: for they shall be called the children of God.

Blessed are they which are persecuted for righteousness' sake: for theirs is the kingdom of heaven.

Blessed are ye, when men shall revile you, and persecute you, and shall say all manner of evil against you falsely, for my sake. Rejoice, and be exceeding glad: for great is your reward in heaven: for so persecuted they the prophets which were before you.

Ye are the salt of the earth: but if the salt have lost his savor, wherewith shall it be salted? it is thenceforth good for nothing, but to be cast out, and to be trodden under foot of men.

Ye are the light of the world. A city that is set on a hill cannot be hid. Neither do men light a candle, and put it under a bushel, but on a candlestick; and it giveth light unto all that are in the house. Let your light so shine before men, that they may see your good works, and glorify your Father which is in heaven.

Think not that I am come to destroy the law, or the prophets: I am not come to destroy, but to fulfil. For verily I say unto you, Till heaven and earth pass, one jot or one tittle shall in no wise pass from the law, till all be fulfilled. Whosoever therefore shall break one of these least commandments, and shall teach men so, he shall be called the least in the kingdom of heaven: but whosoever shall do and teach them, the same shall be called great in the kingdom of heaven. For I say unto you, That except your righteousness shall exceed the righteousness of the scribes and Pharisees, ye shall in no case enter into the kingdom of heaven.[2]

[2] Matthew 4, 5.

DIONYSOS (DIONYSUS)
Greek

Dionysos, like Jesus, must struggle with unbelievers. His is the traditional agon *between one who knows the way and those who do not.*

The vengeance of Hera caught up with Dionysus during his youth and he went mad. He ran away from his nurses and wandered through Egypt, Syria, and other lands. Some say that he went to Dodona in order to consult the oracle there, and perhaps also because, according to this tale, his nurses had originally come from there. Two asses who carried the god across the river were rewarded by being placed in the stars. To one of them the god gave a human voice, which may later have led to his death at the hands of Dionysus' son Priapus.

At length Dionysus came to Phrygia. There Cybele, whom the Greeks identified with Rhea, purified him and presumably cured him of his madness. It was while he was in Phrygia that he adopted the oriental costume that he and his followers affected; there also he instituted many of his own rites, some of which resemble those of Cybele.

Precisely at what point the mortal-born Dionysus became a full-fledged god is not certain. Unlike Heracles, another mortal who achieved divine status, he did not wait for death to receive it. When Dionysus left Phrygia to establish his own worship in much of the region of the eastern Mediterranean, there is no doubt that he was already a god. Wherever people honored him and observed his rites he rewarded them with many blessings, particularly the knowledge of the cultivation of the grape and the pleasures of wine. Where he encountered opposition, he brought terrible destruction on those who defied him.

Dionysus traveled with a strange company of maenads, satyrs, and seileni. Male as well as female votaries dressed in flowing garments that seemed effeminate to the Greeks. During their revels they wore animal skins and carried *thyrsi,* poles twined with ivy and grapevines and often surmounted with pine cones. They worshiped the god, or achieved communion with him, in orgiastic, often nocturnal, rites on the mountains. When these revels reached their peak, under the influence of religious frenzy (and probably of wine, as well), the revelers often had visions of their god, who might appear in the form of a bull or a goat. The women suckled kids or fawns, and sometimes tore them apart with their bare hands and ritually ate them. To judge from characteristic representations of satyrs in art, sexual license may also have been a part of the rites. [5]

Dionysus first met violent opposition at the hands of Lycurgus, son of Dryas. Lycurgus was king of the Edonians, who lived on the river Strymon, in Thrace. He drove away the god and his "nurses" with an ox-goad. The terrified Dionysus, and perhaps all but one of his nurses as well, took refuge in the depths of the [10] sea with Thetis. According to Homer [*Iliad* 6.119–143], Lycurgus' behavior angered the other gods. Zeus blinded him and he did not live long thereafter. Later writers report the king's punishment in more detail, and in a variety of ways. In all of the accounts Dionysus used against the king his infallible weapon: [15] madness. Some say that he imprisoned Lycurgus in a cave until he came to his senses. Others claim that, while mad or drunk, the king tried to destroy with an ax the vines that the god had taught his people to plant. Instead, he hacked to death his son, Dryas, or his wife and son, and cut off his own or his son's feet. [20] Lycurgus recovered his senses, but the land produced no crops. Through his oracle, Dionysus declared that it would remain barren as long as the king lived. The Edonians thereupon bound Lycurgus on Mount Pangaeus and caused him to be killed by horses, or else the god threw him to his panthers on Mount [25] Rhodope.

Dionysus next came to his birthplace, Thebes. Because his mother's sisters had refused to acknowledge his divinity after Semele's death, he drove them and all the women of Thebes mad. (This harshness toward all three sisters seems to conflict with [30] Dionysus' gratitude, in other accounts, toward Ino for having nursed him.) They deserted their homes and rushed off to the slopes of Mount Cithaeron to join his maenads in their wild rites. Old King Cadmus, who had abdicated the throne in favor of his grandson, Pentheus, accepted the god, as did the seer Teiresias. [35] The young Pentheus, however, was outraged by what seemed to him the excesses of the god's strange band of votaries, and by their unsettling influence on the local women. He had the maenads imprisoned, together with a young priest, their leader.[1]

[1] Edward Tripp, ed., *Crowell's Handbook of Classical Mythology*, pp. 205–207.

186

Guards lead in Dionysus: Pentheus reappears from the palace.

Guard. Pentheus, the errand that you charged us with
 Is done—and here is the quarry that we caught,
 A gentle creature, that did not even flee!
 Of his own will he held out both his hands   5
 And waited there. Easy he made my errand.
 Ruddy as wine, his cheek still kept its colour,
 As, with a smile, he bade us take and lead him.
 I felt ashamed, and said: 'By no will of mine
 I seize you, stranger. These are Pentheus' orders.'   10
  But as for the Maenads that you caught and shut,
 Fast chained, in our common prison—they are vanished!
 Freed from their fetters, through the mountain glades
 They dance with loud cries to Bromius divine.
 For, of themselves, the gyves slipped from their ankles,   15
 The bolts slid back untouched by human hand.
 Marvels indeed this stranger has brought to Thebes!
 The rest, my lord, your judgment must decide.
Pentheus. Let go his hands. Now that I have him snared,
 Whatever his swiftness, he shall not escape me.   20
  Indeed your looks are not unhandsome, stranger,
 At least for women (and for *them* you come).
 Never from wrestling grew those flowing ringlets—
 Lovelocks low-curling all about your cheek.
 And what a white complexion, kept with care   25
 In pleasant shades, where never sun should burn it!
 A comely fellow, that quests the Queen of Love!
 First tell me—what's your country?
Dionysus. Gladly I tell it. That is easy said.
 You must have heard of the flower-grown slopes of Tmolus? 30
Pentheus. I have—the heights that girdle Sardis city.
Dionysus. There lies my home. My land is Lydia.
Pentheus. How comes it, then, you bring these rites to Hellas?
Dionysus. Bacchus Himself so taught me, the son of Zeus.
Pentheus. Is there some Zeus there, that begets new gods?   35
Dionysus. No, the same Zeus as here loved Semele.
Pentheus. In dream did your God constrain you? Or awaking?
Dionysus. Yes, face to face. And gave me His holy rites.
Pentheus. What manner of holy rites?
Dionysus. *That* none may know, except the initiate.   40
Pentheus. What profit are they to the worshippers?

187

Dionysus. You may not hear it—though well worth the hearing!
Pentheus. Ah, you are cunning to make me curious.
Dionysus. His rites abhor the heart irreverent.
Pentheus. You say you saw the God? And in what likeness?
Dionysus. Such likeness as He pleased. Not mine to choose.   5
Pentheus. Once more, well parried—with mere empty words!
Dionysus. To ignorance, the wisest words seem folly.
Pentheus. And was it first to Thebes you brought your God?
Dionysus. All the barbarian lands dance in His worship.
Pentheus. Being duller, far, than Hellenes.   10
Dionysus. Wiser in this; though different their customs.
Pentheus. Is it by day or night ye celebrate?
Dionysus. Mostly, by night. Night hath solemnity.
Pentheus. Ah yes, for women, here is shrewd corruption.
Dionysus. Foulness can be contrived no less by day.   15
Pentheus. You shall pay dearly for your cursed quibbles!
Dionysus. And you for your blindness and your blasphemy.
Pentheus. How bold our Bacchant is!—and skilled in speaking!
Dionysus. Tell me my doom now—what dire penalty?
Pentheus. First, I will shear away those delicate tresses.   20
Dionysus. My hair is holy. I keep it for the God.

> [*A guard cuts it off.*

Pentheus. And hand me over, next, your sacred staff.
Dionysus. Take it yourself. It is Dionysus' own.

> [*Pentheus takes it.* 25

Pentheus. Your body we shall keep in close confinement.
Dionysus. The God Himself shall free me, when I will.
Pentheus. He *may,* when you are safe among your Maenads!
Dionysus. He is here—beside me—seeing what I suffer.
Pentheus. And where then? Nowhere that eyes of mine can see. 30
Dionysus. With *me.* But *your* impiety is blind.
Pentheus (to his guard). Seize him! This is contempt of me and
    Thebes.
Dionysus. I, sane, to ye, grown senseless, say: 'Forbear!'
Pentheus. And *I* say: 'Bind him'—with a better right!   35
Dionysus. You know not what you live for—do—or are.
Pentheus. I?—Pentheus, son of Agave and Echion.
Dionysus. Unhappiness lives in your very name.
Pentheus. Go! Shut him in the stables hard at hand—
    Let him contemplate their darkness!   40
    There you can dance! As for these women here

That follow you, as your accomplices,
They shall be sold to bondage—or myself
Will turn their hands from thumping the hide of timbrels
To labour at my loom.
Dionysus. So be it, I go. What is not fated me,   5
    I cannot suffer. Yet shall Dionysus,
    Whom thou deniest, for this sacrilege
    Hound thee to retribution!
For, wronging *me*, thou hast led *Him* in chains.
The guards lead Dionysus away. Pentheus re-enters the palace. 10
                                      strophe.

Chorus.
    Daughter of Achelous,
      Dirce, maiden and queen,
    Washed of old in thy waters   15
      The babe of God hath been,
    That day when his Heavenly Father
      Forth from the quenchless fire
    Snatched the child and laid him
      In the thigh of his own sire.   20
'Come,' He cried, 'come, Dithyrambus,
      In thy father's womb lie sealed.
By that name all Thebes shall know thee,
    Bacchus, whom I have revealed.'
      Why then, O blessed Dirce,   25
        When here with wreath on brow
      I dance, wilt thou reject me—
      Deny me—shun me now?
Nay, by His own vine's clustering grace,
To Bacchus yet thou shalt turn thy face!   30
                         antistrophe.

    This Pentheus once begotten
      Of Echion, son of earth,
    This scion of earth and dragon—
      His rage well shows his birth!   35
    No mortal, but a monster,
      Savage and grim to see
    As the red Giants that challenged
      The high Gods' sovereignty!
Soon about me, Bacchus' servant,   40
    Shall the tyrant's bonds be tied;

Even now the priest, our comrade,
  Shadows of his prison hide.
    Our martyrdom that preach Thee,
      O Lord, canst Thou behold?
    Rise up, O Dionysus,   5
      And shake Thy staff of gold!
Come Thou from Heaven's height to seize
This murderer in his blasphemies.

                                                    epode.
    Where art hidden, Dionysus?   10
    Leadest Thou Thy mystic band
  Through beast-haunted glens of Nysa?—
  Where the Crags Corycian stand?—
Or amid the forest-coverts
  Of Olympus, where of old   15
With his harp by hill and hollow
Orpheus drew the trees to follow,
  Drew the beasts of wild and wold?
  Blest art thou, Pieria,
Cherished by the God of Gladness;   20
He shall bring His holy madness
  For thy dancing, from afar,
With His Maenads round Him whirling,
Over Axius swiftly swirling,
Over Lydias, fairest river,   25
  Where the steeds graze in their pride,
Of all happiness the giver
  To the dwellers by his tide.
Dionysus (within). Ho!
  Hark to my voice now, harken,   30
  O Bacchanals, O Bacchanals!
One of the Chorus. Whence comes this sound around me
  Of the voice of God that calls?
Dionysus (within). Ho, again I call to ye—
  The Son of Zeus and Semele.   35
Another. Ah my Master, ah my Master!
  Hither, hither!—join with us,
  Bromius, Bromius!
Dionysus (within). Spirit of Earthquake, upheave thou the land!
                                    [*The earth trembles.* 40

Another. Ah, ah!
 Swiftly now shall Pentheus' hall
 Shudder to its final fall.
Another. There within moves Bacchus—now!
 Worship Him!
Another.   To Him we bow.
Another. Look, where the palace-columns rise,
 The marble lintel splits and falls!
 Loud and clear behind its walls,
 'Victory!' our Master cries.
Dionysus (*within*). Thunderbolt, fall glittering!
 Kindle the palace of the King!

                                        [*Lightning*.

One of the Chorus. See the sacred tomb where slumbers
 Semele!—high round it glare
 Heaven's fires that, since they smote her,
 Smouldered there.
 Cast ye down, with bodies trembling!
 Down, ye Maenads! From on high
 To this house, all things confounding,
 Sure the Son of God draws nigh.
  They prostrate themselves and Dionysus enters.
Dionysus. Lie ye on the earth prostrated, with your terrors thus
   aghast,
 Asia's daughters? Sure, ye saw it, how Lord Dionysus cast
 To the earth King Pentheus' palace? None the less, with
   better cheer,
 From the dust upraise your bodies—tremble now no more
   with fear.
Leader. Ah thou saving light and glory of our joyous ecstasy,
 How my heart, that was so lonely, gladdens now at sight of
   thee!
Dionysus. Was your courage, then, so broken, when the guards
   led me away
 To the dungeon of King Pentheus, darkened from the light
   of day?
Leader. Could I help it? Hadst thou perished, who was left to
   save me still?
 How wast thou delivered—tell us!— from that man of evil
   will?

5
10
15
20
25
30
35
40

191

Dionysus. I alone, without an effort, made my own way back to 15
    light.

Leader. Had he not, then, bound together both thy hands with
    cords drawn tight?

Dionysus. Thus it was that I befooled him. Binding me, indeed, 5
    he seemed,

    Yet he never grasped nor touched me, feeding but on fancies
      dreamed.

    In the stable where he shut me, as it chanced, a bull he found;

    Knees and hoofs, he sought to bind it, with a rope fast knotted 10
      round.

    Wildly panting in his frenzy, deep he gnawed his nether lip,

    While I calmly sat beside him, from his body watching drip

    Streams of sweat—so hard he laboured. Then it was that
      Bacchus came— 15

    Made the palace quake, and kindled on His mother's tomb
      the flame.

    Fearing that his hall was burning, hither, thither rushed the
      King,

    Shouting madly to his servants, calling to his men to bring 20

    Water, while with idle efforts all his henchmen ran and cried.

    Then, persuaded I had vanished, all his labour cast aside,

    In he rushed to search the palace, snatching up a blue sword-
      blade.

    What there followed next, I know not. But it seems that 25
      Bacchus made

    In the court a phantom like me. Then on that bright shape of
      air

    Pentheus sprang and hewed and stabbed it, passionate to
      slay me there. 30

    Next, Lord Dionysus smote him with a new indignity,

    Toppling all his house to earthward. Ruined it lies for him
      to see—

    Bitter end to my enchaining! Dropped now from his fainting
      hand 35

    In the dust his sword is lying. Fool, that dared in fight to stand

    Man with God! But I, arising, passed from out his royal hall,

    Calm and undisturbed, to join ye, heeding Pentheus not at all.

    Hark! If I am not mistaken, near the door his footstep rings.

    Forth he comes! What will he say now, after these strange 40
      happenings?

Unperturbed I will await him, stormy though his anger be.
Wise the heart that, still unshaken, keeps its equanimity.
Pentheus (*opening the palace-door*). Monstrous! The stranger
　　　　I had confined in durance,
Has slipped from out my grasp!　　　　　　　　　　　　　5

　　　　　　　　　　　　　　　　[*Seeing Dionysus.*

　　Ha!
　Here is the fellow. What means *this*? How come you
　Walking abroad in the court before my palace?
Dionysus. Stay now!—and give your rage an easier pace.　　10
Pentheus. How come you here at large—my prison broken?
Dionysus. Said I not—heard you not—that One would free me?
Pentheus. And who then? Still these strange, new-fangled
　　　　speeches!
Dionysus. He that has given men His clustering vine.　　15
Pentheus. A famous feat—for Dionysus' shame!
　　　[*One or more lines probably missing.*]
　(*To his guards.*) Shut every gateway in the city-wall.
Dionysus. What use? Can even walls confine the Gods?
Pentheus. So wise, so wise!—except where wisdom's needed.　　20
Dionysus. I have the wisdom that is needed most.[2]

[Dionysus] working his influence on the king himself, persuaded him to accompany him, dressed as a maenad, to spy on
the women at their revels. Pentheus climbed a pine tree on the　25
mountain to watch them as they danced and tore animals limb
from limb. They soon discovered him and uprooted the tree.
Believing him in their frenzy to be a lion, they tore him into
pieces, which they scattered about the mountainside. Agave,
Pentheus' mother, triumphantly returned to Thebes with her　30
son's head impaled on her thyrsus. Only then did she come to her
senses and realize what she had done. Dionysus exiled Agave
and both her parents from Thebes because of their long reluc-
tance to acknowledge him. Cadmus and Harmonia also were
exiled. In the land of the Encheleans they were changed into　35
serpents by Dionysus or Ares and eventually went to the Elysian
Fields.
　　Thebes became the principal Greek center of the god's cult.
Pentheus was succeeded by his uncle, Polydorus. It was perhaps

---

[2] Euripides, *The Bacchae*, translated by F. L. Lucas, lines 434–656.

this king who officially instituted the god's rites at Thebes. It is recorded that he enshrined a log that had mysteriously fallen from heaven at the time that Semele was blasted by the thunderbolt. Polydorus had the log ornamented with bronze and it was thereafter honored as Dionysus Cadmus.

The daughters of Minyas, king of nearby Orchomenus, were no more willing to accept Dionysus than Cadmus' daughters had been. Denying that he was a god, they remained in the palace and busied themselves with what had always been regarded as the proper tasks of women, rather than dressing in animal skins and dancing in the woods. Dionysus punished them in his usual way. In their madness they tore to pieces the infant son of one of the sisters, after choosing the victim by lot. Dionysus changed them into bats.

The god next came to Argos, where either Proetus or Anaxagoras was king. Proetus (in that version of the tale) had three daughters, Lysippe, Iphinoe, and Iphianassa. Like the three daughters of Cadmus, and of Minyas, they refused to worship the new god. In the protracted fit of madness with which he afflicted them, they roamed the mountains in a disheveled state, imagined themselves to be cows, and ate the children that they suckled at their breasts. Some say that this disease affected all the Argive women, or that it was sent by Hera, not Dionysus. In any case, the Argive men called in the seer Melampus from Pylus to cure the women. He did so for a fee that amounted to a sizable share of the kingdom.

According to an entirely different tradition, Dionysus came to Argos in company with a band of women from the Aegean islands, whom the Argives dubbed Haliae (Sea-women). Perseus, king of Mycenae, went to war with them and killed many, burying them in a mass grave at Argos. (Some very late Classical writers say that he killed Dionysus himself.) The Argives of Pausanias' day claimed, on the other hand, that Perseus and the god were reconciled and that the latter was worshiped at Argos as the Cretan Dionysus. There was a tomb of Dionysus' wife Ariadne at Argos.

During the reign of Pandion, Dionysus came to Attica. Instead of seeking a direct confrontation with the king, however, he chose to teach the culture of the vine to a man named Icarius and his daughter, Erigone. Icarius was delighted with this boon to mankind, but when he gave some wine to the local peasants they thought themselves poisoned and killed Icarius. Erigone hanged herself. Dionysus drove the women of Attica mad and they too began hanging themselves. Their husbands, after consulting an oracle, punished Icarius' murderers and instituted an annual "swinging festival" in Erigone's honor. Dionysus relented and the women of Attica regained their sanity. He placed Icarius, Erigone, and even their dog, Maeara, in the stars as the constellations Bootes, Virgo, and Canicula or Procyon.

When the god went to Aetolia he met with a hospitable welcome from King Oeneus. Not only did he entertain Dionysus, but, on realizing that his guest wanted to sleep with his wife, Althaea, he found a pretext to leave town for a discreet interval. When he returned, Althaea was pregnant (and later gave birth to a daughter, Deianeira). Dionysus rewarded Oeneus' generosity, or prudence, with the gift of the vine and went on his way.

Dionysus' triumphant travels carried him to many parts of the world. He is said, for example, to have routed the Amazons before Heracles made his famous expedition to their country. The god also led his followers (whom late Classical writers often conceived of as an army) into Egypt. There they were lost for a time in the desert without water. Either the god or some of the army spied a stray ram and followed it. It vanished, but on the spot where it was last seen they discovered a spring. To commemorate this event, Dionysus established a shrine of the ram-headed god Ammon. Furthermore, he placed the ram in the stars as the constellation Aries.

Dionysus' most distant expedition led him as far as the Ganges River, in India. In order to cross the Euphrates River, he constructed a bridge with cables plaited of ivy and vine strands. Seilenus, his old companion, disappeared one day as Dionysus' army was crossing Phrygia, or possibly Macedonia. He reappeared some days later with an honor guard sent along by Midas, king of the Mygdonians. The king, or some of his peasants, had easily captured the ever-thirsty old man by setting out bowls of wine. Midas had entertained him with splendid hospitality, and Dionysus rewarded him by offering to grant any boon that he asked. Midas foolishly requested that everything he touched should turn to gold. The god reluctantly consented, but was not surprised when Midas, starving because he could not eat gold, returned to ask that the gift be withdrawn. Even a god cannot 20 rescind his own vows, but Dionysus told Midas how to wash away his "golden touch" by bathing in the river Pactolus.

Before going to India Dionysus had left Nysus in charge of Thebes. Nysus (who, according to this rather obscure tale, had 5 been the god's nurse on Mount Nysa) refused to turn over the rule again on Dionysus' return. The god was unusually patient with him. After waiting three years he ostensibly made up their quarrel and received permission to celebrate his rites at Thebes. He then dressed his soldiers as maenads and seized the throne 10 in a coup. . . .[3]

[3] Edward Tripp, ed., *Crowell's Handbook of Classical Mythology*, pp. 207-209.

THE SUMMER OF LIFE:
Commentary on Part 4

Many of the better-known quest-labor stories are not included in this collection because of their great length. These stories — epics for the most part — had best be read in full. The seminal quest story is Homer's *Odyssey*, which has modern counterparts in James Joyce's *Ulysses* and Nikos Kazantzakis's *The Odyssey: A Modern Sequel.* Jason's quest for the Golden Fleece, as told of by Apollonius of Rhodes, is also basic, as is Virgil's *Aeneid,* the record of the quest for a new Troy. Nearly all of the great epics — *Beowulf, Paradise Lost, The Cid, The Divine Comedy* — are quest stories.

This leads us to a point which must be established before we proceed further. The quest myth in one sense is the *only* myth — that is, all other myths are a part of the quest myth. The hero's whole life from birth to apotheosis is a quest, whether for an actual place or object in this world, as is the case with Odysseus and Jason, or for eternal life in another world, as is the case with the great religious leaders such as Jesus and Quetzalcoatl. Psychologically all heroes, as we have seen, represent man's search for the self. The birth, childhood, withdrawal, death, underworld, rebirth, and apotheosis myths are really only aspects of this central quest. Northrop Frye, writing from his own specialized point of view, suggests, for instance, that "all literary genres are derived from the quest myth."[1]

While admitting the all-encompassing quality of the quest myth, we can properly consider the motif of the quest or labor within the larger myth — the particular quest or task which is but a stage or aspect of the hero's many-faceted adventure. Although the whole life of Heracles can be read as a quest, the twelve labors are only a part of his life. Aeneas's search for the Golden Bough before he can descend to the underworld is another example of the quest within the larger quest. Jesus's overall mission is to achieve the Kingdom of God for man, yet his actual sermons on that subject are isolated incidents in his life.

In this section the stories collected are best considered in turn. The psychological basis for all of them is every human's need to define or "prove" himself — to suffer the agony of adult

---

[1] Northrop Frye, *Fables of Identity: Studies in Poetic Mythology*, p. 17.

life, to gain its rewards, and to "make a name." The hero—our representative—has established his origins, found divine destiny within himself, and now must act on that destiny. To leave the cave of meditation and embark on the quest is to move from the inner sufferings of adolescence to the active pursuits of the prime of life.

For certain heroes—Heracles, Theseus, and Kutoyis among them—this stage involves immense tasks which, when completed, serve as proof of supreme manhood. These are educative tasks in the sense that the hero voyages to the borders of the environment. Kutoyis's refrain is, "Where are there any people? I want to visit all the people." Heracles' travels take him to the very ends of the universe. Theseus seeks the Minotaur in the depths of the labyrinth; his is a quest which strikes the chords of several motifs in addition to the quest: the underworld descent, the withdrawal into the self, and the child-hero monster-slaying. Dionysus's quest, too, makes him an explorer. His proselytizing takes him as far from Greece as India. For Dionysos the quest is literally for the realization of man. He is the fertility god of wine which is symbolic of his role as mystery god who, as Nietzsche saw, was the impulse of life through all things.[2] His struggles with unbelievers were struggles to bring life to all peoples. This was the *agon*—the struggle between priest and unbeliever, actor and audience, to discover the truth of life however ecstatic, however painful.

The theme of the quest for the essence of life is openly expressed in the various stories of the elixir of life. The search for the Holy Grail, as Jessie Weston established in *From Ritual to Romance,* combines the Christian idea of eternal life through communion with Christ with the older fertility cults of death and rebirth. The mythic reality in the legend lies in the hero's bringing new life to the Fisher King and his barren land, which T. S. Eliot immortalized in "The Waste Land." In the Gilgamesh epic the hero searches for and finds the plant of eternal life only to lose it carelessly. This, like Percival's failure in the Grail story, would seem to reflect man's fear that the goal might be unattainable in any worldly sense. The Gilgamesh quest, like Hiiaka's, is also a descent tale, as the search takes the hero to a kind of underworld. This is appropriate since the underworld myth, like the

[2] See *The Birth of Tragedy,* in Friedrich Nietzsche, *The Philosophy of Nietzsche.*

quest myth, is concerned with the attempt to overcome death, and since the voyage to the underworld is in itself a voyage and quest.

The Quetzalcoatl legend included here is the beginning of a death sequence, but it does include the elixir thirst. Even the wise man is tricked by the promise of being "made a child" again.

Jesus, too, was concerned with man's hope for eternal life and tried through his teaching to describe the means of spiritually achieving that state. His death and resurrection are meant to demonstrate the truth of his way. In this sense the deaths and rebirths of Osiris, Attis, Adonis, and Dionysos are in the nature of quests for eternal life as well.

The Faust legend is in one way a more cynical expression of the same quest. Magic is employed as a means of avoiding the inevitable. But more important is the human yearning to break free which is behind Faust's sins.

Seth seeks the oil of mercy and Kyazimba the land of eternal prosperity "where the sun rises" — the pot at the end of the rainbow. We can feel the significance of these quests.

The Prometheus story contains an aspect of the quest myth even though it occurs in one place. Like Faust, Prometheus pitches himself against the omnipotent force of the universe; he longs to be both himself and totally free. "My mind remains immortal and unsubdued," he cries. Prometheus's defiant cry is man's assertion that he possesses immortality within — that self-identification is the means to eternal life. The quest myth to be drawn from all of these stories — stories of the summer of life — is firmly based in that assertion. The quest myth is the humanistic myth.

Campbell, in *The Hero with a Thousand Faces*, provides much insight into the hero's quest. A perceptive literary approach is that taken by Northrop Frye. His essay "The Archetypes of Literature" (in *Fables of Identity: Studies in Poetic Mythology*) owes something to Frazer and Jung, and it involves a challenging quest for understanding on the reader's part — a quest which is well worth the labor. Jessie Weston's *From Ritual to Romance* concentrates on the Grail stories but in so doing tells us much about the quest myth in general.

5

DEATH AND THE SCAPEGOAT

Crucifix: The cross and the X here are symbolic, as they always have
been, of the hero's crossing from one sphere of existence to another—of
his confronting that which takes life but in so doing defines it. [Thomas
Chimes, *Crucifixion* (1961), oil on canvas, 36 x 36 in. Collection, The
Museum of Modern Art, New York. Larry Aldrich Foundation Fund.
Reproduced with permission.]

ATTIS
Phrygian

The story of the death of Attis is the narrative form of the ritual of the year-god, the hero-king who dies and is reborn in the spring. The year-god is dismembered—in this case castrated— and buried. His death is associated with a tree.

Attis was a boy of marvellous beauty. The tale goes on that Agdistis fell in love with him. The savage deity took the grown lad out hunting, led him into the most inaccessible wildernesses and gave him spoils of the chase. Midas, King of Pessinous, sought to separate Attis from Agdistis, and to this end gave the boy his own daughter to wife. Agdistis appeared at the wedding and drove the participants mad with the notes of a syrinx. Attis castrated himself beneath a pine-tree, crying out: "Unto thee, Agdistis!" And thus he died.[1]

[Sir James Frazer tells us of the ritual connected with the death of Attis.]

On the twenty-second day of March, a pine-tree was cut in the woods and brought into the sanctuary of Cybele, where it was treated as a great divinity. The duty of carrying the sacred tree was entrusted to a guild of Tree-bearers. The trunk was swathed like a corpse with woollen bands and decked with wreaths of violets, for violets were said to have sprung from the blood of Attis, as roses and anemones sprang from the blood of Adonis; and the effigy of a young man, doubtless that of Attis himself, was tied to the middle of the stem.

On the second day of the festival, the twenty-third of March, the chief ceremony seems to have been a blowing of trumpets.

The third day, the twenty-fourth of March, was known as the Day of Blood: the Archigallus or high-priest drew blood from his arms and presented it as an offering. Nor was he alone in making this bloody sacrifice. Stirred by the wild barbaric music of clashing cymbals, rumbling drums, droning horns, and screaming flutes, the inferior clergy whirled about in the dance with waggling heads and streaming hair, until, rapt into a frenzy of ex-

[1] C. Kerényi, *The Gods of the Greeks*, p. 90.

citement and insensible to pain, they gashed their bodies with potsherds or slashed them with knives in order to bespatter the altar and the sacred tree with their flowing blood. The ghastly rite probably formed part of the mourning for Attis and may have been intended to strengthen him for the resurrection. . . . 5

Further, we may conjecture, though we are not expressly told, that it was on the same Day of Blood and for the same purpose that the novices sacrificed their virility. Wrought up to the highest pitch of religious excitement they dashed the severed portions of themselves against the image of the cruel goddess. 10 These broken instruments of fertility were afterwards reverently wrapt up and buried in the earth or in subterranean chambers sacred to Cybele, where, like the offering of blood, they may have been deemed instrumental in recalling Attis to life and hastening the general resurrection of nature, which was then bursting into 15 leaf and blossom in the vernal sunshine. . . .

. . . in the similar worship of Cybele the sacrifice of virility took place on the Day of Blood at the vernal rites of the goddess, when the violets, supposed to spring from the red drops of her wounded lover, were in bloom among the pines. Indeed the story 20 that Attis unmanned himself under a pine-tree was clearly devised to explain why his priests did the same beside the sacred violet-wreathed tree at his festival.

At all events, we can hardly doubt that the Day of Blood witnessed the mourning for Attis over an effigy of him which was 25 afterwards buried. The image thus laid in the sepulchre was probably the same which had hung upon the tree. Throughout the period of mourning the worshippers fasted from bread, nominally because Cybele had done so in her grief for the death of Attis, but really perhaps for the same reason which induced 30 the women of Harran to abstain from eating anything ground in a mill while they wept for Tammuz. To partake of bread or flour at such a season might have been deemed a wanton profanation of the bruised and broken body of the god. Or the fast may possibly have been a preparation for a sacramental meal.[2] 35

[2] Sir James Frazer, *The New Golden Bough,* edited by Theodor H. Gaster, pp. 370–373.

ADONIS AND APHRODITE (VENUS)
Greek and Babylonian

*In a sense Adonis is a Greco-Babylonian form of Attis. As Attis
is associated with the mother goddess, he is Aphrodite's lover.
And, as in the case of Attis, his death results from a wound in
the loins.*

"Time slipped away: there's nothing more elusive
Than Time in flight, more swift in flight than he
Who steals our years and months, our days and hours.
Son of a sister whom he never saw,
Son of a grandfather who cursed his being,   5
Child of a tree, Adonis grew to boyhood—
And lovelier than any man on earth.
When Venus looked at him, his mother's guilt
Seemed like an old and half-forgotten story,
And on that day as Eros stooped to kiss her,   10
His quiver slipped, an arrow scratched her breast;
She thrust her son aside and shook her head
While that swift cut went deeper than she knew.
She found Adonis beautiful and mortal
And lost her taste for old immortal places: 15
The shores of Cythera, the sea-green harbours
Where Paphos floated like a jewel-set finger,
Cnidos, the rocks where wheeling fishes spawn,
Even Amathus streaked in rich gold and bronze,
And she was bored with living in the skies.   20
On Earth she took Adonis for an airing,
An arm around his waist, and thought this better
Than golden afternoons on Mount Olympus.
Before she met him she used to lie on grasses
To rest in shade and wreath herself with flowers,   25
But now she walked abroad through brush and briar,
Climbed rocks and hills, and, looking like Diana,
She wore short dresses, poised as a mistress out
To lead the hunt—yet she sought harmless game,
The nervous rabbit and high-antlered deer.   30
Her rule was to keep shy of savage brutes—
The lunging boar, the wolf, the bear, the lion—

All those who lived by killing men and cattle,
Who smelled of blood. Adonis had her warning,
If any warning could have held him back.
She told him, 'Save your valour for the timid—
The wild and large are much too wild for you;   5
My dear, remember that sweet Venus loves you,
And if you walk in danger, so does she.
Nature has armed her monsters to destroy you—
Even your valour would be grief to me.
What Venus loves—the young, the beautiful—   10
Mean less than nothing to huge, hungry creatures
Who tear and bite and have wide, staring eyes:
The boar whose crooked teeth are lightning flashes,
The stormy lion and his raging jaws.
They have my fears and hates; I know them well.'   15

     *   *   *

These beasts, like others of their kind, attack
Breast forward, tearing at all things they meet
And you, Adonis, should keep far away
Whenever lions roar across the path.
Your efforts to be brave will find no glory;   20
Your death will be an end of both of us.'

     *   *   *

  "Since she believed her warning had been heard,
The goddess yoked her swans and flew toward heaven—
Yet the boy's pride and manliness ignored it.
His hunting dogs took a clear path before them   25
And in the forest waked a sleeping boar;
As he broke through his lair within a covert,
Adonis pricked him with a swift-turned spear.
The fiery boar tore out the slender splinter
And rushed the boy, who saw his death heave toward him.   30
With one great thrust he pierced the boy's white loins
And left him dying where one saw his blood
Flow into rivulets on golden sands.[1]

[1] Ovid, *Metamorphoses*, 10, translated by Horace Gregory.

TAMMUZ AND INANNA (ISHTAR)
Sumerian and Babylonian

Tammuz is still another form of the year-god. The woman figure here is Ishtar or Inanna. Tammuz, too, dies and is buried. His death results in a loss of fertility, as the lament in the story tells us. Hope for new life lies in his resurrection.

Then he brought me to the door of the gate of the LORD's house which was toward the north; and, behold, there sat women weeping for Tammuz.[1]

In the religious literature of Babylonia Tammuz appears as the youthful spouse or lover of Ishtar, the great mother goddess, the embodiment of the reproductive energies of nature. The references to their connexion with each other in myth and ritual are both fragmentary and obscure, but we gather from them that Tammuz was believed to die, passing away from the cheerful earth to the gloomy subterranean world, and that his divine mistress journeyed in quest of him "to the land from which there is no returning, to the house of darkness, where dust lies on door and bolt." During her absence the passion of love ceased to operate: men and beasts alike forgot to reproduce their kinds: all life was threatened with extinction. So intimately bound up with the goddess were the sexual functions of the whole animal kingdom that without her presence they could not be discharged. . . .

Laments for the departed Tammuz are contained in several Babylonian hymns, which liken him to plants that quickly fade. He is

"A tamarisk that in the garden has drunk no water,
   Whose crown in the field has brought forth no blossom.
A willow that rejoiced not by the watercourse,
   A willow whose roots were torn up.
A herb that in the garden had drunk no water."

His death appears to have been annually mourned, to the shrill music of flutes, by men and women about midsummer in the month named after him, the month of Tammuz. The dirges were

[1] Ezekiel 8:14.

207

seemingly chanted over an effigy of the dead god, which was washed with pure water, anointed with oil, and clad in a red robe, while the fumes of incense rose into the air, as if to stir his dormant senses by their pungent fragrance and wake him from the sleep of death.[2]

5

[2] Sir James Frazer, *The New Golden Bough*, edited by Theodor H. Gaster, pp. 341–342.

OSIRIS AND ISIS
Egyptian

Osiris is the Egyptian form of the year-god. He is dismembered; the loss of his genitals is emphasized; a tree is important in the story; his final burial is in the nature of a planting of seeds for a new life; and a woman, Isis, is closely associated with him. The lament is present here, too.

Reigning as a king on earth, Osiris reclaimed the Egyptians from savagery, gave them laws, and taught them to worship the gods. Before his time the Egyptians had been cannibals. But Isis, the sister and wife of Osiris, discovered wheat and barley growing wild, and Osiris introduced the cultivation of these grains 5 amongst his people, who forthwith took kindly to a corn diet. Moreover, Osiris is said to have been the first to gather fruit from trees, to train the vine to poles, and to tread the grapes. Eager to communicate these beneficent discoveries to all mankind, he committed the whole government of Egypt to his wife Isis, and 10 travelled over the world, diffusing the blessings of civilization and agriculture wherever he went. In countries where a harsh climate or niggardly soil forbade the cultivation of the vine, he taught the inhabitants to console themselves for the want of wine by brewing beer from barley. Loaded with the wealth that had 15 been showered upon him by grateful nations, he returned to Egypt, and on account of the benefits he had conferred on mankind he was unanimously hailed and worshipped as a deity. But his brother Set with seventy-two others plotted against him. Having taken the measure of his good brother's body by stealth, the 20 bad brother fashioned and highly decorated a coffer of the same size, and once when they were all drinking and making merry he brought in the coffer and jestingly promised to give it to the one whom it should fit exactly. They all tried one after the other, but it fitted none of them. Last of all Osiris stepped into it and lay 25 down. On that the conspirators ran and slammed the lid down on him, nailed it fast, soldered it with molten lead, and flung the coffer into the Nile. This happened on the seventeenth day of the month Athyr, when the sun is in the sign of the Scorpion, and in the eight-and-twentieth year of the reign or the life of Osiris. 30 When Isis heard of it she sheared off a lock of her hair, put on mourning attire, and wandered disconsolately up and down, seeking the body.

* * *

Meantime the coffer containing the body of Osiris had floated down the river and away out to sea, till at last it drifted ashore at Byblus, on the coast of Syria. Here a fine *erica*-tree shot up suddenly and enclosed the chest in its trunk. The king of the country, admiring the growth of the tree, had it cut down and made into a pillar of his house; but he did not know that the coffer with the dead Osiris was in it. Word of this came to Isis and she journeyed to Byblus, and sat down by the well, in humble guise, her face wet with tears. To none would she speak till the king's handmaidens came, and them she greeted kindly, and braided their hair, and breathed on them from her own divine body a wondrous perfume. When the queen beheld the braids of her handmaidens' hair and smelt the sweet smell that emanated from them, she sent for the stranger woman and took her into her house and made her the nurse of her child. Isis gave the babe her finger instead of her breast to suck, and at night she began to burn all that was mortal of him away, while she herself in the likeness of a swallow fluttered round the pillar that contained her dead brother, twittering mournfully. The queen spied what she was doing and shrieked out when she saw her child in flames, and thereby she hindered him from becoming immortal. Then the goddess revealed herself and begged for the pillar of the roof, and they gave it her, and she cut the coffer out of it, and fell upon it and embraced it and lamented so loud that the younger of the king's children died of fright on the spot. But the trunk of the tree she wrapped in fine linen, and poured ointment on it, and gave it to the king and queen, and the wood stands in a temple of Isis and is worshipped by the people of Byblus to this day. And Isis put the coffer in a boat and took the eldest of the king's children with her and sailed away. As soon as they were alone, she opened the chest, and laying her face on the face of her brother she kissed him and wept. But the child came behind her softly and saw what she was about, and she turned and looked at him in anger, and the child could not bear her look and died; but some say that it was not so, but that he fell into the sea and was drowned. It is he whom the Egyptians sing of at their banquets under the name of Maneros.

But Isis put the coffer by and went to see her son Horus at the city of Buto, and Set found the coffer as he was hunting a boar one night by the light of a full moon. And he knew the body, and rent it into fourteen pieces, and scattered them abroad. But Isis sailed up and down the marshes in a shallop made of papyrus, looking for the pieces; and that is why when people sail in shallops made of papyrus, the crocodiles do not hurt them, for they fear or respect the goddess. And that is the reason, too, why there are many graves of Osiris in Egypt, for she buried each limb as she found it. But others will have it that she buried an image of him in every city, pretending it was his body, in order that Osiris might be worshipped in many places, and that if Set searched for the real grave he might not be able to find it. However, the genital member of Osiris had been eaten by the fishes, so Isis made an image of it instead, and the image is used by the Egyptians at their festivals to this day. "Isis," writes the historian Diodorus Siculus, "recovered all the parts of the body except the genitals; and because she wished that her husband's grave should be unknown and honoured by all who dwell in the land of Egypt, she resorted to the following device. She moulded human images out of wax and spices, corresponding to the stature of Osiris, round each one of the parts of his body. Then she called in the priests according to their families and took an oath of them all that they would reveal to no man the trust she was about to repose in them. So to each of them privately she said that to them alone she entrusted the burial of the body, and reminding them of the benefits they had received she exhorted them to bury the body in their own land and to honour Osiris as a god. She also besought them to dedicate one of the animals of their country, whichever they chose, and to honour it in life as they had formerly honoured Osiris, and when it died to grant it obsequies like his. And because she would encourage the priests in their own interest to bestow the aforesaid honours, she gave them a third part of the land to be used by them in the service and worship of the gods. Accordingly it is said that the priests, mindful of the benefits of Osiris, desirous of gratifying the queen, and moved by the prospect of gain, carried out all the injunctions of Isis. Wherefore to this day each of the priests imagines that Osiris is buried in his country, and they honour the beasts that were consecrated in the beginning, and when the animals die the priests renew at their burial the mourning for Osiris. But the sacred bulls, the one called Apis and the other Mnevis, were dedicated to Osiris, and it was ordained that they should be worshipped as gods in common by all the Egyptians; since these animals above all others had helped the discoverers of corn in sowing the seed and procuring the universal benefits of agriculture."

Such is the myth or legend of Osiris, as told by Greek writers and eked out by more or less fragmentary notices or allusions in native Egyptian literature. A long inscription in the temple at Denderah has preserved a list of the god's graves, and other texts mention the parts of his body which were treasured as holy relics in each of the sanctuaries. Thus his heart was at Athribis, his backbone at Busiris, his neck at Letopolis, and his head at Memphis. As often happens in such cases, some of his divine limbs were miraculously multiplied. His head, for example, was at Abydos as well as at Memphis, and his legs, which were remarkably numerous, would have sufficed for several ordinary mortals.

According to native Egyptian accounts, which supplement that of Plutarch, when Isis had found the corpse of her husband Osiris, she and her sister Nephthys sat down beside it and uttered a lament which in after ages became the type of all Egyptian lamentations for the dead. "Come to thy house," they wailed, "Come to thy house. O god On! come to thy house, thou who hast no foes. O fair youth, come to thy house, that thou mayest see me. I am thy sister, whom thou lovest; thou shalt not part from me. O fair boy, come to thy house. . . . I see thee not, yet doth my heart yearn after thee and mine eyes desire thee. Come to her who loves thee, who loves thee, Unnefer, thou blessed one! Come to thy sister, come to thy wife, to thy wife, thou whose heart stands still. Come to thy housewife. I am thy sister by the same mother, thou shalt not be far from me. Gods and men have turned their faces towards thee and weep for thee together. . . . I call after thee and weep, so that my cry is heard to heaven, but thou hearest not my voice; yet am I thy sister, whom thou didst love on earth; thou didst love none but me, my brother! my brother!"[1]

[1] Sir James Frazer, *The New Golden Bough*, edited by Theodor H. Gaster, pp. 386–388.

PERSEPHONE (PROSERPINA) AND DEMETER (CERES)

Greek and Roman

The search by Demeter for Persephone is analogous to Inanna's search for Tammuz, Aphrodite's for Adonis, and Isis's for Osiris. With the loss of Persephone comes an end of fertility. New life depends on her return. She, too, is a year-god.

" 'Hard by the town of Henna was a lake,
Pergus its name; nor even Cayster's waters
Held in their echoes sweeter songs of swans.
A forest crowned the hills on every side
Where even at sunstruck noonday the cool shores   5
Were green beneath a canopy of leaves,
The lawns, the purling grasses bright with flowers,
And spring the only season of the year.
This was the place where Proserpina played;
She plucked white lily and the violet   10
Which held her mind as in a childish game
To outmatch all the girls who played with her,
Filling her basket, then the hollow of small breasts
With new-picked flowers. As if at one glance, Death
Had caught her up, delighted at his choice,   15
Had ravished her, so quick was his desire,
While she in terror called to friends and mother,
A prayer to mother echoing through her cries.
Where she had ripped the neckline of her dress,
Her flowers had slipped away—and in her childish,   20
Pure simplicity she wept her new loss now
With bitter, deeper sorrow than her tears
For the brief loss of spent virginity.
He who had raped her lashed his horses on
To greater speed, crying the names of each,   25
Shaking black reins across their backs and shoulders;
He stormed his way through waterfalls and canyons
Past the Palici, where fiery thick sulphur bubbled
From split earth to the narrows where men came
(Corinthians who lived between two seas   30
And followed Bacchus) to set up a city
That rose between two jagged rocky harbours.

"'Between Cyane and the spring of Arethusa
There is a bay, a horn-shaped stretch of water
Contained by narrowing peninsulas.
Here lived Cyane, nymph of Sicily
Who gave the place a legend with her name;   5
Waist-high she raised herself above the waves
And at the sight of childlike Proserpina
She called to Death, "Sir, you shall go no farther,
Nor can you be the son-in-law of Ceres
By right of conquest and the use of force;   10
The child deserves a gentle courtly marriage.
If I compare a humble situation
With one of highest birth, then let me say
I once was courted by my lord Anapis,
And gave in to his prayers, but not through terror."   15
With this she spread her arms and barred his way—
Yet Saturn's son lashed at his furious horses
And swung his sceptre overhead, then struck
Through waves and earth as his dark chariot
Roared down that road to deepest Tartarus.   20

"'Cyane grieved at Proserpina's fate,
Her own loss of prestige, her waters tainted
By the wild capture of the youthful goddess,
Nor was consoled; she held her wounds at heart.
Speechless, she flowed in tears, into those waves   25
Where she was known as goddess. There one saw
Her limbs grow flaccid and her bones, her nails
Turn fluid; and her slender gliding features,
Her green hair and her fingers, legs, and feet
Were first to go, nor did her graceful limbs   30
Seem to show change as they slipped in cool waters;
Then shoulders, breasts and sides and back were tears
Flowing in streams and then her living blood
In pale veins ran to clearest, yielding spray—
And nothing there for anyone to hold.   35

"'In all this time the anxious frightened mother
Looked for her daughter up and down the world;
Neither Aurora with dew-wet raining hair
Nor evening Hesperus saw her stop for rest.

214

She lit two torches at the fires of Aetna
And through the frost-cloaked night she walked abroad,
Then, when good-natured day had veiled the stars,
Kept at her rounds from dawn to setting sun.
Spent with her travels and throat dry with thirst   5
(Nor had her lips touched either brook or fountain),
She saw a cottage roofed with straw and knocked
On its frail gate at which an ancient woman
Ambled forward, who when she learned the goddess
Wanted drink brought her a draught of sweetest   10
Barley water. And as the goddess drank
An impudent small boy stared up at her,
Made fun of her, and said she drank too much,
At which she took offense and threw the dregs
Of barley in his face. The boy grew spotted;   15
His arms were legs; between them dropped a tail;
He dwindled to a harmless size, a lizard,
And yet a lesser creature. The old woman
Marvelled at what she saw, then wept, then tried
To capture it; it fluttered under stones.   20
It took a name that fitted to its crime,
Since it was covered with star-shining spots.

   " 'It would take long to list the many names
Of seas and distant lands that Ceres travelled,
But when she found no other place to go,   25
She turned her way again through Sicily
And on this route stood where Cyane flowed.
Though she had much to say and wished to tell it—
Would have told all—Cyane had no speech
But that of water, neither tongue nor lips,
Yet she could bring sign language to the surface,   30
And tossed the girdle Proserpina dropped
Before her mother's eyes. When Ceres saw it,
It was as if the child had disappeared
Today or yesterday: the goddess tore
Her hair and beat her breasts—nor did she know   35
Where the child was, but cursed all earthly places
For lack of pity and ingratitude,
Saying they had disowned the gift of grain,
And worst of these the land of Sicily

Where she had seen the water-drifting ribbon
That Proserpina wore. With savage hands
She smashed the crooked ploughs that turned the soil
And brought dark ruin down on men and cattle;
She then gave orders to tilled field and lawn   5
To blight the seed, betray their duties, and
Unmake their reputation for rich harvest.
Crops died almost at birth, from too much sun,
Or withering rain; even the stars and wind
Unfavored them; birds ate the fallen seed,   10
And weeds and brambles thrived in starving wheat.

   " 'Then Alpheus' daughter, Arethusa, rose
Lifting her face from the Elean waters.
She shook her streaming hair back from her eyes
And cried, "O mother of that lost girl, the child   15
That you have looked for everywhere, mother
Of fruit and field, come rest awhile with me.
Forgive this pious land that worships you—
This countryside is innocent of wrong;
It had been forced to welcome rape—nor do I,   20
Pleading its cause, claim it my native land.
Pisa is mine, my ancestors from Elis,
And as a stranger came to Sicily—
Yet I have learned to love this countryside,
This island more than any place I know.   25
Here is my home—O gracious goddess, bless
The place I live; a proper time will come
To tell you why I came to Sicily,
Steering my course beneath uncharted seas—
A time when you are smiling down at me.   30
Earth opened to me down to deepest dark,
And floating through its underwater channels
I raised my head as if to turn my eyes
Toward stars almost forgotten to my sight,
And as I drifted through the Styx I saw   35
Persephone herself; she seemed in tears,
Even then her face still held its look of terror,
Yet she was like a queen, true wife, regina
Of that dictator who rules underground."
When the mother heard this news, she stood half-dazed   40

216

And stared as if she had been turned to stone,
But when her sorrow turned to active grief,
She stepped aboard her chariot and flew
To heaven itself; there, with dark features
And wild hair, flushed, passionate, she stepped 5
To Jove. She said, "I come to speak aloud,
To plead a case for your child and my own.
If you disown the mother, allow the child
In her distress to move a father's soul,
Nor think the less of her because I gave 10
Her birth, the long-lost daughter who has now
Been found—if one calls finding her sure proof
That she is lost, or if to find is knowing
Where she's gone; I can endure the knowing
She was raped—if he who has her shall return 15
Her to me. Surely any child of yours
Should never take a thief for her true husband."
Then Jupiter exclaimed, "She is our daughter,
The token of our love and ours to cherish,
But we should give the proper names to facts: 20
She has received the gift of love, unhurt,
Nor will he harm us as a son-in-law.
And if he has no other merits, then
It's no disgrace to marry Jove's own brother,
For all he needs is your good will, my dear. 25
His great fault is: he does not hold my place,
His lot is to rule over lower regions
But if your will is fixed on her divorce,
The girl shall rise to heaven on one condition—
That is, if no food touched her lips in Hades 30
For this is law commanded by the Fates."

    "'He had his say, and Ceres was determined
To claim their daughter, yet the Fates said No.
But Proserpina, guileless, innocent,
Had taken refuge in Death's formal gardens 35
And, as she strolled there, plucked a dark pomegranate,
Unwrapped its yellow skin, and swallowed seven
Of its blood-purpled seeds. The one who saw
Her eat was Ascalaphus, said to have been
The son of Orphne—she the not least known 40

Among the pliant ladies of Avernus,
And by her lover, Acheron, conceived him
In the grey forest of the Underworld.
The boy's malicious gossip worked its ill
Preventing Proserpina's step to earth;   5
Then the young queen of Erebus in rage
Changed her betrayer to an obscene bird:
She splashed his face with fires of Phlegethon
Which gave him beak and wings and great round eyes;
Unlike himself he walked in yellow feathers,   10
Half head, half body and long crooked claws,
Yet barely stirred his heavy wings that once
Were arms and hands: he was that hated creature,
Scritch-owl of fatal omen to all men.

   " 'Surely he earned his doom through evil talk,   15
But why are Achelous' daughters wearing
The claws, the feathers of peculiar birds—
And yet they have the faces of young girls?
Was this because, O Sirens of sweet song,
You were among the friends of Proserpina   20
Who joined her in the game of plucking flowers?
However far they travelled, land or sea,
They could not find her; then they begged the gods
To give them wings to skim the waves of ocean,
Renew the search again. The gods were kind,   25
And quickly Siren limbs took golden feathers,
But human, girlish faces did not change,
Nor did their voices cease to charm the air.

   " 'But Jove (with equal justice to his brother
And to his stricken sister) cut the cycle   30
Of the revolving year; and for their claims
Six months to each, with Proserpina goddess
For half the year on earth, the other half
Queen with her husband; then at once her face
And spirit changed, for even dark Death noticed   35
A weary sadness spreading through her veins,
Now changed to joy; who, like the sun when held
Behind grey mist and rain, now showers down
His light through clouds and shows his golden face.[1]

   [1] Ovid, *Metamorphoses*, 5, translated by Horace Gregory.

DIONYSOS (DIONYSUS)
Greek

Dionysos follows the established pattern. In this story the great mother is Hipta or Rhea. The god is dismembered; much is made of the removed genitals, and the implications of fertility and resurrection are clear.

It was told that they [the Titans] surprised the child-god as he was playing with the toys. Jealous Hera had instigated them to this: . . . The Titans had whitened their faces with chalk. They came like spirits of the dead from the Underworld, to which Zeus had banished them. They attacked the playing boy, tore him into seven pieces and threw these into a cauldron standing on a tripod. When the flesh was boiled, they began roasting it over the fire on seven spits.

. . . When Zeus smote the Titans with his lightning they had already eaten the flesh of Dionysos. They must have been hurled back into the Underworld, since . . . they are invoked as the subterranean ancestors of mankind. . . .

The boiled limbs of the god were burnt — with the exception of a single limb — and we may presume that the vine arose from the ashes. [The limb] was devoured neither by the Titans nor by the fire nor by the earth. . . . A goddess was present at the meal — in later tales, the goddess Pallas Athene — and she hid the limb in a covered basket. Zeus took charge of it. It was said to have been Dionysos's heart. This statement contains a pun: for it was also said that Zeus entrusted the *kradiaios Dionysos* to the goddess Hipta [the mother goddess] [or great mother Rhea], so that she might carry it on her head . . . *kradiaios* is a word of double meaning: it can be derived both from *kradia*, "heart," and from *krade*, "fig-tree," in which latter derivation it means an object made of fig-wood. The basket on Hipta's head was a *liknon:* a winnowing-fan, such as was carried on the head at festal processions, and contained a phallus hidden under a pile of fruit — Dionysos himself having made the phallus of fig-wood. . . .[1]

---

[1] C. Kerényi, *The Gods of the Greeks*, pp. 254–256.

ORPHEUS
Greek and Roman

*Orpheus can be seen as a form of Dionysos. He represents
youth and fertility. Women are associated with him; they perform the traditional dismemberment.*

The songs that Orpheus sang brought creatures round him,
All beasts, all birds, all stones held in their spell.
But look! There on a hill that overlooked the plain,
A crowd of raging women stood, their naked breasts
Scarce covered by strips of fur. They gazed at Orpheus   5
Still singing, his frail lyre in one hand.
Her wild hair in the wind, one naked demon cried,
"Look at the pretty boy who will not have us!"
And shouting tossed a spear aimed at his mouth.
The leaf-grown spear scratched his white face,   10
Nor bruised his lips, nor was the song unbroken.
Her sister threw a stone, which as it sailed
Took on his music's charm, wavered and swayed;
As to beg free of its mistress' frenzy,
Fell at the poet's feet. At this the women   15
Grew more violent and madness flamed among the crowd:
A cloud of spears were thrown which flew apart
And dropped to earth, steered by the singer's voice.
The screams of women, clapping of hands on breasts and thighs,
The clattering tympanum soon won their way   20
Above the poet's music; spears found their aim,
And stones turned red, streaked by the singer's blood.
No longer charmed by music now unheard,
The birds, still with the echoes of Orpheus' music
Chiming through their veins, began to fly away—   25
Then snakes and wild things (once his pride to charm)
Turned toward their homes again and disappeared.
Now, as wild birds of prey swoop down to kill
An owl struck by a blinding light at noon,
Or as when dawn breaks over an open circus   30
To show a stag bleeding and put to death by dogs,
Such was the scene as Maenads came at Orpheus,
Piercing his flesh with sharpened boughs of laurel,
Tearing his body with blood-streaming hands,
Whipping his sides with branches torn from trees;   35

He was stoned, beaten, and smeared with hardened clay.
Yet he was still alive; they looked for deadlier weapons,
And in the nearby plains, they saw the sweating peasants
And broad-shouldered oxen at the plough.
As they rushed toward them, peasants ran to shelter,   5
Their rakes and mattocks tossed aside
As the maddened women stormed the helpless oxen
To rip their sides apart, tear out their horns.
Armed with this gear they charged on Orpheus
Who bared his breast to them to cry for mercy   10
(A prayer that never went unheard before);
They leaped on him to beat him into earth.
Then, O by Jupiter, through those same lips,
Lips that enchanted beasts, and dying rocks and trees,
His soul escaped in his last breath   15
To weave invisibly in waves of air.

    The saddened birds sobbed loud for Orpheus;
All wept: the multitude of beasts,
Stones, and trees, all those who came to hear   20
The songs he sang, yes, even the charmed trees
Dropped all their leaves as if they shaved their hair.
Then it was said the rivers swelled with tears,
That dryads, naiads draped their nakedness
In black and shook their hair wild for the world to see.
Scattered in blood, and tossed in bloody grasses,   25
Dismembered arm from shoulder, knee from thigh,
The poet's body lay, yet by a miracle the River Hebrus
Caught head and lyre as they dropped and carried them
Midcurrent down the stream. The lyre twanged sad strains,
The dead tongue sang; funereally the river banks and reeds   30
Echoed their music. Drifting they sang their way
To open sea, and from the river's mouth
The head and lyre met salt sea waves that washed them up
On shores of Lesbos, near Methymna: salt spray in hair,
The head faced upward on strange sands, where a wild snake   35
Came at it to pierce its lips and eyes, to strike:
Phoebus was quicker, for as the snake's tongue flickered
He glazed the creature into polished stone,
And there it stayed, smiling wide-open-jawed.[1]

   [1] Ovid, *Metamorphoses*, 11, translated by Horace Gregory.

KUTOYIS
Blackfoot Indian

This American Indian Dionysos-Orpheus allows himself to be dismembered, as if to follow a ritual. In keeping with tradition he is accompanied by a female figure — in this case a child.

. . . Again he went on, and after a while he came to a big camp. This was the place of a man-eater. Kutoyis called a little girl he saw near by, and said to her: "Child, I am going into that lodge to let that man-eater kill and eat me.

Watch close, therefore, and when you can get hold of one of [5] my bones, take it out and call all the dogs, and when they have all come up to you, throw it down and cry out, 'Kutoyis, the dogs are eating your bones!'"

Then Kutoyis entered the lodge, and when the man-eater saw him, he cried out, *"O'ki, O'ki,"* and seemed glad to see him, [10] for he was a fat young man. The man-eater took a large knife, and went up to Kutoyis, and cut his throat, and put him into a great stone kettle to cook. When the meat was cooked, he drew the kettle from the fire, and ate the body, limb by limb, until it was all eaten up. . . .[1]   [15]

---

[1] George Bird Grinnell, *Blackfoot Lodge Tales*, pp. 37–38.

WANJIRU
African

*The maiden Wanjiru is a tribal scapegoat whose ritual death in
the sacred circle will result in the flowing of the waters.*

The sun was very hot and there was no rain, so the crops died
and hunger was great. This happened one year; and it happened
again a second, and even a third year, that the rain failed. The
people all gathered together on the great open space on the hill-
top, where they were wont to dance, and they said to each other, 5
"Why does the rain delay in coming?" And they went to the
Medicine-Man and they said to him, "Tell us why there is no rain,
for our crops have died, and we shall die of hunger."

And he took his gourd and poured out its contents. This he did
many times; and at last he said, "There is a maiden here who 10
must be bought if rain is to fall, and the maiden is named Wanjiru. The day after tomorrow let all of you return to this place, and
every one of you from the eldest to the youngest bring with him a
goat for the purchase of the maiden."

On the day after the morrow, old men and young men all 15
gathered together, and each brought in his hand a goat. Now they
all stood in a circle, and the relations of Wanjiru stood together,
and she herself stood in the middle. As they stood there, the feet
of Wanjiru began to sink into the ground, and she sank in to her
knees and cried aloud, "I am lost!" 20

Her father and mother also cried and exclaimed, "We are
lost!"

Those who looked on pressed close and placed goats in the
keeping of Wanjiru's father and mother. Wanjiru sank lower to
her waist, and again she cried aloud, "I am lost, but much rain 25
will come!"

She sank to her breast; but the rain did not come. Then she
said again, "Much rain will come."

Now she sank in to her neck, and then the rain came in great
drops. Her people would have rushed forward to save her, but 30
those who stood around pressed upon them more goats, and they
desisted.

Then Wanjiru said, "My people have undone me," and she
sank down to her eyes. As one after another of her family stepped

forward to save her, someone in the crowd would give to him or her a goat, and he would fall back. And Wanjiru cried aloud for the last time, "I am undone, and my own people have done this thing." Then she vanished from sight; the earth closed over her, and the rain poured down, not in showers, as it sometimes does, 5 but in a great deluge, and all the people hastened to their own homes.[1]

[1] Paul Radin and James J. Sweeney, eds., *African Folktales and Sculpture*, p. 272.

JESUS
Christian

The Christian man-god is executed on a tree and lamented by women. His burial is an act of planting in which lies man's hope of new life.

And the first day of unleavened bread, when they killed the passover, his disciples said unto him, Where wilt thou that we go and prepare that thou mayest eat the passover? And he sendeth forth two of his disciples, and saith unto them, Go ye into the city, and there shall meet you a man bearing a pitcher of water: follow 5 him. And wheresoever he shall go in, say ye to the goodman of the house, The Master saith, Where is the guest chamber, where I shall eat the passover with my disciples? And he will show you a large upper room furnished and prepared: there make ready for us. And his disciples went forth, and came into the city, and found 10 as he had said unto them: and they made ready the passover.

And in the evening he cometh with the twelve. And as they sat and did eat, Jesus said, Verily I say unto you, One of you which eateth with me shall betray me. And they began to be sorrowful, and to say unto him one by one, Is it I? and another said, Is it I? 15 And he answered and said unto them, It is one of the twelve, that dippeth with me in the dish. The Son of man indeed goeth, as it is written of him: but woe to that man by whom the Son of man is betrayed! good were it for that man if he had never been born. 20

And as they did eat, Jesus took bread, and blessed, and brake it, and gave to them, and said, Take, eat; this is my body. And he took the cup, and when he had given thanks, he gave it to them: and they all drank of it. And he said unto them, This is my blood of the new testament, which is shed for many. Verily I say unto 25 you, I will drink no more of the fruit of the vine, until that day that I drink it new in the kingdom of God.

And when they had sung a hymn, they went out into the mount of Olives.

And they came to a place which was named Gethsemane: 30 and he saith to his disciples, Sit ye here, while I shall pray. And he taketh with him Peter and James and John, and began to be sore amazed, and to be very heavy; and saith unto them, My soul is exceeding sorrowful unto death: tarry ye here, and watch.[1]

Then the band and the captain and officers of the Jews took Jesus, and bound him, and led him away to Annas first; for he was father-in-law to Caiaphas, which was the high priest that same year. Now Caiaphas was he, which gave counsel to the Jews, that it was expedient that one man should die for the people.

The high priest then asked Jesus of his disciples, and of his doctrine. Jesus answered him, I spake openly to the world; I ever taught in the synagogue, and in the temple, whither the Jews always resort; and in secret have I said nothing. Why askest thou me? ask them which heard me, what I have said unto them: behold, they know what I said. And when he had thus spoken, one of the officers which stood by struck Jesus with the palm of his hand, saying, Answerest thou the high priest so? Jesus answered him, If I have spoken evil, bear witness of the evil: but if well, why smitest thou me? Now Annas had sent him bound unto Caiaphas the high priest.

Then led they Jesus from Caiaphas unto the hall of judgment: and it was early; and they themselves went not into the judgment hall, lest they should be defiled; but that they might eat the passover. Pilate then went out unto them, and said, What accusation bring ye against this man? They answered and said unto him, If he were not a malefactor, we would not have delivered him up unto thee. Then said Pilate unto them, Take ye him, and judge him according to your law. The Jews therefore said unto him, It is not lawful for us to put any man to death: that the saying of Jesus might be fulfilled, which he spake, signifying what death he should die.

Then Pilate entered into the judgment hall again, and called Jesus, and said unto him, Art thou the King of the Jews? Jesus answered him, Sayest thou this thing of thyself, or did others tell it thee of me? Pilate answered, Am I a Jew? Thine own nation and the chief priests have delivered thee unto me: what hast thou done? Jesus answered, My kingdom is not of this world: if my kingdom were of this world, then would my servants fight, that I should not be delivered to the Jews: but now is my kingdom not from hence. Pilate therefore said unto him, Art thou a king then? Jesus answered, Thou sayest that I am a king. To this end was

[1] Mark 14.

I born, and for this cause came I into the world, that I should bear witness unto the truth. Every one that is of the truth heareth my voice. Pilate saith unto him, What is truth?

And when he had said this, he went out again unto the Jews, and saith unto them, I find in him no fault at all. But ye have a custom, that I should release unto you one at the passover: will ye therefore that I release unto you the King of the Jews? Then cried they all again, saying, Not this man, but Barabbas. Now Barabbas was a robber.

Then Pilate therefore took Jesus, and scourged him.[2]

Then the soldiers of the governor took Jesus into the common hall, and gathered unto him the whole band of soldiers. And they stripped him, and put on him a scarlet robe. And when they had platted a crown of thorns, they put it upon his head, and a reed in his right hand: and they bowed the knee before him, and mocked him, saying, Hail, King of the Jews! And they spit upon him, and took the reed, and smote him on the head. And after that they had mocked him. . . .[3]

Pilate therefore went forth again, and saith unto them, Behold, I bring him forth to you, that ye may know that I find no fault in him. Then came Jesus forth, wearing the crown of thorns, and the purple robe. And Pilate saith unto them, Behold the man! When the chief priests therefore and officers saw him, they cried out, saying, Crucify him, crucify him. Pilate saith unto them, Take ye him, and crucify him: for I find no fault in him. The Jews answered him, We have a law, and by our law he ought to die, because he made himself the Son of God. When Pilate therefore heard that saying, he was the more afraid; and went again into the judgment hall, and saith unto Jesus, Whence art thou? But Jesus gave him no answer. Then saith Pilate unto him, Speakest thou not unto me? knowest thou not that I have power to crucify thee, and have power to release thee? Jesus answered, Thou couldest have no power at all against me, except it were given thee from above: therefore he that delivered me unto thee hath the greater sin.

And from thenceforth Pilate sought to release him: but the Jews cried out, saying, If thou let this man go, thou art not

[2] John 18, 19.
[3] Matthew 27.

227

Caesar's friend: whosoever maketh himself a king speaketh against Caesar. When Pilate therefore heard that saying, he brought Jesus forth, and sat down in the judgment seat in a place that is called the Pavement, but in the Hebrew, Gabbatha. And it was the preparation of the passover, and about the sixth hour: and he saith unto the Jews, Behold your King! But they cried out, Away with him, away with him, crucify him. Pilate saith unto them, Shall I crucify your King? The chief priests answered, We have no king but Caesar. Then delivered he him therefore unto them to be crucified. And they took Jesus, and led him away.

And he bearing his cross went forth into a place called the place of a skull, which is called in the Hebrew Golgotha.[4]

And there followed him a great company of people, and of women, which also bewailed and lamented him. But Jesus turning unto them said, Daughters of Jerusalem, weep not for me, but weep for yourselves, and for your children. For, behold, the days are coming, in the which they shall say, Blessed are the barren, and the wombs that never bare, and the paps which never gave suck. Then shall they begin to say to the mountains, Fall on us; and to the hills, Cover us. For if they do these things in a green tree, what shall be done in the dry?

And there were also two others, malefactors, led with him to be put to death. And when they were come to the place, which is called Calvary, there they crucified him, and the malefactors, one on the right hand, and the other on the left. Then said Jesus, Father, forgive them; for they know not what they do. And they parted his raiment, and cast lots. And the people stood beholding. And the rulers also with them derided him, saying, He saved others; let him save himself, if he be Christ, the chosen of God. And the soldiers also mocked him, coming to him, and offering him vinegar, and saying, If thou be the King of the Jews, save thyself. And a superscription also was written over him in letters of Greek, and Latin, and Hebrew, THIS IS THE KING OF THE JEWS.

And one of the malefactors which were hanged railed on him, saying, If thou be Christ, save thyself and us. But the other answering rebuked him, saying, Dost not thou fear God, seeing thou art in the same condemnation? And we indeed justly; for we receive the due reward of our deeds: but this man hath done

[4] John 19.

nothing amiss. And he said unto Jesus, Lord, remember me when thou comest into thy kingdom. And Jesus said unto him, Verily I say unto thee, Today shalt thou be with me in paradise.

And it was about the sixth hour, and there was a darkness over all the earth until the ninth hour. And the sun was darkened, [5] and the veil of the temple was rent in the midst. And when Jesus had cried with a loud voice, he said, Father, into thy hands I commend my spirit: and having said thus, he gave up the ghost. Now when the centurion saw what was done, he glorified God, saying, Certainly this was a righteous man. And all the people [10] that came together to that sight, beholding the things which were done, smote their breasts, and returned. And all his acquaintance, and the women that followed him from Galilee, stood afar off, beholding these things.

And, behold, there was a man named Joseph, a counselor; [15] and he was a good man, and a just: (the same had not consented to the counsel and deed of them:) he was of Arimathea, a city of the Jews; who also himself waited for the kingdom of God. This man went unto Pilate, and begged the body of Jesus. And he took it down, and wrapped it in linen, and laid it in a sepulchre that [20] was hewn in stone, wherein never man before was laid. And that day was the preparation, and the sabbath drew on. And the women also, which came with him from Galilee, followed after, and beheld the sepulchre, and how his body was laid. And they returned, and prepared spices and ointments; and rested the [25] sabbath day according to the commandment.[5]

[5] Luke 23.

ODIN
Norse

The story of Odin contains basic elements of the Christian ritual sacrifice: the tree, the spear wound, and the hope for spiritual fertility.

I know that I hung
on the windswept tree
for nine full nights,
wounded with a spear
and given to Odin,   5
myself to myself;
on that tree
of which none know
from what roots it rises.

They did not comfort me with bread,   10
and not with the drinking horn;
I peered downward,
I grasped the 'runes,'
screeching I grasped them;
I fell back from there.   15

I learned nine mighty songs
from the famous son
of Bolthor, father of Bestla,
and I got a drink
of the precious mead,   20
I was sprinkled with Odrerir.

Then I began to be fruitful
and to be fertile,
to grow and to prosper;
one word sought   25
another word from me;
one deed sought
another deed from me.[1]

[1] *Havamal*, in E. O. G. Turville-Petre, *Myth and Religion of the North: The Religion of Ancient Scandinavia.*

DEATH AND THE PROMISE OF NEW LIFE:
Commentary on Part 5

The stories of this section are really a part of a death-underworld-resurrection pattern, a consideration of which will be continued in the next two chapters. Emerging from the stories of Part 5 alone is a myth of the death of the hero by some violent means — hanging, dismemberment, castration, or rape. Sometimes the death is self-inflicted. In the wake of the hero's departure from life comes a loss of fertility; the land, as in the story of the Fisher King, dies.[1] This point is specifically made in the Attis, Tammuz, and Persephone tales and in several others not included here such as the one about the Hittite fertility figure, Telipinu, who leaves the earth in a temper and thus throws the seasons out of balance.[2] The point is implied in all of the stories of this section. The death is followed by a lament for the loss of the hero and the barrenness of the land. The lament is almost always expressed by women.

The dominant presence of women in the myth — Isis, Cybele, Ishtar (Inanna), Aphrodite, Hipta, the Marys, Demeter, the Maenads, and Anat in the story of Baal (not included here)[3] — gives us a clue as to much of the basic myth's significance. The lament by a woman who is a fertility-earth-mother goddess — as the women in these stories usually are — and the woman's active search for the dead hero imply the possibility of his being found and resurrected, as he almost always is. Mythologically these women must be seen in connection with the ritual sowing of the seed by fertile women in planting cultures. The death of the hero and his association with the female force holds promise of new life. Thus, out of the bodies of Attis, Adonis, and Dionysos spring flowers and the vine; the body of the dismembered Osiris is literally planted by his sister-wife, Isis, and the world is renovated by the Osiris religion which grows out of these ritual burials; Attis is buried in the chambers sacred to the earth mother, Cybele, and thus returned to his mother he can be reborn as Spring.

It was Sir James Frazer who did the pioneer work on the connection between the dying heroes and fertility. Jung added

---

[1] Flood myths are cosmological equivalents of death myths; see Appendix 3.
[2] See Theodor H. Gaster, *The Oldest Stories in the World*, pp. 99–103.
[3] See Gaster, *The Oldest Stories in the World*, pp. 218–223.

significantly to the subject. Among a great many other things he recognized the prominence of the tree in the myth—Osiris is buried in a tree; Adonis is born of one; Attis, Odin, and Jesus are hanged on trees; the Norse god Balder is killed by the mistletoe from a tree; and Dionysos, who carves a phallus out of a fig tree, was called in Boetia, "he in the tree."[4] Jung saw in the association of hero and tree the sacred burial of the hero in the great mother—the tree being the world tree with its roots in the depths of man's subconscious mind. Not only is the tree the world navel and the world heart, it springs as a phallic symbol from the world womb. As it is the place of Adam and Eve's first sin, so it is the place of the death out of which will grow new life. Alan Watts interprets the tree as follows:

The symbolism of the tree is quite clearly the world—Life itself—having its stem rooted in the unknown. Its branches, leaves, flowers and fruit form the multiplicity of creatures—"I am the vine; ye are the branches" —which blossom from the ever-fertile source of life. The wood of the tree is matter, *prima materia,* out of which all things are made. . . .[5]

This brings us to the phallic motif so important to the death myth. The genitals of Osiris are lost; the phallus of Dionysos is carried in procession as a sacred object; Attis and his priests are castrated; and Adonis is struck by the boar in his loins. This motif can be traced to the role of the male in the fertilization process. The hero-god dies as he gives his sex to the mother in whose sacred precinct he is buried. Also involved here is the fact that reproduction and death depend on each other. Modern ecologists are well aware of this fact. "The hero of yesterday becomes the tyrant of tomorrow, unless he crucifies himself today," writes Joseph Campbell.[6]

The hero's death, then, is an act of positive benefit to mankind. Sir James Frazer writes at length of this scapegoat aspect of the hero's death. He tells us of kings who in certain societies were killed at the end of pre-ordained reigns or at such times as the societies required very special sacrifices. This led eventually to the tradition of the substitute king who would replace the real king for a short time on the throne in return for replacing him

[4] Carl Gustav Jung, *Symbols of Transformation,* p. 425.
[5] Alan Watts, *Myth and Ritual in Christianity,* p. 160.
[6] Joseph Campbell, *The Hero with a Thousand Faces,* p. 353.

finally on the scaffold. In one sense or another each of the heroes in this section and the next two plays the role of the mock king. Each is a scapegoat for the guilt and the fears of a society. One need but think of the trial of Jesus—the crown of thorns, the purple robes, and the mocking by those present.

And this brings us to the immediate meaning of the myth. The hero faces death and dies for us. In so doing he holds out a promise of new life through his sacrifice. He thus also teaches us something of the positive nature of death as the catalyst for a new birth through the spirit. As always, the hero is the symbol of man in search of himself. At this stage in his voyage the hero is man in the later part of life when death becomes increasingly our measuring rod. The hero stands physically annihilated at the edge of the Kingdom of Death. The time of life's prime has passed; the process of individuation moves away from the deeds of the body back to those of the spirit. The hero stands with man face to face with the unknown. The voyage into that unknown is initiated by death. The voyage itself is the subject of Part 6.

A list of important books on the death myth must begin with Frazer's *The Golden Bough*—especially the sections on the dying god, the scapegoat, Attis, Osiris and Adonis, and Balder—which is now available in a single volume edited by Theodor H. Gaster (*The New Golden Bough*). Jung's *Symbols of Transformation* is a crucial work on the subject with its pertinent chapter on the sacrifice. In Campbell's *Masks of God: Primitive Mythology* the death myth is associated with rituals still practiced by "primitive" peoples today. A useful source book with commentary is *The Wisdom of the Serpent: The Myths of Death, Rebirth, and Resurrection*, by Joseph Henderson and Maud Oakes.

6

THE DESCENT
TO THE UNDERWORLD

The Anxious Journey: A symbol of the energies of our society, the locomotive wanders among classical forms, perhaps searching like the hero of old for destiny and meaning among shades of the past. [Giorgio de Chirico, *The Anxious Journey* (1913), oil on canvas, 29¼ x 42 in. Collection, The Museum of Modern Art, New York. Acquired through the Lillie P. Bliss Bequest. Reproduced with permission.]

INANNA (ISHTAR)
Babylonian and Sumerian

The Sumerian Inanna story contains the basic elements of the Ur-myth of the descent: the search for a loved one and the struggle with and conquering of death in the underworld.

Inanna, queen of heaven, the goddess of light and love and life, has set her heart upon visiting the nether world, perhaps in order to free her lover Tammuz. She gathers together all the appropriate divine decrees, adorns herself with her queenly robes and jewels, and is ready to enter the "land of no return." Queen 5
of the nether world is her elder sister and bitter enemy Ereshkigal, the goddess of darkness and gloom and death. Fearing lest her sister put her to death in the nether world, Inanna instructs her messenger, Ninshubur, who is always at her beck and call, that if after three days she shall have failed to return, he is to go to 10
heaven and set up a hue and cry for her in the assembly hall of the gods. Moreover, he is to go to Nippur, the very city where our tablets have been excavated, and there weep and plead before the god Enlil to save Inanna from Ereshkigal's clutches. If Enlil should refuse, he is to go to Ur, Ur of the Chaldees, whence ac- 15
cording to Biblical tradition Abraham migrated to Palestine, and there repeat his plea before Nanna, the great Sumerian moon-god. If Nanna, too, refuses, he is to go to Eridu, the city in which Sumerian civilization is said to have originated, and weep and plead before Enki, the "god of wisdom." And the latter, "who 20
knows the food of life, who knows the water of life," will restore Inanna to life.

Having taken these precautions, Inanna descends to the nether world and approaches Ereshkigal's temple of lapis lazuli. At the gate she is met by the chief gatekeeper, who demands to 25
know who she is and why she came. Inanna concocts a false excuse for her visit, and the gatekeeper, upon instructions from his mistress Ereshkigal, leads her through the seven gates of the nether world. As she passes through each of the gates part of her robes and jewels are removed in spite of her protest. Finally after 30
entering the last gate she is brought stark naked and on bended knees before Ereshkigal and the seven Anunnaki, the dreaded judges of the nether world. These latter fasten upon Inanna their

"look of death," whereupon she is turned into a corpse and hung from a stake.

So pass three days and three nights. On the fourth day, Ninshubur, seeing that his mistress has not returned, proceeds to make the rounds of the gods in accordance with his instructions. As Inanna had foreseen, both Enlil of Nippur and Nanna of Ur refuse all help. Enki, however, devises a plan to restore her to life. He fashions the *kurgarru* and *kalaturru*, two sexless creatures, and entrusts to them the "food of life" and the "water of life," with instructions to proceed to the nether world and to sprinkle this food and this water sixty times upon Inanna's suspended corpse. This they do and Inanna revives. As she leaves the nether world, however, to reascend to the earth, she is accompanied by the shades of the dead and by the bogies and harpies who have their home there. Surrounded by this ghostly, ghastly crowd, she wanders through Sumer from city to city.[1]

---

[1] S. N. Kramer, *Sumerian Mythology*, pp. 86–87. For complete text see Kramer, pp. 88–96.

HIIAKA AND LOHIAU
Polynesian

Hiiaka, like Inanna, descends to the Underworld to retrieve her lover — in this case the betrayed husband of her sister, the fire goddess Pele.

After celebrating his recovery with feasts and sacrifices to the gods, Lohiau announced to the chiefs of his kingdom that he was about to visit his wife, whose home was on Hawaii, and that he should leave the government of the island in the hands of his friend, the high chief Paoa, to whom he enjoined the fealty and respect of all during his absence.

In a magnificent double canoe, bearing the royal standard, and suitably equipped, Lohiau set sail for Hawaii, accompanied by Hiiaka' and her companions, his high priest, chief navigator, and the customary staff of personal attendants.

Touching at Oahu, Hiiaka' ascended the Kaala Mountains, and saw that her beautiful *lehua* and *hala* groves near the beach of Puna, on the distant island of Hawaii, had been destroyed by a lava-flow. Impatient at the long absence of Hiiaka', and unreasoningly jealous, Pele in a paroxysm of rage had destroyed the beautiful shore-retreat of her faithful sister. She had little doubt that Hiiaka' had dared to love Lohiau, and in her caves of fire chafed impatiently for her return.

After bewailing her loss, Hiiaka' rejoined her companions, and Lohiau embarked for Hawaii. Landing at Kohala, the Prince ordered his attendants to remain there until his return, and started overland for Kilauea with Hiiaka' and her companions. Before reaching the volcano Hiiaka' learned yet more of the jealous rage of Pele, and finally from an eminence saw her dear friend Hopoe suffering, near the beach of Puna, the cruel tortures of volcanic fire, which ended in her being turned into stone.

Approaching the crater with apprehension, Hiiaka' sent Pauo-palae and Omeo in advance to announce to Pele her return with Lohiau; but Pele in her wrath ordered the messengers to be slain at once, and resolved to treat her lover in the same manner. Aware of this heartless resolution, but unable to avert his fate, on their arriving at the verge of the crater Hiiaka' threw her arms around the neck of the Prince, whom she had learned to love, yet without wrong to her sister, and, telling him of his impending fate, bade him a tender farewell. On the fiery brink, in the open view of the court of Pele, Hiiaka', in resentment of the broken faith of her sister, and in defiance of her power, invited and received from Lohiau the kisses and dalliance which till that time both had repelled.

This scene was witnessed by Pele, and it did not serve to soften her resolution. Enraged beyond measure, she caused a gulf of molten lava to open between Hiiaka' and the Prince, and then ordered the instant destruction of Lohiau by fire. While the sisters of Pele were ascending the walls of the crater to carry out her command Lohiau chanted a song to the goddess, avowing his innocence and praying for mercy; but the sound of his voice added to her rage, and she was deaf to his entreaties.

Approaching Lohiau, and pitying him in their hearts, the sisters merely touched the palms of his hands, and turned them into lava, and retired. Observing this, Pele ordered them to return at once and consume the body of her lover. Lohiau again appealed to her, but her only answer was an impatient signal to her sisters to complete their work of destruction. In his despair he turned to Hiiaka', but she answered in agony that she could do nothing.

The sisters returned to Lohiau, and reluctantly touched his feet, which became stone; then his knees, his thighs, his breast. Hiiaka' could at least render the body of the Prince insensible to pain, and this she did; and it was therefore without suffering that he felt his joints hardening to stone under the touch of the sympathizing sisters.

Before he was quite turned to lava, Hiiaka' said to Lohiau, "Listen! When you die, go to leeward, and I shall find you!" The next moment he was a lifeless pillar of stone.

Seeing that all that now remained of Lohiau was a black mass of lava, Hiiaka' caused the earth to open at her feet, and started downward at once for the shadowy realms of Milu, to overtake the soul of Lohiau and with the consent of the god of death to restore it to its body.

The god welcomed her, and, answering her inquiry, said that the soul of Lohiau had not yet reached the realm of spirits. Having no desire to return to earth without him, Hiiaka' accepted the invitation of Milu, and, waiting and watching for Lohiau, remained awhile in the land of shades.

The attendants of Lohiau remained in Kohala until they

learned of his fate at the hands of Pele, when they returned to Kauai and related the story of his death.

Enraged and desperate, Paoa, the faithful and manly chief to whom Lohiau had confided the government of his kingdom, started at once for Hawaii with a small body of retainers, determined, even at the risk of his life, to denounce the powers that had slain his friend.

Landing on the coast of Puna, he ascended the crater of Kilauea, and, standing upon the brink of the seething lake of fire, denounced the cruelty of Pele and defied her power. He contemptuously threw to her offerings unfit for sacrifice, and stigmatized all the volcanic deities as evil spirits who had been driven with Kanaloa from the presence of Kane and the society of the gods.

Paoa expected instant destruction, and recklessly courted and awaited death. The brothers and sisters of Pele were momentarily expecting a command from the goddess to consume the audacious mortal. Never before had such words of reproach and defiance been uttered by human tongue, and they could not doubt that swift vengeance would overtake the offender.

But Pele, in one of her sudden and unpredictable revulsions of feeling, refused to harm the desperate champion of Lohiau. Convinced of the innocence of the gentle Hiiaka' and the fidelity of the Prince, instead of punishing the brave Paoa Pele and her relatives received him with friendship, chided him for his words of insult and defiance, but disarmed his anger by forgiving the offence. It is said, too, that Paoa, who was a skilful actor, by his dancing and his prayer-song, both of which were used in the *hula* named after the goddess, not only appeased her, but won her.

Satisfied that she had wronged her sister, and longing for her quiet presence again in the caves of the crater, Pele restored Pauo-palae and Omeo to life, and sent Omeo down to the realm of shades to induce Hiiaka' to return to earth. Milu, however, did not wish that his visitor should depart, and gave no assistance in the search of Omeo for Hiiaka'; indeed, he attempted to deceive her by saying that Hiiaka' had already returned and was on a visit to relatives in Kahiki.

Omeo was about to return, disappointed, to earth, when she discovered Hiiaka' as she was listlessly emerging from a thick grove of trees where she had spent most of her time since her arrival in quest of the soul of Lohiau. Their greeting was most friendly; and when Omeo informed her of what had occurred at the volcano since her departure she consented to leave the land of death and rejoin her relatives in the crater. Her brothers and sisters were overjoyed at her return, and Pele herself welcomed her with assurances of restored affection. Paoa was still there. He was recognized by Hiiaka', and next day she descended from Kilauea and embarked with him for Kauai in search of the soul of Lohiau.

The canoe of Paoa had barely left the shores of Puna when a strange craft swung in on the sweep of the ocean, and was beached at the spot at which Paoa and Hiiaka' had embarked. It was a huge cowrie-shell, dazzling in the brilliancy of its colours, and capable of indefinite expansion or contraction. Its masts were of ivory; its sails and mats were white as milk. Both seemed rather for ornament than for use, since the shell moved as quickly through the water without wind as with it.

The sole occupant of this strange but beautiful vessel was the god Kane-milohai, a relative of the Pele family, who had come from Kahiki on a visit to the volcanic gods of Hawaii. It appears that Pele had been expelled from her native land Honua-mea, in Kahiki, because of her insubordination and disrespect. She voyaged north. Her first stop was at the little island of Kaula, in the Hawaiian group. She tunneled into the earth, but the ocean poured in and put a stop to her work. The same occurred on Lehua, on Nihau, and on the large island Kauai. She then moved on to Oahu, hoping for better results; but though she tried both sides of the island, first Mount Kaala, the fragrant, and then Kona-hua-nui, she still found conditions unsatisfactory. She passed on to Molokai, thence to Lanai, to West Maui, digging at the last place the immense pit of Hale-a-ka-la; but everywhere she was unsuccessful. Still journeying east and south, she crossed the wide Ale-nui-haha channel and came to Hawaii, and, after exploring in all directions, was satisfied to make her home in Kilauea. Here is the navel of the earth (*ka piko o ka honua*), a name also applied to Rapanui (Easter Island). . . .

Proceeding in a direct route, when about midway between the two islands the god Kane-milohai caught the soul of Lohiau, which had misunderstood the final instructions of Hiiaka', and was on its way to Kauai. Not having gone to the land of spirits, it had been searching and searching for Hiiaka', and at last was taking flight for Kauai when intercepted by the god. He returned to the crater with the captured spirit, and, finding the pillar of

242

stone which was once the body of Lohiau, he restored the Prince to life. As he recovered his consciousness he recognized Pele, who stood before him; and not knowing all that had taken place in the meantime, and apprehensive of further persecution, he was about to appeal again for mercy, when she said in a tone as tender 5 as that in which she had first replied to his welcome on the beach at Kaena:

"Fear me no longer. I have been unjust to you and to Hiiaka'. After what I have done I cannot expect you to love me. She loves you, and knows better than myself how to be kind to a mortal." 10

Lohiau would have thanked the goddess, but she was gone, and where she had stood now stood Kane-milohai, who bade him take the shell vessel he would find on the beach below, and proceed to Kauai, where he would probably meet Hiiaka' and his friend Paoa. 15

Lohiau hesitated, for there was something in the presence of Kane-milohai that inspired a feeling of awe.

"Go, and fear nothing," said the god, who knew the thoughts of the Prince; "the shell was not fashioned in the sea or by human hands, but it will bear you safely on your journey, no matter how 20 rough the seas or how great its burden."

"The coast of Puna is a day's journey in length," said Lohiau. "Where and how shall I find the shell?"

"Hasten to the shore at Keauhou," rejoined the god. "You will see me there." 25

Arrived at the beach, the Prince found the god already there; and his wonder was great when the god took from a crevice in the rocks a shell that could lie in the palm of his hand, and passed it to him, saying that it was the vessel in which he was to sail to Kauai. 30

The god bade him place the shell at the edge of the water. He did so, and was surprised when he saw before him the beautiful craft in which the god had made his journey from Kahiki. To the Prince was given the power of causing the boat to expand or contract at pleasure; he entered, and directing its course simply by 35 pointing with his finger he set out, and was borne swiftly forward on the ocean.

Rounding the southern cape of Hawaii, Lohiau thought of proceeding directly to Kauai; but he pointed too far northward, and the next morning sighted Oahu. Passing the headland of 40 Leahi, he turned and entered the harbour of Hou. Landing, he re-

duced his boat to the size of a limpet, and hid it in the rocks. He
went to the village, where he learned to his great joy that Hiiaka'
and Paoa were there on a visit. Hou was at the time the scene of
great merriment and feasting. It had become the temporary resi-
dence of the high chiefs, the wise men, and adventurers and
noted surf-riders and *hula* performers had gathered there from
all parts of the island. Ascertaining that an entertainment of
great magnificence was that evening to be given by a distinguished chiefess in honour of Hiiaka' and Paoa, Lohiau resolved
to be present. Had he made himself known he would have been
entitled to the highest consideration; would have been the guest
of the *alii-nui* (high chief), with the right of entry anywhere; but
fancy induced him to conceal his rank and appear among the
revellers in disguise.

Early in the evening the grounds of the chiefess were lighted
with hundreds of torches; and under a broad pavilion, festooned
and scented with fragrant vines and flowers, the favoured guests,
enwreathed and crowned with leaf and blossom, were entertained with all the delicacies the sea and land produced. After the
feast came song and music, and bands of gaily decked dancers
kept step among the flaring torches, while around the doors of the
mansion bards chanted wild legends of the past and sang *mele-
inoa* (name songs) of the hostess and her guests.

In the midst of this inspiring revelry the guests divided into
groups, some strolling among the dancers, others listening to the
bards; and one party, including Hiiaka', Paoa, and their hostess,
entered to engage in the game of *kilu*. It was a pastime in which
singing or chanting formed a part, and the chiefess was noted for
her excellence in this amusement.

Lohiau entered the grounds toward the close of the feast, and
stood watching when the party of *kilu*-players retired. He had
turned inward the feathers of his royal yellow mantle, and with
his long hair falling over his face and shoulders was readily mis-
taken for a *kahuna* (*tohunga*, wise man, priest).

A number of people thronged round the *kilu*-players to see the
game, and Lohiau entered with them, standing concealed behind
two old chiefs who were watching like himself.

The game went on, until the *kilu* fell to Hiiaka'; and as she
threw it she chanted a song of her own composing, in which she
mentioned the name of Lohiau with tenderness. The song ceased,
and from among the onlookers came the answering song of the

Prince. As he sang he brushed back the hair from his face, and turned outward the yellow feathers of his mantle. The throng divided before him, the singer advanced, and before the players stood Lohiau, the Prince of Kauai.

He was recognized at once. Hiiaka' threw herself into his arms, and the faithful Paoa wept with joy. The guests vied with each other in showing him honour. The festivities were renewed and carried far into the night. Learning of his presence, the *alii-nui* wished to entertain him in a befitting manner; but Lohiau was anxious to return to his people, and set sail for Kauai at once in the shell boat of Kane-milohai, expanded flower-like so as to accommodate Hiiaka' and Paoa.

Although Hiiaka' soon after returned to Hawaii and effected a complete reconciliation with her sister, while Lohiau lived she spent much of her time in Kauai. Hopoe her friend was restored to life, and Omeo, because of what she had done, was given an immortal form, and thereafter became a mediator between the volcanic deities.[1]

[1] Johannes Andersen, *Myths and Legends of the Polynesians*, pp. 274–283.

WANJIRU
African

The maiden, having been sacrificed for rain, is retrieved from the Underworld by her lover, who reenacts her ritual death.

Now there was a young warrior who loved Wanjiru and he lamented continually, saying, "Wanjiru is lost, and her own people have done this thing." And he said, "Where has Wanjiru gone? I will go to the same place." So he took his shield and spear. And he wandered over the country day and night until, at last, as the dusk fell, he came to the spot where Wanjiru had vanished. Then he stood where she had stood and, as he stood, his feet began to sink as hers had sunk; and he sank lower and lower until the ground closed over him, and he went by a long road under the earth as Wanjiru had gone and, at length, he saw the maiden. But, indeed, he pitied her sorely, for her state was miserable, and her raiment had perished. He said to her, "You were sacrificed to bring the rain; now the rain has come, and I shall take you back." So he took Wanjiru on his back as if she had been a child and brought her to the road he had traversed, and they rose together to the open air, and their feet stood once more on the ground.

Then the warrior said, "You shall not return to the house of your people, for they have treated you shamefully." And he bade her wait until nightfall. When it was dark he took her to the house of his mother and he asked his mother to leave, saying that he had business, and he allowed no one to enter.

But his mother said, "Why do you hide this thing from me, seeing I am your mother who bore you?" So he suffered his mother to know, but he said, "Tell no one that Wanjiru has returned."

So she abode in the house of his mother. He and his mother slew goats, and Wanjiru ate the fat and grew strong. Then of the skins they made garments for her, so that she was attired most beautifully.[1]

---

[1] Paul Radin and James J. Sweeney, eds., *African Folktales and Sculpture*, p. 272.

DIONYSOS (DIONYSUS)
Greek

Dionysos descends to the underworld on the traditional mission of retrieval. His object is his mother, whom he successfully rescues from death.

When Dionysus had firmly established his worship throughout the lands of the eastern Mediterranean and as far east as India, he withdrew from earth and took his place with the other gods on Mount Olympus. First, however, he descended into Hades to bring up his mother. Several Greek cities later claimed that this memorable event had occurred in their territory. Instead of going by a land route, Dionysus apparently dived into the water, either the bottomless Alcyonian Lake, at Lerna, or the bay of Troezen. He was shown this route by a native guide named Prosymnus, Polymnus, or Hypolipnus. On meeting the handsome young god, the guide demanded that he lie with him. Dionysus, unwilling to delay his rescue of his mother,[1] vowed to pay Prosymnus on his return. When the time came, Prosymnus was dead. The god discharged his debt by whittling out of fig-wood an image of the organ that the guide had admired, and leaving it at the tomb.[2]

[1] Semele in this version. See the Dionysos story in Part 7.
[2] Edward Tripp, ed., *Crowell's Handbook of Classical Mythology*, p. 209.

247

JESUS
Christian

According to tradition, Jesus, too, descended into hell before the resurrection. Like so many other heroes, he went to overcome death and to retrieve a loved one — mankind in the form of Adam.

After the resurrection from the dead of our Lord Jesus Christ, Bartholomew came unto the Lord and questioned him, saying: Lord, reveal unto me the mysteries of the heavens.

Jesus answered and said unto him: If I put not off the body of the flesh, I shall not be able to tell them unto thee. 5

Bartholomew therefore drew near unto the Lord and said: I have a word to speak unto thee, Lord.

And Jesus said to him: I know what thou art about to say; say then what thou wilt, and I will answer thee.

And Bartholomew said: Lord, when thou wentest to be 10 hanged upon the cross, I followed thee afar off and saw thee hung upon the cross, and the angels coming down from heaven and worshipping thee. And when there came darkness, I beheld, and I saw thee that thou wast vanished away from the cross, and I heard only a voice in the parts under the earth, and great wailing 15 and gnashing of teeth on a sudden. Tell me, Lord, whither wentest thou from the cross?

And Jesus answered and said: Blessed art thou, Bartholomew, my beloved, because thou sawest this mystery; and now will I tell thee all things whatsoever thou askest me. For when I van- 20 ished away from the cross, then went I down into Hades that I might bring up Adam and all them that were with him, according to the supplication of Michael the archangel.

Then said Bartholomew: Lord, what was the voice which was heard? 25

Jesus saith unto him: Hades said unto Beliar: As I perceive, a God cometh hither.

And the angels cried unto the powers, saying: Remove your gates, ye princes, remove the everlasting doors, for behold the King of Glory cometh down. Hades said: Who is the King of Glory, 30 that cometh down from heaven unto us?

And when I had descended five hundred steps, Hades was troubled, saying: I hear the breathing of the Most High, and I cannot endure it. But the devil answered and said: Submit not thyself, O Hades, but be strong: for God himself hath not descended upon the earth. But when I had descended yet five hundred steps, the angels and the powers cried out: Take hold, remove the doors, for behold the King of Glory cometh down. And Hades 5 said: O, woe unto me, for I hear the breath of God.

And Beliar said unto Hades: Look carefully who it is that cometh, for it is Elias, or Enoch, or one of the prophets that this man seemeth to me to be. But Hades answered Death and said: Not yet are six thousand years accomplished. And whence are 10 these, O Beliar; for the sum of the number is in mine hands.

And Beliar said unto Hades: Be not troubled, make safe thy gates and strengthen thy bars: consider, God cometh not down upon the earth.

Hades saith unto him: These be no good words that I hear 15 from thee: my belly is rent, and mine inward parts are pained: it cannot be but that God cometh hither. Atlas, whither shall I flee before the face of the power of the great King? Suffer me to enter into myself: for before thee was I formed.

Then did I enter in and scourged him and bound him with 20 chains that cannot be loosed, and brought forth thence all the patriarchs and came again unto the cross.

Bartholomew saith unto him: Tell me, Lord, who was he whom the angels bare up in their hands, even that man that was very great of stature? 25

Jesus answered and said unto him: It was Adam the first-formed, for whose sake I came down from heaven upon earth. And I said unto him: I was hung upon the cross for thee and for thy children's sake. And he, when he heard it, groaned and said: So was thy good pleasure, O Lord. 30

Again Bartholomew said: Lord, I saw the angels ascending before Adam and singing praises. But one of the angels which was very great, above the rest, would not ascend up with them: and there was in his hand a sword of fire, and he was looking steadfastly upon thee only. And all the angels besought him that 35 he would go up with them, but he would not. But when thou didst command him to go up, I beheld a flame of fire issuing out of his hands and going even unto the city of Jerusalem.

And Jesus said unto him: Blessed art thou, Bartholomew my beloved, because thou sawest these mysteries. This was one of 40 the angels of vengeance which stand before my Father's throne:

and this angel sent he unto me. And for this cause he would not ascend up, because he desired to destroy all the powers of the world. But when I commanded him to ascend up, there went a flame out of his hand and rent asunder the veil of the temple, and parted it in two pieces for a witness unto the children of 5 Israel for my passion because they crucified me.

And when he had thus spoken, he said unto the apostles: Tarry for me in this place, for to-day a sacrifice is offered in paradise. And Bartholomew answered and said unto Jesus: Lord, what is the sacrifice which is offered in paradise? And Jesus said: 10 There be souls of the righteous which to-day have departed out of the body and go unto paradise, and unless I be present they cannot enter into paradise.

And Bartholomew said: Lord, how many souls depart out of the world daily? Jesus said unto him: Thirty thousand. 15

Bartholomew saith unto him: Lord, when thou wast with us teaching the word, didst thou receive the sacrifices in paradise? Jesus answered and said unto him: Verily I say unto thee, my beloved, that I both taught the word with you and continually sat with my Father, and received the sacrifices in paradise every 20 day. Bartholomew answered and said unto him: Lord, if thirty thousand souls depart out of the world every day, how many souls out of them are found righteous? Jesus saith unto him: Hardly fifty my beloved. Again Bartholomew saith: And how do three only enter into paradise? Jesus saith unto him: The three 25 enter into paradise or are laid up in Abraham's bosom: but the others go into the place of the resurrection, for the three are not like unto the fifty.

Bartholomew saith unto him: Lord, how many souls above the number are born into the world daily? Jesus saith unto him: 30 One soul only is born above the number of them that depart.

And when he had said this he gave them the peace, and vanished away from them.[1]

[1] "The Apocryphal New Testament," in R. O. Ballou, ed., *The Bible of the World*, pp. 1268–1270.

HERACLES (HERCULES)
Greek

The descent of Heracles to the underworld is his twelfth and ultimate labor. Like most other heroes of the descent, he must struggle with the forces of death, and, also like the others, he rescues a fellow human being, Theseus, from these forces.

Now had come the time for the twelfth and last of the labours that Hercules did for his master Eurystheus. This labour would seem to anyone by far the hardest; for the hero was commanded to descend into the lower world, and bring back with him from the kingdom of Proserpine the terrible three-headed watch-dog Cerberus.

Hercules took the dark path which before him had been trodden only by Orpheus and Theseus and Pirithous. Orpheus had returned. Theseus and Pirithous, for their wicked attempt, were still imprisoned.

Hercules passed the Furies, undaunted by the frightful eyes beneath the writhing serpents of their hair. He passed the great criminals, Sisyphus, Tantalus and the rest. He passed by his friend, the unhappy Theseus, who was sitting immovably fixed to a rock, and he came at last into the terrible presence of black Pluto himself, who sat on his dark throne with his young wife Proserpine beside him. To the King and Queen of the Dead Hercules explained the reason of his coming. "Go," said Pluto, "and, so long as you use no weapon, but only your bare hands, you may take my watch-dog Cerberus to the upper air."

Hercules thanked the dreadful king for giving him the permission which he had asked. Then he made one more request which was that Theseus, who had sinned only by keeping his promise to his friend, might be allowed to return again to life. This, too, was granted him. Theseus rose to his feet again and accompanied the hero to the entrance of hell, where the huge dog Cerberus, with his three heads and his three deep baying voices, glared savagely at the intruders. Even this tremendous animal proved no match for Hercules, who with his vice-like grip stifled the breath in two of the shaggy throats, then lifted the beast upon his shoulders and began to ascend again, Theseus following close behind, the path that leads to the world of men. They say that when he carried Cerberus to Mycenae, Eurystheus fled in terror to another city and was now actually glad that Hercules had completed what might seem to have been twelve impossible labours. Cerberus was restored to his place in Hell and never again visited the upper world. Nor did Hercules ever go down to the place of the dead, since, after further trials, he was destined to live among the gods above.[1]

[1] Rex Warner, *The Stories of the Greeks*, pp. 101–102.

KUTOYIS

Blackfoot Indian

This descent story contains the traditional struggle and re-trieval. Added to it is the motif in which hell is the inside of a monster. The inside of the whale is a hell for Jonah in the biblical story.

Then he asked them where there were some more people. They told him that there were some people down the river, and some up in the mountains. But they said: "Do not go there, for it is bad, because Aisinokoki (Wind Sucker) lives there. He will kill you." It pleased Kutoyis to know that there was such a person, [5] and he went to the mountains. When he got to the place where Wind Sucker lived, he looked into his mouth, and could see many dead people there, — some skeletons and some just dead. He went in, and there he saw a fearful sight. The ground was white as snow with the bones of those who had died. There were bodies [10] with flesh on them; some were just dead, and some still living. He spoke to a living person, and asked, "What is that hanging down above us?" The person answered that it was Wind Sucker's heart. Then said Kutoyis: "You who still draw a little breath, try to shake your heads (in time to the song), and those who are still [15] able to move, get up and dance. Take courage now, we are going to have the ghost dance." So Kutoyis bound his knife, point up-ward, to the top of his head and began to dance, singing the ghost song, and all the others danced with him; and as he danced up and down, the point of the knife cut Wind Sucker's heart and [20] killed him. Kutoyis took his knife and cut through Wind Sucker's ribs, and freed those who were able to crawl out, and said to those who could still travel to go and tell their people that they should come here for the ones who were still alive but unable to walk.[1]

[1] George Bird Grinnell, *Blackfoot Lodge Tales*, pp. 35–36.

ORPHEUS AND EURYDICE
Greek and Roman

*The descent into the underworld is not always totally success-
ful. The Orpheus tale is the prototype of the tragic failure to
follow the proper ritual and the resulting loss of the loved one
who was almost saved.*

When his farewells were said at Iphis' wedding,
Hymen leaped into space toward blue uncharted skies,
His golden-amber colours gliding up,
Till he sailed over Thrace where Orpheus hailed him
(But not entirely to his advantage)   5
To bless another wedding celebration.
Though Hymen came to help him at the feast
And waved his torch, its fires guttered out
In coiling smoke that filled the eyes with tears.
Then on the morning after, things went wrong: 10
While walking carelessly through sun-swept grasses,
Like Spring herself, with all her girls-in-waiting,
The bride stepped on a snake; pierced by his venom,
The girl tripped, falling, stumbled into Death.
Her bridegroom, Orpheus, poet of the hour,   15
And pride of Rhadope, sang loud his loss
To everyone on earth. When this was done,
His wailing voice, his lyre, and himself
Came weaving through the tall gates of Taenarus
Down to the world of Death and flowing Darkness   20
To tell the story of his grief again.
He took his way through crowds of drifting shades
Who had escaped their graves to hear his music
And stood at last where Queen Persephone
Joined her unyielding lord to rule that desert   25
Which had been called their kingdom. Orpheus
Tuned up his lyre and cleared his throat to sing:
"O King and Queen of this vast Darkness where
All who are born of Earth at last return,
I cannot speak half flattery, half lies;   30
I have not come, a curious, willing guest
To see the streets of Tartarus wind in Hell,

Nor have I come to tame Medusa's children,
Three-throated beasts with wild snakes in their hair.
My mission is to find Eurydice,
A girl whose thoughts were innocent and gay,
Yet tripped upon a snake who struck his poison   5
Into her veins—then her short walk was done.
However much I took her loss serenely,
A god called Love had greater strength than I;
I do not know how well he's known down here,
But up on Earth his name's on every tongue,   10
And if I'm to believe an ancient rumour,
A dark king took a princess to his bed,
A child more beautiful than any queen;
They had been joined by Love. So at your mercy,
And by the eternal Darkness that surrounds us,   15
I ask you to unspin the fatal thread
Too swiftly run, too swiftly cut away,
That was my bride's brief life. Hear me, and know
Another day, after our stay on Earth,
Or swift or slow, we shall be yours forever,   20
Speeding at last to one eternal kingdom—
Which is our one direction and our home—
And yours the longest reign mankind has known.
When my Eurydice has spent her stay on Earth,
The child, a lovely woman in your arms,   25
Then she'll return and you may welcome her.
But for the present I must ask a favour;
Let her come back to me to share my love,
Yet if the Fates say 'No,' here shall I stay—
Two deaths in one—my death as well as hers."   30

    Since these pathetic words were sung to music
Even the blood-drained ghosts of Hell fell weeping:
Tantalus no longer reached toward vanished waves
And Ixion's wheel stopped short, charmed by the spell;
Vultures gave up their feast on Tityus' liver   35
And cocked their heads to stare; fifty Belides
Stood gazing while their half-filled pitchers emptied,
And Sisyphus sat down upon his stone.
Then, as the story goes, the raging Furies
Grew sobbing-wet with tears. Neither the queen

Nor her great lord of Darkness could resist
The charms of Orpheus and his matchless lyre.
They called Eurydice, and there among
The recent dead she came, still hurt and limping
At their command. They gave him back his wife   5
With this proviso: that as he led her up
From where Avernus sank into a valley,
He must not turn his head to look behind him.
They climbed a hill through clouds, pitch-dark and gloomy,
And as they neared the surface of the Earth,   10
The poet, fearful that she'd lost her way,
Glanced backward with a look that spoke his love —
Then saw her gliding into deeper darkness,
As he reached out to hold her, she was gone;
He had embraced a world of emptiness.   15
This was her second death — and yet she could not blame him
(Was not his greatest fault great love for her?)
She answered him with one last faint "Good-bye,"
An echo of her voice from deep Avernus.
                                                                 20
    When Orpheus saw his wife go down to Death,
Twice dead, twice lost, he stared like someone dazed.
He seemed to be like him who saw the fighting
Three-headed Dog led out by Hercules
In chains, a six-eyed monster spitting bile;
The man was paralyzed and fear ran through him   25
Until his very body turned to stone.
Or rather, Orpheus, was not unlike
Lethaea's husband, who took on himself
The sin of being proud of his wife's beauty,
Of which that lady bragged too much and long,   30
Yet since their hearts were one (in their opinion)
They changed to rocks where anyone may see them
Hold hands and kiss where Ida's fountains glitter.
Soon Orpheus went "melancholy-mad":
As often as old Charon pushed him back,   35
He begged, he wept to cross the Styx again.
Then for a week he sat in rags and mud,
Nor ate nor drank; he lived on tears and sorrow.
He cried against the gods of black Avernus
And said they made him suffer and go wild;

Then, suddenly, as if his mood had shifted,
He went to Thrace and climbed up windy Haemus.

   Three times the year had gone through waves of Pisces,
While Orpheus refused to sleep with women;
Whether this meant he feared bad luck in marriage,   5
Or proved him faithful to Eurydice,
No one can say, yet women followed him
And felt insulted when he turned them out.
Meanwhile he taught the men of Thrace the art
Of making love to boys and showed them that   10
Such love affairs renewed their early vigour,
The innocence of youth, the flowers of spring.

   One day while walking down a little hill
He sloped upon a lawn of thick green grasses,   15
A lovely place to rest—but needed shade.
But when the poet, great-grandson of the gods,
Sat down to sing and touched his golden lyre,
There the cool grasses waved beneath green shadows,
For trees came crowding where the poet sang,   20
The silver poplar and the bronze-leaved oak,
The swaying lina, beechnut, maiden-laurel,
Delicate hazel and spear-making ash,
The shining silver fir, the ilex leaning
Its flower-weighted head, sweet-smelling fir,   25
The shifting-coloured maple and frail willow
Whose branches trail where gliding waters flow;
Lake-haunted lotus and the evergreening boxwood,
Thin tamarisk and the myrtle of two colours,
Viburnum with its darkly shaded fruit.   30
And with them came the slender-footed ivy,
Grapevine and vine-grown elms and mountain ash,
The deeply wooded spruce, the pink arbutus,
The palm whose leaves are signs of victory,
And the tall pine, beloved of Cybele   35
Since Attis her loyal priest stripped off his manhood,
And stood sexless and naked as that tree. [1]

After his death Orpheus returned to the underworld.

[1] Ovid, *Metamorphoses*, 10, translated by Horace Gregory.

257

THE YOUNG COMANCHE
Comanche Indian

The Young Comanche is a North American Indian Orpheus.
His mistake, like his prototype's, is reminiscent of Gilgamesh's
loss of the elixir of life.

A young man loved his wife dearly. When she died, he therefore resolved to follow her, and got ready his horse and suitable
equipment. Then he set out westwards, and rode thus for months.
He journeyed over the mountains, but all he had with him was
worn out there, finally even his horse, and he arrived on foot in   5
the realm of the dead. The children there skipped around him and
shouted: "Look, there is a raw one!" He soon found the lodge of
his father-in-law, where his deceased wife also lived. She was
now torn with conflicting feelings: she did not wish to return,
for she was happy where she was, but at the same time she loved   10
her husband dearly. At last her father settled the matter. He said
to the husband: "Well, go back with her. But remember this:
when you leave the camp you must go eastward. And you must
not touch her before you come to the place where the buffalo is.
You must give her a buffalo's kidney to eat. When she eats this   15
she will become flesh, and after that she can live with you as
your wife. But you must never strike her. If you strike her she
will come back to us."

So they set off. After a time they came to the buffalo plains.
The husband slew a young buffalo and gave the kidney to his   20
wife, who now became a living human being. They both kissed
and embraced each other, and they forgot all about the life in
the world of the dead. Then they went on, and soon reached the
camp of the living.

This happened in the spring. When autumn came round all   25
was still well between the two. One day they lay together in their
lodge, and the man grasped the buffalo hide and wanted to draw
it over himself and his wife to warm their bodies. But his hand
slipped and hit his wife hard. She shrieked: "You struck me on
the head, now I must return to the dead!" The unhappy husband   30
heard his wife's voice fading and finally dying away altogether.[1]

[1] Åke Hultkrantz, *The North American Indian Orpheus Tradition*, pp. 17–
18.

HERMODR AND BALDER
Icelandic

This story also contains the unsuccessful rescue. The implication here, however, is that death is irreversible.

But to speak now of Hermodr: he rode nine days and nights down ravines ever darker and deeper, meeting no one, until he came to the banks of the river Gjoll which he followed as far as the Gjoll Bridge: this bridge is roofed with burning gold. Modgudr is the maiden's name who guards the bridge. She asked him his name or lineage, saying only the day before five droves of dead men had passed over the bridge, "but the bridge echoed less under them than you. Anyway, you haven't the pallor of a dead man: why are you riding down the Hel Way?"

He replied, "I ride to hel to seek out Balder. You don't happen to have set eyes on Balder on the road to hel?"

She said Balder had already ridden over Gjoll Bridge, "and the road to hel lies down still and to the north."

Hermodr galloped on until he came to Hel Gate Bars, where he stepped down from his horse and tightened the girths. He mounted again and plunged his spurs into the animal's flanks. The stallion leapt so high there was plenty of twilight between him and the bars. And Hermodr rode on to the hall of Hel where he got down and went in to see his brother Balder sitting on a throne. Hermodr stayed with him that night.

Next morning Hermodr begged Hel to let Balder ride back home with him and went on to tell how greatly the gods were grieving. Hel said it would soon be put to the test that Balder was so beloved by all as they make out: "If every single creature up in heaven, dead or alive, really mourns him then he shall be restored to the gods. He stays with Hel if but one alone speaks against him or refuses to mourn."

Hermodr stood up and Balder saw him outside and he pulled off the ring Draupnir and sent it back to Odin for a memento, while Nanna sent some linen and many other gifts to Frigg, and to Fulla a golden ring.

Then rode Hermodr back to Asgard and related all his news, everything he had seen and everything he had heard.

At once, the gods sent messengers to every corner of heaven

asking all to weep Balder un-dead, and everything did so, both men and beasts, earth, stones, trees, and every metal. . . . When at last the messengers came home, having pursued their errand diligently, they passed to a cave where an old witch was crouching. Her name was Pokk and they asked her to mourn for Balder, [5] but she chanted:

> Pokk must drop
> only dry tears
>   for the beautiful Balder's burial:
> living or dead [10]
> I loved not the churl's son;
>   let Hel hold what she has.

Everything guessed this must have been Loki who had done so much evil among the gods.[1]

---

[1] Brian Branston, *Gods of the North*, pp. 274–275.

IZANAGI AND IZANAMI
Japanese

This descent story is traditional in that the hero is in search of his beloved. In keeping with the Orpheus tradition, the quest, for ritualistic reasons, is unsuccessful. The struggle, too, is traditional but for the fact that the combatants are the former lovers.

Izanami continued producing a variety of divinities: the sea, the waves, the mountains, and so on, until finally she brought forth the god of Fire. The private parts of the August Female were so burned in giving birth to this last divinity, that she mortally sickened, and various other divinities came into existence from her vomit (mountains), her offal (mud), and her urine. At last she dies. Izanagi is sick with rage and despair, and as he creeps around her pillow, lamenting, still other divinities spring into existence from his tears. Then he seizes his sword, ten handbreadths long, and cuts off his son's (the Fire god) head; from the blood are born still more deities.

At this point begins one of the most striking sequences in the story. Izanagi, unable to contain his desire to see his dead sister-wife, decides to visit her in the Land of Darkness. There she has built a castle. Izanagi tries to entice her back to the upper world where their creative work is still unfinished. But she hesitates, saying it is too late, for she has eaten the food of the Land of Darkness. She bids her brother not to look upon her and retires into her palace. But Izanagi is impatient. He breaks off the left end-tooth of his comb, ignites it, and enters to discover why she tarries so long. He finds her in a shocking condition of disintegration, covered with maggots, putrescent, and rotting. Frightened at the sight, he turns and flees. But his sister, angry at being discovered in such a shameful state, launches the hags (*shikome*) of the Land of Darkness in his pursuit. As he flees Izanagi takes his headdress and throws it behind him; it immediately turns into grapes, which the hags stop to devour. But the pursuit resumes, and Izanagi snatches from his hair the right comb, which he casts behind him; it immediately turns into bamboo sprouts, which the hags also tear up and eat. Izanami then sends an army of fifteen hundred warriors on her brother's traces. However, the

August Male keeps them at a distance by brandishing his ten-grasp sword. Finally, at the Even Pass between the world of light and the Land of Darkness, he finds three peaches with which he pelts his pursuers so that they are obliged to retreat. Without further ado he blocks the Even Pass with a great rock, from either side of which he and his sister address each other menacingly. She threatens to kill a thousand beings a day in the land of light, to which Izanagi replies that in such a case he will set up fifteen hundred parturition houses, that is, he will cause fifteen hundred births each day, thereby establishing a just proportion between births and deaths. He further severs connection with his sister by pronouncing the formula of divorce.[1]

[1] S. N. Kramer, ed., *Mythologies of the Ancient World*, pp. 419–420.

MOSES
Judaic

The legendary visit of Moses to hell is an educational field trip. God sends the prophet to learn the results of sin.

When Moses was on the point of departing from heaven, a celestial voice announced: "Moses, thou camest hither, and thou didst see the throne of My glory. Now thou shalt see also Paradise and hell," and God dispatched Gabriel on the errand of showing hell to him. Terrified by its fires, when he caught sight of them 5 as he entered the portals of hell, Moses refused to go farther. But the angel encouraged him, saying, "There is a fire that not only burns but also consumes, and that fire will protect thee against hell fire, so that thou canst step upon it, and yet thou wilt not be seared." 10

As Moses entered hell, the fire withdrew a distance of five hundred parasangs, and the Angel of Hell, Nasargiel, asked him, "Who art thou?" and he answered, "I am Moses, the son of Amram."

Nasargiel: "This is not thy place, thou belongest in Paradise." 15

Moses: "I came hither to see the manifestation of the power of God."

Then said God to the Angel of Hell, "Go and show hell unto Moses, and how the wicked are treated there." Immediately he went with Moses, walking before him like a pupil before his 20 master, and thus they entered hell together, and Moses saw men undergoing torture by the Angels of Destruction: some of the sinners were suspended by their eyelids, some by their ears, some by their hands, and some by their tongues, and they cried bitterly. And women were suspended by their hair and by their breasts, 25 and in other ways, all on chains of fire. Nasargiel explained: "These hang by their eyes, because they looked lustfully upon the wives of their neighbors, and with a covetous eye upon the possessions of their fellow-men. These hang by their ears because they listened to empty and vain speech, and turned their ear away 30 from hearing the Torah. These hang by their tongues, because they talked slander, and accustomed their tongue to foolish babbling. These hang by their feet, because they walked with them in order to spy upon their fellow-men, but they walked not to the synagogue, to offer prayer unto their Creator. These hang by their hands, because with them they robbed their neighbors of their possessions, and committed murder. These women hang by their hair and their breasts, because they uncovered them in the presence of young men, so that they conceived desire unto them, and fell into sin." 5

Moses heard Hell cry with a loud and a bitter cry, saying to Nasargiel: "Give me something to eat, I am hungry."—Nasargiel: "What shall I give thee?"—Hell: "Give me the souls of the pious." —Nasargiel: "The Holy One, blessed be He, will not deliver the 10 souls of the pious unto thee."

Moses saw the place called 'Alukah, where sinners were suspended by their feet, their heads downward, and their bodies covered with black worms, each five hundred parasangs long. They lamented, and cried: "Woe unto us for the punishment of 15 hell. Give us death, that we may die!" Nasargiel explained: "These are the sinners that swore falsely, profaned the Sabbath and the holy days, despised the sages, called their neighbors by unseemly nicknames, wronged the orphan and the widow, and bore false witness. Therefore hath God delivered them to these 20 worms."

Moses went thence to another place, and there he saw sinners prone on their faces, with two thousand scorpions lashing, stinging, and tormenting them, while the tortured victims cried bitterly. Each of the scorpions had seventy thousand heads, each 25 head seventy thousand mouths, each mouth seventy thousand stings, and each sting seventy thousand pouches of poison and venom, which the sinners are forced to drink down, although the anguish is so racking that their eyes melt in their sockets. Nasargiel explained: "These are the sinners who caused the Israelites 30 to lose their money, who exalted themselves above the community, who put their neighbors to shame in public, who delivered their fellow-Israelites into the hands of the Gentiles, who denied the Torah of Moses, and who maintained that God is not the Creator of the world." 35

Then Moses saw the place called Tit ha-Yawen, in which the sinners stand in mud up to their navels, while the Angels of Destruction lash them with fiery chains, and break their teeth with fiery stones, from morning until evening, and during the night they make their teeth grow again, to the length of a para- 40 sang, only to break them anew the next morning. Nasargiel explained: "These are the sinners who ate carrion and forbidden flesh, who lent their money at usury, who wrote the Name of God on amulets for Gentiles, who used false weights, who stole money from their fellow-Israelites, who ate on the Day of Atonement, who ate forbidden fat, and animals and reptiles that are an abomination, and who drank blood."

Then Nasargiel said to Moses: "Come and see how the sinners are burnt in hell," and Moses answered, "I cannot go there," but Nasargiel replied, "Let the light of the Shekinah precede thee, and the fire of hell will have no power over thee." Moses yielded, and he saw how the sinners were burnt, one half of their bodies being immersed in fire and the other half in snow, while worms bred in their own flesh crawled over them, and the Angels of Destruction beat them incessantly. Nasargiel explained: "These are the sinners who committed incest, murder, and idolatry, who cursed their parents and their teachers, and who, like Nimrod and others, called themselves gods." In this place, which is called Abaddon, he saw the sinners taking snow by stealth and putting it in their armpits, to relieve the pain inflicted by the scorching fire, and he was convinced that the saying was true, "The wicked mend not their ways even at the gate of hell."

As Moses departed from hell, he prayed to God, "May it be Thy will, O Lord my God and God of my fathers, to save me and the people of Israel from the places I have seen in hell." But God answered him, and said, "Moses, before Me there is no respecting of persons and no taking of gifts. Whoever doeth good deeds entereth Paradise, and he that doeth evil must go to hell."[1]

---

[1] Louis Ginzberg, *The Legends of the Jews*, vol. 2, pp. 309–313.

ODYSSEUS
Greek

Odysseus is one of many heroes who visits the dead to gain knowledge of his destiny. His descent is a forerunner to similar trips by Aeneas and Dante.

At length we were at the shore where lay the ship. Promptly we launched her into the divine sea, stepped the mast, made sail and went: not forgetting the sheep, though our hearts were very low and big tears rained down from our eyes. Behind the dark-prowed vessel came a favourable wind, our welcomed way-fellow, whom we owed to Circe, the kind-spoken yet awesome Goddess: so when each man had done his duty by the ship we could sit and watch the wind and the helmsman lead us forward, day-long going steadily across the deep, our sails cracking full, till sundown and its darkness covered the sea's illimitable ways. We had attained Earth's verge and its girdling river of Ocean, where are the cloud-wrapped and misty confines of the Cimmerian men. For them no flashing Sun-God shines down a living light, not in the morning when he climbs through the starry sky, nor yet at day's end when he rolls down from heaven behind the land. Instead an endless deathful night is spread over its melancholy people.

"We beached the ship on that shore and put off our sheep. With them we made our way up the strand of Ocean till we came to the spot which Circe had described. There Perimedes and Eurylochus held the victims while I drew the keen blade from my hip, to hollow that trench of a cubit square and a cubit deep. About it I poured the drink-offerings to the congregation of the dead, a honey-and-milk draught first, sweet wine next, with water last of all: and I made a heave-offering of our glistening barley; invoking the tenuous dead, in general, for my intention of a heifer-not-in-calf, the best to be found in my manors when I got back to Ithaca; which should be slain to them and burnt there on a pyre fed high with treasure: while for Teiresias apart I vowed an all-black ram, the choicest male out of our flocks.

"After I had been thus instant in prayer to the populations of the grave I took the two sheep and beheaded them across my pit in such manner that the livid blood drained into it. Then from out of Erebus they flocked to me, the dead spirits of those who had died. Brides came and lads; old men and men of sad experience; tender girls aching from their first agony; and many fighting men showing the stabbed wounds of brazen spears — war-victims, still in their blooded arms. All thronged to the trench and ranged rest- lessly this side of it and that with an eerie wailing. Pale fear gripped me. Hastily I called the others and bade them flay and burn with fire the sheep's bodies which lay there, slaughtered by my pitiless sword. They obeyed, conjuring without cease the Gods, great Hades and terrible Persephone, while I sat over the pit holding out my sharp weapon to forbid and prevent this shambling legion of the dead from approaching the blood till I had had my answer from Teiresias.

. . . Then advanced the spirit of my mother who had died, even Anticleia, daughter of kindly Autolycus. I had left her alive when I started for the sacred city of Ilios, so now the sight of her melted my heart and made me weep with quick pain. Nevertheless I would not let her near to touch the blood, for I awaited Teiresias to speak with me. And at last he came, the spirit of Theban Teire- sias, gold sceptre in hand. He knew me and said, 'Heaven-born Odysseus, what now? O son of misfortune, why leave the lambent sunshine for this joyless place where only the dead are to be seen? Stand off from the pit and put up your threatening sword that I may drink blood and declare to you words of truth.' So he said and I stepped back, thrusting my silver-hilted sword home into its scabbard: while he drank of the blackening blood. Then did the blameless seer begin to say: —

" 'You come here, renowned Odysseus, in quest of a com- fortable way home. I tell you the God will make your way hard. I tell you that your movements will not remain secret from the Earth-shaker, whose heart is bitter against you for the hurt you did him in blinding the Cyclops, his loved son. Yet have you a chance of surviving to reach Ithaca, despite all obstacles, if you and your followers can master your greed in the island of Thrina- cia, when your ship first puts in there for refuge from the lower- ing sea. For in that island you will find at pasture the oxen and wonderful sheep of Helios our Sun, who oversees and overhears all things. If you are so preoccupied about returning as to leave these beasts unhurt, then you may get back to Ithaca, very toil- worn, after all: but if you meddle with them, then I certify the doom of your men and your ship; and though yourself may escape alive, it will not be till after many days, in a ship of strangers, alone and in sorry plight, that you win back, having suffered the loss of all your company: while in your house you shall find trouble awaiting you, even overbearing men who devour your substance on pretext of courting your worshipful wife and chaffering about her marriage dues. Yet at your coming shall you visit their violence upon them, fatally. After you have killed these suitors, either by cunning within the house or publicly with the stark sword, then go forth under your shapely oar till you come to a people who know not the sea and eat their victuals unsavoured with its salt: a people ignorant of purple-prowed ships and of the smoothed and shaven oars which are the wings of a ship's flying. I give you this token of them, a sign so plain that you cannot miss it: you have arrived when another wayfarer shall cross you and say that on your doughty shoulder you bear the scatterer of haulms, a winnowing-fan. Then pitch in the earth your polished oar and sacrifice goodly beasts to King Poseidon, a ram and a bull and a ramping boar. Afterward turn back; and at home offer hecatombs to the Immortal Gods who possess the broad planes of heaven: to all of them in order, as is most seemly. At the last, amidst a happy folk, shall your own death come to you, softly, far from the salt sea, and make an end of one utterly weary of slipping downward into old age. All these things that I relate are true.'

"So he prophesied and I, answering, said: 'O Teiresias, surely these things are threads of destiny woven in the Gods' design. Yet tell to me one other thing. Before me is the ghost of my mother, dead. Lo there, how she crouches by the blood and will not look upon me nor address me one word. Tell me, King, how shall she know that I am her son?' So I said and he replied, 'A simple thing for my saying and your learning. Any of these ghosts of the dead, if you permit them to come near the blood, will tell you truth: and to whomsoever you begrudge it, he shall go back, away.' The spirit of King Teiresias ended his soothsaying and departed to the House of Hades, but I remained firmly there, while my mother came up and drank of the storm-dark blood. Then at once she knew me and wailed aloud, crying to me winged words: 'My child, what brings you to visit here, a quick man in this darkness of the shadow? It is sore travail for the living to see such things, because of the wide rivers and fearful waters that run between: especially Ocean's flood, that mortals cannot cross on foot but only by ship, in a well-found ship. Are you still errant, you and your men, from

Troy? The time has been long if you have not yet reached Ithaca nor seen your wife in the house.'

"So she said and I returned: 'My mother, I had no choice but to come down to Hades. I must needs consult the spirit of Theban Teiresias, inasmuch as I have not yet drawn nigh Achaea, not yet set foot upon my own land, but have strayed ever painfully from that day I followed great Agamemnon to fight the Trojans at Ilios of the fine horses. But tell me now plainly—by what fateful agency did Death strike you down? Was it a slow disease, or did arrow-loving Artemis slay you with a stroke of her gentle darts? Inform me of the father and son I left. Is my position still safe in their keeping, or has a stranger assumed it on the rumour that I shall not return? Also of my wife—what is her mood and conduct? Does she abide by the child and guard all things as they were, or has she married some noble Achaean?' My lady mother exclaimed: 'Why, she is ever in your house, most patiently. The nights drag through for her heavily and her days are wet with tears. Your fair position has not fallen to another. Telemachus holds the estate unchallenged, feasting amongst his peers at all such entertainments as magistrates may properly attend. He is invited everywhere. For your father—he now-a-days dwells wholly in the country and does not come to town. Old age grows crankily upon him. He will not suffer for his own use any bed or couch, quilts or glossy blankets: nor aught but rags upon his body. In winter-time he sleeps at home as bondmen sleep, by the hearth in the ashes of the fire: but when the summer brings its rush of harvest-tide and all through his rich vine-terraces the dead leaves are strewn for him in ground-carpets, upon them will he lie distressfully, sighing for your return with a sorrow that ever waxes in his heart. Also my death and doom were of that sort. No archer-goddess with piercing sight came upon me in the house and felled me with gentle arrows: nor any set disease, with a sorry wasting to drain the life from my limbs. Rather it was my longing for you—your cunning ways, O my wonderful Odysseus, and your tenderness—which robbed me of the life that had been sweet.'

"She ceased her say. While my heart pondered the word a longing rose in me to take in my arms this spirit of my mother, though she were dead. Thrice I stepped toward her for an embrace, and thrice she slipped through my grasp like a shadow or a dream. The pain conceived in my heart grew very bitter and I cried to her in piercing words: 'Mother mine, can you not abide the loving arms of one who yearns so sorely after you, that here, even here in Hades, we may tearfully sate ourselves with icy shuddering grief? Or are you only some phantasm which great Persephone has sent to increase the misery of my pain?' So I said; but my mother lamented: 'Alas my hapless child! Here is no ⁵ mockery from Persephone, daughter of Zeus: it is the common judgement upon all mortals when they die. Then the nerves will no more bind flesh and frame into one body. for the terrible intensity of searing fire subdues them till they vanish, as the quickening spirit vanishes from the white bones and the soul flies out, ¹⁰ to hover like a dream. Therefore make your best speed back into daylight, noting all things as you go, for rehearsal hereafter to your wife.'"[1]

---

[1] Homer, *The Odyssey of Homer*, translated by T. E. Shaw, book XI, pp. 152–158.

AENEAS

Roman

Aeneas must enter the underworld to find his father and through him the destiny of Rome.

The journey from Carthage to the west coast of Italy was easy as compared with what had gone before. A great loss, however, was the death of the trusty pilot Palinurus who was drowned as they neared the end of their perils by sea.

Aeneas had been told by the prophet Helenus as soon as he [5] reached the Italian land to seek the cave of the Sibyl of Cumae, a woman of deep wisdom, who could foretell the future and would advise him what to do. He found her and she told him she would guide him to the underworld where he would learn all he needed to know from his father Anchises, who had died just before the [10] great storm. She warned him, however, that it was no light undertaking: —

Trojan, Anchises' son, the descent of Avernus is easy.
All night long, all day, the doors of dark Hades stand open.
But to retrace the path, to come up to the sweet air of heaven, [15]
That is labor indeed.

Nevertheless, if he was determined she would go with him. First he must find in the forest a golden bough growing on a tree, which he must break off and take with him. Only with this in his hand would he be admitted to Hades. He started at once to look [20] for it, accompanied by the ever-faithful Achates. They went almost hopelessly into the great wilderness of trees where it seemed impossible to find anything. But suddenly they caught sight of two doves, the birds of Venus. The men followed as they flew slowly on until they were close to Lake Avernus, a dark foul- [25] smelling sheet of water where the Sibyl had told Aeneas was the cavern from which the road led down to the underworld. Here the doves soared up to a tree through whose foliage came a bright yellow gleam. It was the golden bough. Aeneas plucked it joyfully and took it to the Sibyl. Then, together, prophetess and hero [30] started on their journey.

Other heroes had taken it before Aeneas and not found it especially terrifying. The crowding ghosts had, to be sure, finally frightened Ulysses,[1] but Theseus, Hercules, Orpheus, Pollux, had apparently encountered no great difficulty on the way. Indeed, the timid Psyche had gone there all alone to get the beauty charm for Venus from Proserpine and had seen nothing worse than the three-headed dog Cerberus, who had been easily mollified by a bit of cake. But the Roman hero found horrors piled upon horrors. The way the Sibyl thought it necessary to start was calculated to frighten any but the boldest. At dead of night in front of the dark cavern on the bank of the somber lake she slaughtered four coal-black bullocks to Hecate, the dread Goddess of Night. As she placed the sacrificial parts upon a blazing altar, the earth rumbled and quaked beneath their feet and from afar dogs howled through the darkness. With a cry to Aeneas, "Now will you need all your courage," she rushed into the cave, and undaunted he followed her. They found themselves soon on a road wrapped in shadows which yet permitted them to see frightful forms on either side, pale Disease and avenging Care, and Hunger that persuades to crime, and so on, a great company of terrors. Death-dealing War was there and mad Discord with snaky, bloodstained hair, and many another curse to mortals. They passed unmolested through them and finally reached a place where an old man was rowing a boat over a stretch of water. There they saw a pitiful sight, spirits on the shore innumerable as the leaves which fall in the forest at the first cold of winter, all stretching out their hands and praying the ferryman to carry them across to the farther bank. But the gloomy old man made his own choice among them; some he admitted to his skiff, others he pushed away. As Aeneas stared in wonder the Sibyl told him they had reached the junction of two great rivers of the underworld, the Cocytus, named of lamentation loud, and the Acheron. The ferryman was Charon and those he would not admit to his boat were the unfortunates who had not been duly buried. They were doomed to wander aimlessly for a hundred years, with never a place to rest in.

Charon was inclined to refuse Aeneas and his guide when they came down to the boat. He bade them halt and told them he did not ferry the living, only the dead. At sight of the golden bough, however, he yielded and took them across. The dog Cerberus was there on the other bank to dispute the way, but they

[1] Odysseus.

followed Psyche's example. The Sibyl, too, had some cake for him and he gave them no trouble. As they went on they came to the solemn place in which Minos, Europa's son, the inflexible judge of the dead, was passing the final sentence on the souls before him. They hastened away from that inexorable presence and found themselves in the Fields of Mourning, where the unhappy lovers dwelt who had been driven by their misery to kill themselves. In that sorrowful but lovely spot, shaded with groves of myrtle, Aeneas caught sight of Dido. He wept as he greeted her. "Was I the cause of your death?" he asked her. "I swear I left you against my will." She neither looked at him nor answered him. A piece of marble could not have seemed less moved. He himself, however, was a good deal shaken, and he continued to shed tears for some time after he lost sight of her.

At last they reached a spot where the road divided. From the left branch came horrid sounds, groans and savage blows and the clanking of chains. Aeneas halted in terror. The Sibyl, however, bade him have no fear, but fasten boldly the golden bough on the wall that faced the crossroads. The regions to the left, she said, were ruled over by stern Rhadamanthus, also a son of Europa, who punished the wicked for their misdeeds. But the road to the right led to the Elysian Fields where Aeneas would find his father. There when they arrived everything was delightful, soft green meadows, lovely groves, a delicious life-giving air, sunlight that glowed softly purple, an abode of peace and blessedness. Here dwelt the great and good dead, heroes, poets, priests, and all who had made men remember them by helping others. Among them Aeneas soon came upon Anchises, who greeted him with incredulous joy. Father and son alike shed happy tears at this strange meeting between the dead and the living whose love had been strong enough to bring him down to the world of death.

They had much, of course, to say to each other. Anchises led Aeneas to Lethe, the river of forgetfulness, of which the souls on their way to live again in the world above must all drink. "A draught of long oblivion," Anchises said. And he showed his son those who were to be their descendants, his own and Aeneas', now waiting by the river for their time to drink and lose the memory of what in former lives they had done and suffered. A magnificent company they were—the future Romans, the masters of the world. One by one Anchises pointed them out, and told of the deeds they would do which men would never through all time forget. Finally, he gave his son instructions how he would best establish his home in Italy and how he could avoid or endure all the hardships that lay before him.

Then they took leave of each other, but calmly, knowing that they were parting only for a time. Aeneas and the Sibyl made their way back to the earth and Aeneas returned to his ships. Next day the Trojans sailed up the coast of Italy looking for their promised home.[2]

[2] Edith Hamilton, *Mythology*, pp. 226–230.

THE NIGHT JOURNEY OF THE SOUL:
Commentary on Part 6

In the universal myth of the descent into the underworld the hero finds himself an explorer in the province of death itself. This is the continuance of the scapegoat process, in which the hero, as man's agent, faces in depth what man himself so fears. The hero is our hope of overcoming death and understanding its meaning. The specific purpose of the voyage is usually to retrieve a loved one, to attain knowledge of personal or racial destiny, or simply to complete a great task. Whatever the reason, the myth involves the hero's suffering or witnessing the actual torments of the underworld before defeating death definitively in rebirth or resurrection. Usually the quest is successful, although in the Orpheus tradition the loved one is retrieved only to be lost again.

Much of the underworld myth's meaning lies in the fact of the hero's return to the inner earth — to the natural mother. This is the stage of the germinating seed; the hero must spend the allotted time in the world womb before he can be born again in his role as divine hero who has truly broken through the local and material barriers of human life to become the Son of Man. The descent into the underworld is a rite of passage carrying the hero and man past the monster guardians of the higher truth which the underworld contains. As the voyager enters Death's kingdom, he leaves temporal and physical things behind, and he emerges later as literally a new being.

The psychological reality behind this and all mythological processes is the process of self-realization. The voyage to the underworld is the "night journey" or "dark night of the soul" — the second and final stage of meditation. It is the crucial stage of self-exploration in the face of a life already lived. The hero is the archetype of the self, and, as Jung wrote, "the archetype of the self has, functionally, the significance of a ruler of the inner world, i.e., of the collective unconscious."[1] Thus Inanna, "goddess of light and love and life," must confront in the nether world her sister Ereshkigal, "goddess of darkness and gloom and death" — the dark side of her own self. And Jesus descends to conquer Hell and to retrieve the other side of himself. For Christ and Adam are theologically and psychologically parts of the same

[1] Carl Gustav Jung, *Symbols of Transformation*, p. 368.

being: Christ as Son of Man, as redeemer of Adam's sin, is the New Adam.

This sense of recognizing and retrieving the various parts of the self—the evil and the good, the flesh and the spirit, the light and the dark—is at the very essence of the underworld myth. A comment by Alan Watts will help to clarify this point:

... the descent into the depths is almost invariably one of the great tasks of "the hero with a thousand faces," of the Christ in his many forms. Hades or Hell may here be understood as the Valley of the Shadow, the experience of impotence and despair in which "I" die and Christ comes to life. The descent is likewise a figure of the descent of consciousness into the unconscious, of the necessity of knowing one's very depths. For so long as the unconscious remains unexplored it is possible to retain the naïve feeling of the insularity and separateness of the conscious ego. Its actions are still taken to be free and spontaneous movements of the "will," and it can congratulate itself upon having motivations which are purely "good," unaware of the "dark" and hidden forces of conditioning which actually guide them.[2]

Full self-realization demands that we move beyond traditional ideas of good and evil to an acknowledgment and understanding of ourselves as both Adam and Christ, Inanna and Ereshkigal. The descent into the underworld is a pilgrimage which the true hero cannot avoid, for only after the pilgrimage can the new complete self be born in the act of rebirth.

Works of interest to the student of the descent myth include Jung's *Answer to Job* and *Symbols of Transformation*, parts of Alan Watts's *Myth and Ritual in Christianity* and Joseph Campbell's *The Hero with a Thousand Faces*, and Henderson and Oakes's *The Wisdom of the Serpent*.

[2] Alan Watts, *Myth and Ritual in Christianity*, p. 168.

7

RESURRECTION
AND
REBIRTH

Spiraling out the cresecent moon — usually a female symbol — is a seed of
life. The painting is a joyful — even playful — celebration of the eternal
cycle. [Joan Miró, *Landscape; The Hare* (1927), oil on canvas, 51 x 76⁵/₈
in. Collection, The Solomon R. Guggenheim Museum, New York. Photo:
Robert E. Mates. Reproduced with permission.]

HERACLES (HERCULES)
Greek

The comic story of the mock rebirth of Heracles is symbolic of an important rite of passage. Through his rebirth the hero breaks through his personal and local limitations and approaches godhead.

Now, Zeus had destined Heracles as one of the Twelve Olympians, yet was loth to expel any of the existing company of gods in order to make room for him. He therefore persuaded Hera to adopt Heracles by a ceremony of rebirth: namely, going to bed, pretending to be in labour, and then producing him from beneath her skirts — which is the adoption ritual still in use among many barbarian tribes. Henceforth, Hera regarded Heracles as her son and loved him next only to Zeus.[1]

5

[1] Robert Graves, *The Greek Myths*, vol. 2, p. 203.

DIONYSOS (DIONYSUS)
Greek

Like Heracles, Dionysos, in this version of his birth story, is re-born of the gods. When he springs from the thigh of Zeus, he joins Athena, who was born miraculously from Zeus's head, as one of the most favored gods.

It was told that when Zeus came to Semele, this was not a divine mating. He had prepared a potion from the heart of Diony-sos, and this he gave Semele to drink. The potion made the girl pregnant. When Hera heard of this, she tried to prevent the birth. She disguised herself as Semele's nurse, . . . when Zeus first came 5 to Semele he did not do so in the form of the lightning-bearing god of Heaven. The shape which Semele's secret husband had as-sumed was a mortal guise. Led astray by her pretended nurse, Semele asked Zeus to grant her just one wish. Zeus promised to do so, and when his beloved wished that he would appear to her 10 as he did to Hera, he visited her with lightning. . . . The lightning struck her and she descended into the Underworld. Zeus rescued from her body the unripe fruit, the child Dionysos.

The Father sheltered the prematurely born god in his own thigh . . . by sewing the child into it. . . . His father bore him, when 15 the proper time for his birth had come, far away to the east, on Mount Nysa. Zeus then . . . entrusted Dionysos to the divine nurses who were to look after him in the cave. . . .[1]

---

[1] C. Kerényi, *The Gods of the Greeks*, pp. 257–258.

HYACINTH
Greek and Roman

This traditional form of rebirth probably has its origins in the
practice of sacrificing youths to bring good crops.

"Phoebus[1] himself was charmed by Hyacinthus,
And if the Fates had given him more time,
And space as well, Apollo would have placed him
Where stars break out in heaven. Anyhow,
The boy became immortal. Now as often   5
As spring rides down the frosted reign of winter,
And leaping Ram runs after diving Pisces,
Frail Hyacinthus rises from green earth.
My father loved the boy; he thought him sweeter
Than any living creature of his kind—   10
And Delphi, capital of sacred glory,
Was like a tomb, deserted by Apollo.
The god went ranging after boyish pleasures
And strolled suburban Sparta, field and river.
Bored with the arts of music and long bow,   15
He found distraction near his lover's home.
Humble as any mountain guide or shepherd,
He carried bird nets, tended dogs and leashed them,
And joined the boy in day-long mountain climbing.
This native life stirred Phoebus' appetite   20
And made the boy more charming now than ever.
When Phoebus-Titan came at noon, half way
Between grey morning and the evening's pallor,
The lovers, naked, sleeked themselves with oil,
And stood at discus-throw. Phoebus came first,   25
And like a shot he whirled the disk midair
To cut a cloud in two. It disappeared;
It looked as if the thing had gone forever—
And eager to retrieve it, Hyacinthus
Ran out to meet it where it seemed to fall.   30
Then like a ricochetting wheel of fire,
It glanced a rock and struck the boy full face.
As pale as Death itself, the god rushed toward him,

[1] Apollo.

To fold the shrinking creature in his arms,
To bind his broken features with sweet grasses,
To cure his ragged lips and sightless eyes.
But all of Phoebus' healing arts were useless:
As in a garden, if one breaks a flower,   5
Crisp violet or poppy or straight lily
Erect with yellow stamens pointed high,
The flower wilts, head toppled into earth,
So bent the dying face of Hyacinthus,
Staring at nothingness toward breast and shoulder.   10
'Even now, my child, your hour is passed, is run,'
Cried Phoebus, 'and my hand your murderer,
And yet its crime was meeting yours at play.
Was that a crime? Or was my love to blame—
The guilt that follows love that loves too much?   15
You should have lived forever in my sight,
Your life well-earned, and my life given for it—
But this runs far beyond the laws of Fate,
Yet certain accents of your name shall echo
"Ai, Ai," within the music of my lyre   20
And shall be printed letters on frail flowers.
And Ajax, hero of a time to come
Will wear a name that calls your name to mind.'
As God Apollo spoke his prophecies,
The blood that filled the grasses at his feet   25
Turned to a brighter dye than Tyrian purple,
And from its lips there came a lily flower,
And yet, unlike the silver-white of lilies,
Its colour was a tinted, pinkish blue.
Nor was this miracle enough for Phoebus;   30
He wrote the words 'Ai, Ai' across its petals,
The sign of his own grief, his signature.
And now, the very gentlemen of Sparta
Give honours to the memory of their son,   35
And like their ancestors, each year they gather
To make a feast on Hyacinthus day.²

---

² Ovid, *Metamorphoses*, 10, translated by Horace Gregory.

ADONIS AND APHRODITE (VENUS)
Babylonian and Greek

*Adonis, too, is reborn as a flower. Like Hyacinth and most gods
who are reborn, he is a fertility spirit.*

As Cytherea sailed midair near Cyprus,
She overheard, as from far distance, echoes
Of her beloved's voice; swiftly she steered
Her circling swans above the boy's pale body.
She stepped to earth and when she saw his blood   5
She cried against blind Fate, then slowly said,
'But even Fate shan't have eternal will;
My sorrow shall have tribute to its own.
Each year will bring memorials of this death,
And where its blood has stained the earth, a flower.   10
Do I remember this? Persephone
Once had the gift of Heaven to change a nymph
Into a plant that's called sweet-smelling mint—
And if she held that gift, it's mine as well.'
She cupped her hands and poured bright streams of nectar   15
Above the pale remains of Cinyras' son,
And as low fountains spring from yellow sands,
The drops of nectar seemed to move, and flutter,
Red as the pomegranate seed in fruit.
Soft echoes of the wind—'anemone'—   20
Are in the flower's name; yet at one touch,
The fading petals scatter—all too soon."[1]

    Aphrodite was thus compelled to mourn for Adonis before
she could truly possess him. The festivals at which her woeful
love was celebrated were held in commemoration of the day of 25
the love-goddess's parting from her young lord. He lay there
wounded unto death, loved and wept over by Aphrodite. In vain
she tried to hold him back. On the next day he soared away
through sea and air. It used to be said, however, that he was still

---

[1] Ovid, *Metamorphoses*, 10, translated by Horace Gregory.

alive. Women brought him little "gardens"—a symbol and pic-turesque expression, which was common in our tongue, as in others, for their own femininity. In eastern shrines they gave themselves to strangers. Whoever did not do this must at least sacrifice her hair to Adonis.[2]

5

[2] C. Kerényi, *The Gods of the Greeks*, p. 76.

TELIPINU

Hittite

*When the god Telipinu disappears, the earth becomes barren.
The effect of his disappearance is much like Persephone's. With
his return comes a revival of nature symbolized by the newborn
lamb, so important later to Christianity as well.*

Thereupon the goddess [Kamrusepa] summoned an eagle
and told it to go forth along with the bee and bring Telipinu back.

"But that," she added, "is only the first step. He is still furious
and in a temper, and it will need high magic both in heaven and
on earth to drive out his wrath!"   5

Across the hills and over the dales flew the eagle and the bee,
while the gods clustered about the ramparts of heaven, waiting
with bated breath for the moment of their return.

It was a long and anxious wait, but at last what seemed like a
small black cloud rolled up on the horizon; and even as it ap- 10
peared there was a rumble of thunder and a flash of lightning, and
the air was rent with loud and angry cries.

The gods huddled together.

Louder and louder grew the thunder, more strident the cries,
more dazzling and more frequent the lightning, until it seemed as 15
though heaven and earth were locked in combat.

Suddenly, above the din and clamor, came the steady drone
of a bee in flight, and the black cloud began to take on a familiar
shape. When the gods looked closer, there, winging toward them,
was the eagle, with Telipinu poised upon its pinion, and the little 20
bee buzzing and humming around it, partly in triumph, partly in
fear.

In a few moments the bird had alighted, and immediately a
train of servants moved forward, bearing in their hands goblets
of nectar, jars of cream and honey, and baskets of fruit; and as 25
they set them before Telipinu the great goddess Kamrusepa stood
beside them and made sweet music, crooning over each a little
snatch of song.

Over the figs she sang:

"Bitter figs turn sweet with age.   30
  Be turn'd to sweet thy bitter rage!"

And over the grapes and olives:

"As the olive's with oil, the grape's with wine,
  With grace be fill'd that heart of thine!"   5

And over the cream and honey:

"Be smooth as cream, as honey sweet.
  Now from thine angry mood retreat!"

    Although they sounded to Telipinu like prayers and petitions,
these words were really magic spells—for Kamrusepa was the 10
mistress of the black art—and so no sooner had the angry god
tasted a few bites of the food and quaffed a few sips of the drink
than he was instantly bewitched. All the rage and fury which had
been seething within him seemed of a sudden to vanish, and in
its place there stole over him a warm and gentle glow of benevo- 15
lence. The more he ate and the more he drank, the more kindly he
became, for every time the enchanted fare touched his lips grace
abounding entered his soul.
    At length, when the gods saw that his anger had altogether
departed and that he was filled with love and tenderness toward 20
them, they redecked the tables and replaced the benches and re-
sumed the banquet which had been so rudely interrupted. There
they sat as before, feasting and carousing—the gods of field, crop,
and grain, and the goddesses of birth and of fate—but now, in the
center, sat Telipinu himself, gaily receiving and returning their 25
toasts.
    Meanwhile, down on earth, mortals too were bestirring them-
selves to remove the god's displeasure, but because of the blight
and the famine they could not offer him food and drink, as did his
brothers and sisters in heaven. So in every house they flung open 30
the doors and windows and chanted in chorus:

"Out of the house and thro' the window,
  Out of the window and thro' the yard,
  Out of the yard and thro' the gate,

  Out of the gate and down the path   35
  Go the fury, the rage, the wrath!

Down the path and straight ahead,
Nor turn aside to garden-bed
Or field or orchard-close, but hie
To where the earth doth meet the sky,
And, like the setting sun at night,   5
Sink and disappear from sight!"

   Then they went out into the yard and emptied into large bins
all the ashes and garbage which had gathered during the winter
months, and as they did so they again chanted in chorus:

"Ash and trash and rag and clout,   10
  In it goes and never out!
  Toss thy temper in the bin;
  Let it stay and rot therein!"

   Finally they washed and scoured the insides of their houses
and then tossed the pails of sullied water upon the stones, while 15
they sang:

"Water pour'd upon the floor
  To the pail returns no more.
  Pour the temper from thy heart,
  Likewise let it now depart!"   20

   Now although they sounded to Telipinu like prayers and petitions, the words they chanted were also really magic spells, and
suddenly the cold winter winds seemed to abate, and through the
open doors and windows stole the first breezes of spring. On the
branches of the trees and in the hedgerows a promise of green   25
began to appear and, as if in a moment, field and woodland were
alive with a thousand sounds — the purling of brooks, the scamper-
ing of tiny feet, the first hesitant notes of fledgling birds.
   A few days later a tall pole was set up in the courtyard of the
temple, and from it was hung, in honor of Telipinu, the snow-   30
white fleece of a newborn lamb.[1]

---

[1] Theodor H. Gaster, *The Oldest Stories in the World*, pp. 103–106.

AMATERASU AND SUSANOWA
Japanese

In this story of the sun goddess we are provided with an expla-
nation for the day-night phenomenon and for the male-female
conflict on which it is said to be based.

From his contact with death and the defiled nether land,
Izanagi proceeds to purify himself. This he does in a small river
in Tsukushi (i.e., Kyūshū). As he throws his clothing on the
ground some twelve deities are born of the individual garments
and jewelry. Avoiding the water of the upper river as being too   5
fast and that of the lower river as being too sluggish, he bathes
himself in the middle course, and from the maculations on his
body are born other divinities — some fourteen in all. At last, from
his left eye is born the sun goddess, Amaterasu, the "Heaven
Shining," and from his right eye, the moon god. From his nose is   10
born Susanowo, the "Impetuous Male." Of these three divinities,
Amaterasu and Susanowo are to occupy henceforth the central
place in the legend; the moon god fades rapidly from the account.

Amaterasu is resplendent and shining; Izanagi places under
her domination the Plain of High Heaven and bestows upon her a   15
necklace of jewels. Susanowo is impetuous and dark, and to him
is given the rule of the Sea Plain. But the Impetuous Male is dis-
consolate; he weeps and laments loudly without ceasing until the
mountains wither and the seas dry up. All the gods are baffled and
distracted. At last, Izanagi questions him on his clamorous de-   20
spair, to which, indeed, he seems more devoted than to his duties
as ruler of the Sea Plain. Susanowo answers that he is lamenting
because he wishes to visit his mother (Izanami) in the Land of
Darkness, and that such is the cause of his distress. Izanagi is
furious at such impertinence and as punishment banishes him   25
from the land.

Susanowo resolves then to take leave of his sister the sun
goddess and sets off for her realm in the heavens. But so boister-
ous is his approach that the sun goddess is frightened lest his arrival mean a coming encroachment on her own domains. So she   30
prepares herself for meeting him. She slings a thousand-arrow
quiver on her back, and another holding five hundred, and, grasping her bow, she takes her stance with such vigor that her legs
sink to the thighs in the ground, and her appearance is that of a
mighty warrior. Face to face with this formidable amazon, Su-   35

sanowo assures her he has come only to take his leave, that he ar-rives with "no strange intentions." In order that she may know the sincerity of his motives, he suggests they take an oath to-gether and produce children, which they do. She accepts the ten-grasp sword he gives her and, breaking it into three pieces, puts them in her mouth and chews them. He does the same with the jewels she has presented to him. And as they spew out the bits, numerous divinities come into being.

In spite of all his assurances, the Impetuous Male does not give up his rude ways. In fact, in certain respects his behavior worsens. He breaks down the divisions in the rice fields, which had been laid out by Amaterasu, fills the irrigation ditches, defiles her dwelling place with excrement. Curiously enough, she at first excuses him, blaming his actions on drunkenness. But when he flays a piebald colt with a backward flaying and flings it into the weaving hall where she is working with her attendants so that they are fatally wounded in their private parts by the flying shuttles, she is profoundly annoyed. To underline her displeasure, she retires into a rock cave and makes the entrance fast.

With the retirement of the sun goddess, light leaves the world, and the alternation of day and night ceases. The myriads of divinities are deeply perturbed at this turn of events and gather in the river bed of heaven to consult among themselves as how best to entice the goddess from her hiding place. They place long-singing night birds (i.e., roosters?) near the entrance of the cave and cause them to crow; they suspend from a tree a string of curved jewels, a mirror, and offerings of white cloth, and they all recite official liturgies (norito). But what is to prove finally ef-ficacious is a lascivious, madcap dance performed by the goddess Ama no uzume, who, stamping loudly on the ground, pulling the nipples of her breasts, and lowering her skirt, so delights the as-sembled gods that they break out in raucous and appreciative laughter. Piqued with understandable curiosity, the sun goddess peers out of the cave, whereupon the mirror is pushed to the door and the goddess, intrigued with her own image, gradually steps out. A rope is passed in back of her, beyond which she is forbidden to return. With the appearance of the sun, light returns once again to the world, and the alternation of night and day recom-mences.[1]

[1] E. Dale Saunders, "Japanese Mythology," in S. N. Kramer, *Mythology of the Ancient World*, pp. 420–422.

BUDDHA
Indian

This story of rebirth is a preface to the story of the Buddha's birth included in Part 1. For the Buddha each birth is a rebirth, and each death a preface to life.

Now while the future Buddha was still dwelling in the city of the Tusita gods, the "Buddha-Uproar," as it is called, took place. For there are three uproars which take place in the world, — the Cyclic-Uproar, the Buddha-Uproar, and the Universal-Monarch-Uproar. They occur as follows:

When it is known that after the lapse of a hundred thousand years the cycle is to be renewed, the gods called Loka-byuhas, inhabitants of a heaven of sensual pleasure, wander about through the world, with hair let down and flying in the wind, weeping and wiping away their tears with their hands, and with their clothes red and in great disorder. And thus they make announcement:

"Sirs, after the lapse of a hundred thousand years, the cycle is to be renewed; this world will be destroyed; also the mighty ocean will dry up; and this broad earth, and Sineru, the monarch of the mountains, will be burnt up and destroyed, — up to the Brahma heavens will the destruction of the world extend. Therefore, sirs, cultivate friendliness; cultivate compassion, joy, and indifference; wait on your mothers; wait on your fathers; and honour your elders among your kinsfolk."

This is called the Cyclic-Uproar.

Again, when it is known that after a lapse of a thousand years an omniscient Buddha is to arise in the world, the guardian angels of the world wander about, proclaiming:

"Sirs, after the lapse of a thousand years a Buddha will arise in the world."

This is called the Buddha-Uproar.

And lastly, when they realize that after the lapse of a hundred years a universal monarch is to arise, the terrestrial deities wander about, proclaiming:

"Sirs, after the lapse of a hundred years a universal monarch is to arise in the world."

This is called the Universal-Monarch-Uproar. And these three are mighty uproars.

When of these three uproars they hear the sound of the Buddha-Uproar, the gods of all ten thousand worlds come together into one place, and having ascertained what particular being is to be the Buddha, they approach him, and beseech him to become one. But it is not till after omens have appeared that they beseech him.

At that time, therefore, having all come together in one world, with the Chatum-Maharajas, and with the Sakka, the Suyama, the Santusita, the Paranimmita-Vasavatti, and the Maha-Brahma of each several world, they approached the future Buddha in the Tusita heaven, and besought him, saying,

"Sir, it was not to acquire the glory of a Sakka, or of a Mara, or of a Brahma, or of a universal monarch, that you fulfilled the ten perfections; but it was to gain omniscience in order to save the world, that you fulfilled them. Sir, the time and fit season for your Buddhaship has now arrived."

But the great being, before assenting to their wish, made what is called the five great observations. He observed, namely, the time, the continent, the country, the family, and the mother of her span of life.

Having thus made the five great observations, he kindly made the gods the required promise, saying,

"Sirs, you are right. The time has come for my Buddhaship."

Then, surrounded by the gods of the Tusita heaven, and dismissing all the other gods, he entered the Nandana Grove of the Tusita capital, — for in each of the heavens there is a Nandana Grove. And here the gods said, "Attain in your next existence your high destiny," and kept reminding him that he had already paved the way to it by his accumulated merit. Now it was while he was thus dwelling, surrounded by these deities, and continually reminded of his accumulated merit, that he died, and was conceived in the womb of queen Maha-Maya.[1]

---

[1] From the introduction to the *Jataka,* in Henry Clarke Warren, trans., *Buddhism in Translations.*

OSIRIS AND ISIS
Egyptian

The rebirth of Osiris is a revivification or resurrection. It symbolizes the hope for eternal life for all people and the hope for abundant crops.

The lamentations of the two sad sisters were not in vain. In pity for her sorrow the sun-god Ra sent down from heaven the jackal-headed god Anubis, who, with the aid of Isis and Nephthys, of Thoth and Horus, pieced together the broken body of the murdered god, swathed it in linen bandages, and observed all the other rites which the Egyptians were wont to perform over the bodies of the departed. Then Isis fanned the cold clay with her wings: Osiris revived, and thenceforth reigned as king over the dead in the other world. There he bore the titles of Lord of the Underworld, Lord of Eternity, Ruler of the Dead. There, too, in the great Hall of the Two Truths, assisted by forty-two assessors, one from each of the principal districts of Egypt, he presided as judge at the trial of the souls of the departed, who made their solemn confession before him, and, their heart having been weighed in the balance of justice, received the reward of virtue in a life eternal or the appropriate punishment of their sins.

In the resurrection of Osiris the Egyptians saw the pledge of a life everlasting for themselves beyond the grave. They believed that every man would live eternal in the other world if only his surviving friends did for his body what the gods had done for the body of Osiris. Hence the ceremonies observed by the Egyptians over the human dead were an exact copy of those which Anubis, Horus, and the rest had performed over the dead god. "At every burial there was enacted a representation of the divine mystery which had been performed of old over Osiris, when his son, his sisters, his friends were gathered round his mangled remains and succeeded by their spells and manipulations in converting his broken body into the first mummy, which they afterwards reanimated and furnished with the means of entering on a new individual life beyond the grave. The mummy of the deceased was Osiris; the professional female mourners were his two sisters Isis and Nephthys; Anubis, Horus, all the gods of the Osirian legend gathered about the corpse."

Thus every dead Egyptian was identified with Osiris and bore his name. From the Middle Kingdom onwards it was the regular practice to address the deceased as "Osiris So-and-So," as if he were the god himself, and to add the standing epithet "true of speech," because true speech was characteristic of Osiris. The thousands of inscribed and pictured tombs that have been opened in the valley of the Nile prove that the mystery of the resurrection was performed for the benefit of every dead Egyptian; as Osiris died and rose again from the dead, so all men hoped to arise like him from dead to life eternal. In an Egyptian text it is said of the departed that "as surely as Osiris lives, so shall he live also; as surely as Osiris did not die, so shall he not die; as surely as Osiris is not annihilated, so shall he too not be annihilated." The dead man, conceived to be lying, like Osiris, with mangled body, was comforted by being told that the heavenly goddess Nut, the mother of Osiris, was coming to gather up his poor scattered limbs and mould them with her own hands into a form immortal and divine. "She gives thee thy head, she brings thee thy bones, she sets thy limbs together and puts thy heart in thy body." Thus the resurrection of the dead was conceived, like that of Osiris, not merely as spiritual but also as bodily. "They possess their heart, they possess their senses, they possess their mouth, they possess their feet, they possess their arms, they possess all their limbs."[1]

[1] Sir James Frazer, *The New Golden Bough,* edited by Theodor H. Gaster, pp. 388–390.

KUTOYIS

Blackfoot Indian

In this final segment of the Kutoyis story, the dismembered hero, like Osiris, is revived with the assistance of his female companion.

Then the little girl, who was watching, came up to him, and said, "Pity me, man-eater, my mother is hungry and asks you for those bones." So the old man bunched them up together and handed them to her. She took them out, and called all the dogs to her, and threw the bones down to the dogs, crying out, "Look out, 5 Kutoyis; the dogs are eating you!" and when she said that, Kutoyis arose from the pile of bones.

Again he went into the lodge, and when the man-eater saw him, he cried out, "How, how, how! the fat young man has survived," and seemed surprised. Again he took his knife and cut 10 Kutoyis' throat, and threw him into the kettle. Again, when the meat was cooked, he ate it up, and again the little girl asked for the bones, which he gave her; and, taking them out, she threw them to the dogs, crying, "Kutoyis, the dogs are eating you!" and Kutoyis again arose from the bones. 15

When the man-eater had cooked him four times, he again went into the lodge, and, seizing the man-eater, he threw him into the boiling kettle, and his wives and children too, and boiled them to death.

The man-eater was the seventh and last of the bad animals 20 and people who were destroyed by Kutoyis.[1]

[1] George Bird Grinnell, *Blackfoot Lodge Tales*, p. 38.

BEAR MAN

Cherokee Indian

The bear follows Osiris and Kutoyis as a resurrected god figure. Like the others, he represents the possibility of eternal life for those who will learn from him.

A man went hunting in the mountains and came across a black bear, which he wounded with an arrow. The bear turned and started to run the other way, and the hunter followed, shooting one arrow after another into it without bringing it down. Now, this was a medicine bear, and could talk or read the thoughts of people without their saying a word. At last he stopped and pulled the arrows out of his side and gave them to the man, saying, "It is of no use for you to shoot at me, for you can not kill me. Come to my house and let us live together." The hunter thought to himself, "He may kill me;" but the bear read his thoughts and said, "No, I won't hurt you." The man thought again, "How can I get anything to eat?" but the bear knew his thoughts, and said, "There shall be plenty." So the hunter went with the bear.

They went on together until they came to a hole in the side of the mountain, and the bear said, "This is not where I live, but there is going to be a council here and we will see what they do." They went in, and the hole widened as they went, until they came to a large cave like a townhouse. It was full of bears—old bears, young bears, and cubs, white bears, black bears, and brown bears —and a large white bear was the chief. They sat down in a corner, but soon the bears scented the hunter and began to ask, "What is it that smells bad?" The chief said, "Don't talk so; it is only a stranger come to see us. Let him alone." Food was getting scarce in the mountains, and the council was to decide what to do about it. They had sent out messengers all over, and while they were talking two bears came in and reported that they had found a country in the low grounds where there were so many chestnuts and acorns that mast was knee deep. Then they were all pleased, and got ready for a dance, and the dance leader was the one the Indians call Kalas-gunahita, "Long Hams," a great black bear that is always lean. After the dance the bears noticed the hunter's bow and arrows, and one said, "This is what men use to kill us. Let us see if we can manage them, and may be we can fight man with his own weapons." So they took the bow and arrows from the hunter to try them. They fitted the arrow and drew back the string, but when they let go it caught in their long claws and the arrows dropped to the ground. They saw that they could not use the bow and arrows and gave them back to the man. When the dance and the council were over, they began to go home, excepting the White Bear chief, who lived there, and at last the hunter and the bear went out together.

They went on until they came to another hole in the side of the mountain, when the bear said, "This is where I live," and they went in. By this time the hunter was very hungry and was wondering how he could get something to eat. The other knew his thoughts, and sitting up on his hind legs he rubbed his stomach with his forepaws—so—and at once he had both paws full of chestnuts and gave them to the man. He rubbed his stomach again—so—and had his paws full of huckleberries, and gave them to the man. He rubbed again—so—and gave the man both paws full of blackberries. He rubbed again—so—and had his paws full of acorns, but the man said that he could not eat them, and that he had enough already.

The hunter lived in the cave with the bear all winter, until long hair like that of a bear began to grow all over his body and he began to act like a bear; but he still walked like a man. One day in early spring the bear said to him, "Your people down in the settlement are getting ready for a grand hunt in these mountains, and they will come to this cave and kill me and take these clothes from me"—he meant his skin—"but they will not hurt you and will take you home with them." The bear knew what the people were doing down in the settlement just as he always knew what the man was thinking about. Some days passed and the bear said again, "This is the day when the Topknots will come to kill me, but the Split-noses will come first and find us. When they have killed me they will drag me outside the cave and take off my clothes and cut me in pieces. You must cover the blood with leaves, and when they are taking you away look back after you have gone a piece and you will see something."

Soon they heard the hunters coming up the mountain, and then the dogs found the cave and began to bark. The hunters came and looked inside and saw the bear and killed him with their arrows. Then they dragged him outside the cave and skinned the body and cut it in quarters to carry home. The dogs kept on barking until the hunters thought there must be another bear in the cave. They looked in again and saw the man away at the farther end. At first they thought it was another bear on account of his long hair, but they soon saw it was the hunter who had been lost the year before, so they went in and brought him out. Then each hunter took a load of the bear meat and they started home again, bringing the man and the skin with them. Before they left the man piled leaves over the spot where they had cut up the bear, and when they had gone a little way he looked behind and saw the bear rise up out of the leaves, shake himself, and go back into the woods. . . .[1]

[1] James Mooney, *Myths of the Cherokee*, pp. 327–329.

ATTIS

Phrygian

The myth of Attis contains the familiar pattern of death and resurrection in the spring and the association with plant and human fertility.

But when night had fallen, the sorrow of the worshippers was turned to joy. For suddenly a light shone in the darkness: the tomb was opened: the god had risen from the dead; and as the priest touched the lips of the weeping mourners with balm, he softly whispered in their ears the glad tidings of salvation. The resur- 5 rection of the god was hailed by his disciples as a promise that they too would issue triumphant from the corruption of the grave.

On the morrow, the twenty-fifth day of March, which was reckoned the vernal equinox, the divine resurrection was celebrated with a wild outburst of glee. At Rome, and probably 10 elsewhere, the celebration took the form of a carnival. It was the Festival of Joy (*Hilaria*). A universal licence prevailed. Every man might say and do what he pleased. People went about the streets in disguise. No dignity was too high or too sacred for the humblest citizen to assume with impunity. 15

Next day, the twenty-sixth of March, was given to repose, which must have been much needed after the varied excitements and fatigues of the preceding days. Finally, the Roman festival closed on the twenty-seventh of March with a procession to the brook Almo. The silver image of the goddess, with its face of 20 jagged black stone, sat in a waggon drawn by oxen. Preceded by the nobles walking barefoot, it moved slowly, to the loud music of pipes and tambourines, out by the Porta Capena, and so down to the banks of the Almo, which flows into the Tiber just below the walls of Rome. There the high-priest, robed in purple, washed 25 the waggon, the image, and the other sacred objects in the water of the stream. On returning from their bath, the wain and the oxen were strewn with fresh spring flowers. All was mirth and gaiety. No one thought of the blood that had flowed so lately. Even the eunuch priests forgot their wounds. 30

Such, then, appears to have been the annual solemnization of the death and resurrection of Attis in spring. But besides these public rites, his worship is known to have comprised certain secret or mystic ceremonies, which probably aimed at bringing the worshipper, and especially the novice, into closer communication with his god. Our information as to the nature of these mysteries and the date of their celebration is unfortunately very scanty, but they seem to have included a sacramental meal and a baptism of blood. In the sacrament the novice became a partaker of the mysteries by eating out of a drum and drinking out of a cymbal, two instruments of music which figured prominently in the thrilling orchestra of Attis. The fast which accompanied the mourning for the dead god may perhaps have been designed to prepare the body of the communicant for the reception of the blessed sacrament by purging it of all that could defile by contact the sacred elements. In the baptism the devotee, crowned with gold and wreathed with fillets, descended into a pit, the mouth of which was covered with a wooden grating. A bull, adorned with garlands of flowers, its forehead glittering with gold leaf, was then driven on to the grating and there stabbed to death with a consecrated spear. Its hot reeking blood poured in torrents through the apertures, and was received with devout eagerness by the worshipper on every part of his person and garments, till he emerged from the pit, drenched, dripping, and scarlet from head to foot, to receive the homage, nay the adoration, of his fellows as one who had been born again to eternal life and had washed away his sins in the blood of the bull. For some time afterwards the fiction of a new birth was kept up by dieting him on milk like a new-born babe. The regeneration of the worshipper took place at the same time as the regeneration of his god, namely at the vernal equinox.[1]

---

[1] Sir James Frazer, *The New Golden Bough*, edited by Theodor H. Gaster, pp. 373–374.

JESUS
Christian

The resurrection of Jesus marks a culmination of the human need which gives us the myth of rebirth. With his great miracle, death is definitively overcome.

Now upon the first day of the week, very early in the morning, they came unto the sepulchre, bringing the spices which they had prepared, and certain others with them. And they found the stone rolled away from the sepulchre. And they entered in, and found not the body of the Lord Jesus. And it came to pass, as they were much perplexed thereabout, behold, two men stood by them in shining garments: and as they were afraid, and bowed down their faces to the earth, they said unto them, Why seek ye the living among the dead? He is not here, but is risen: remember how he spake unto you when he was yet in Galilee, saying, The Son of man must be delivered into the hands of sinful men, and be crucified, and the third day rise again. And they remembered his words, and returned from the sepulchre, and told all these things unto the eleven, and to all the rest. It was Mary Magdalene, and Joanna, and Mary the mother of James, and other women that were with them, which told these things unto the apostles. And their words seemed to them as idle tales, and they believed them not. Then arose Peter, and ran unto the sepulchre; and stooping down, he beheld the linen clothes laid by themselves, and departed, wondering in himself at that which was come to pass.

And, behold, two of them went that same day to a village called Emmaus, which was from Jerusalem about threescore furlongs. And they talked together of all these things which had happened. And it came to pass, that, while they communed together and reasoned, Jesus himself drew near, and went with them. But their eyes were holden that they should not know him. And he said unto them, What manner of communications are these that ye have one to another, as ye walk, and are sad? And the one of them, whose name was Cleopas, answering said unto him, Art thou only a stranger in Jerusalem, and has not known the things which are come to pass there in these days? And he said unto them, What things? And they said unto him, Concerning Jesus of Nazareth, which was a prophet mighty in deed and word before God and all the people: and how the chief priests and our rulers delivered him to be condemned to death, and have crucified him. But we trusted that it had been he which should have redeemed Israel: and beside all this, today is the third day since these things were done. Yea, and certain women also of our company made us astonished, which were early at the sepulchre; and when they found not his body, they came, saying, that they had also seen a vision of angels, which said that he was alive. And certain of them which were with us went to the sepulchre, and found it even so as the women had said: but him they saw not. Then he said unto them, O fools, and slow of heart to believe all that the prophets have spoken: ought not Christ to have suffered these things, and to enter into his glory? And beginning at Moses and all the prophets, he expounded unto them in all the Scriptures the things concerning himself.

And they drew nigh unto the village, whither they went: and he made as though he would have gone further. But they constrained him, saying, Abide with us; for it is toward evening, and the day is far spent. And he went in to tarry with them. And it came to pass, as he sat at meat with them, he took bread, and blessed it, and brake, and gave to them. And their eyes were opened, and they knew him; and he vanished out of their sight. And they said one to another, Did not our heart burn within us, while he talked with us by the way, and while he opened to us the Scriptures? And they rose up the same hour, and returned to Jerusalem, and found the eleven gathered together, and them that were with them, saying, The Lord is risen indeed, and hath appeared to Simon. And they told what things were done in the way, and how he was known of them in breaking of bread.

And as they thus spake, Jesus himself stood in the midst of them, and saith unto them, Peace be unto you. But they were terrified and affrighted, and supposed that they had seen a spirit. And he said unto them, Why are ye troubled? and why do thoughts arise in your hearts? Behold my hands and my feet, that it is I myself: handle me, and see; for a spirit hath not flesh and bones, as ye see me have. And when he had thus spoken, he showed them his hands and his feet. And while they yet believed not for joy, and wondered, he said unto them, Have ye here any meat? And they gave him a piece of a broiled fish, and of a honeycomb. And he took it, and did eat before them.

And he said unto them, These are the words which I spake

unto you, while I was yet with you, that all things must be fulfilled, which were written in the law of Moses, and in the prophets, and in the psalms, concerning me. Then opened he their
understanding, that they might understand the Scriptures, and
said unto them, Thus it is written, and thus it behooved Christ to   5
suffer, and to rise from the dead the third day: and that repentance and remission of sins should be preached in his name
among all nations, beginning at Jerusalem. And ye are witnesses
of these things.[1]

10

[1] Luke 24.

WANJIRU

African

Wanjiru returns to the Dance of Life, which she has preserved by her sacrifice. She now achieves wholeness in the ritual of marriage.

It came to pass that the next day there was a great dance, and her lover went with the throng. But his mother and the girl waited until everyone had assembled at the dance, and all the road was empty. Then they came out of the house and mingled with the crowd. When the relations saw Wanjiru, they said, "Surely that is Wanjiru whom we had lost." 5

And they pressed to greet her, but her lover beat them off, for he said, "You sold Wanjiru shamefully."

Then she returned to his mother's house. But on the fourth day her family again came and the warrior repented, for he said, 10 "Surely they are her father and her mother and her brothers."

So he paid them the purchase price, and he wedded Wanjiru who had been lost.[1]

[1] Paul Radin and James J. Sweeney, eds., *African Folktales and Sculpture*, p. 272.

QUETZALCOATL
Toltec and Aztec

The myth of Quetzalcoatl breaks into the realm of the historical. Quetzalcoatl was presumed dead but expected to return at a prescribed time.

Quetzalcoatl was not dead. In one of his statues he was shown reclining, covered with wrappings, signifying that he was absent or "as one who lays him down to sleep, and that when he should wake from that dream of absence, would rise to rule again the land." He had built mansions underground to the Lord of Mictlan, the lord of the dead, but did not occupy these himself, dwelling, rather, in that land of gold where the sun abides at night. This too, however, is underground. Certain caverns lead to it, one of which, called Cincalco, "To the Abode of Abundance," is south of Chapultepec; and through its gloomy corridors men can reach that happy land, the habitation of the sun, which is still ruled by Quetzalcoatl. Moreover, that land is the land from which he came in the beginning. . . .

All this, which in so many ways parallels the normal imagery of the Old World culture-hero myths, telling of the one who is gone, dwells underground in a happy, timeless land, as lord of the realm of the happy dead, like Osiris, but will arise again, we can read without surprise. But what is surprising indeed was the manner of Quetzalcoatl's actual return. The priests and astrologers did not know in what cycle he was to appear; however, the name of the year within the cycle had been predicted, of old, by Quetzalcoatl himself. Its sign was "One Reed" *(Ce Acatl)*, which, in the Mexican calendar, is a year that occurs only once in every cycle of fifty-two. But the year when Cortes arrived, with his company of fair-faced companions and his standard, the cross, was precisely the year "One Reed." The myth of the dead and resurrected god had circumnavigated the globe.[1]

---

[1] Joseph Campbell, *The Masks of God: Primitive Mythology*, p. 460.

UNION WITH THE CYCLE OF NATURE:
Commentary on Part 7

The outlines of the myth of the rebirth or resurrection are universal and clear. The hero progresses from a state of nonlife to one of life. The miraculous birth is thus repeated. In some stories the Hero—Hyacinth and Adonis, for instance—dies and is turned into a living flower. In others the rebirth is in the nature of a reincarnation. The Buddha and, to a lesser extent, Dionysos fall into this category. But the major motif of the myth is that of the hero who has died violently, visited the underworld, and returned to the earth as a living being. Much of what needs to be said about the rebirth myth has been said in the commentaries of Parts 5 and 6. The myth is the final stage of the scapegoat pattern. The hero finalizes the defeat of death; he completes the cycle of nature by being reborn in the spring. The Easter story reflects the hope of all men.

Not surprisingly this myth very likely originated in the various natural cycles which are so much a part of our existence. Hyacinth and Adonis no doubt spring from rites of sacrifice in which the gods were paid for their gift of plant life with the gift of human life. And the various dismembered gods are frequently vegetation or fertility gods—Osiris, Dionysos, Attis. Often the various pieces of these gods were actually sown in the earth. Not only plant life but nearly everything in the universe contained a symbolic example of how death might be overcome. Seasons when they exist run in cycles, and the solar and lunar cycles are self-evident. The bear myth included in this section is surely the result of early man's fascination with an animal which in the winter descended into the earth only to rise again in the spring. Bear cults still exist in parts of the world.[1] The mystery religions, including Christianity and the Eleusinian cult, have always been much concerned with the cycles, in all of which death or its equivalent plays a positive role as the most necessary step to rebirth. In death is not only pain but the possibility of rejuvenation.

It is worth mentioning in this connection the fetal position of the urn-buried peoples of so many ancient cultures. This position in death is, of course, in keeping with the idea of the return

---

[1] See Rhys Carpenter, *Folk Tale, Fiction, and Saga in the Homeric Epics*.

to the great mother—the world womb—and the rebirth which will result from that return.

Psychologically the rebirth myth is the culmination of the process of self-realization and individuation which produces the new, whole man. The hero has faced and overcome death and has placed man collectively back in the secure fold of the mother's cycle. As plants can be reborn, so now can we. In the underworld the monsters and gargoyles of the infantile, nightmarish past have been defeated, and the individual emerges now in his new form, having experienced the very depths of his and the collective being. The hero "has died as a modern man; but as eternal man—perfected, unspecific, universal man—he has been reborn."[2]

Few major works on mythology ignore the rebirth myth. The Henderson and Oakes book contains valuable information. Alan Watts on the Christian version is perceptive. A classic work is Wallis Budge's *Osiris and the Egyptian Resurrection*. Jung and Kerényi's comments on the Eleusinian mysteries are useful. And Mircea Eliade's *Birth and Rebirth* is still another important study of the subject.

---

[2] Joseph Campbell, *The Hero with a Thousand Faces*, p. 20.

8

ASCENSION, APOTHEOSIS, AND ATONEMENT

Mandalas, general symmetry, a sense of strangely meaningful connections, and upward movement create a sense of apotheosis and wholeness that is the heroic life or human adventure. [Max Ernst, *Men Shall Know Nothing of This* (1923), The Tate Gallery, London. Reproduced with permission. Copyright administered by S.P.A.D.E.M.]

OEDIPUS
Greek

The hero's apotheosis or atonement with the gods is most fre-
quently associated with death. In this story the long-suffering
Oedipus is miraculously taken off to the gods.

Messenger
> Citizens, the briefest way to tell you
> Would be to say that Oedipus is no more;
> But what has happened cannot be told so simply —
> It was no simple thing.   5

Chorus
>   He is gone, poor man?

Messenger
> You may be sure that he has left this world.

Chorus   10
> By God's mercy, was his death a painless one?

Messenger
> That is the thing that seems so marvelous.
>
> You know, for you were witnesses, how he
> Left this place with no friend leading him,   15
> Acting, himself, as guide for all of us.
> Well, when he came to the steep place in the road,
> The embankment there, secured with steps of brass,
> He stopped in one of the many branching paths.
> This was not far from the stone bowl that marks   20
> Theseus' and Pirithous' covenant.
>
> Half-way between that place of stone
> With its hollow pear tree, and the marble tomb,
> He sat down and undid his filthy garments;
> Then he called his daughters and commanded   25
> That they should bring him water from a fountain
> For bathing and libation to the dead.

From there they could see the hill of Demeter,
Freshener of all things: so they ascended it
And soon came back with water for their father;
Then helped him properly to bathe and dress.

When everything was finished to his pleasure,   5
And no command of his remained undone,
Then the earth groaned with thunder from the god below;
And as they heard the sound, the girls shuddered,
And dropped to their father's knees, and began wailing,
Beating their breasts and weeping as if heartbroken.   10
And hearing them cry out so bitterly,
He put his arms around them, and said to them:

"Children, this day your father is gone from you.
All that was mine is gone. You shall no longer
Bear the burden of taking care of me—   15
I know it was hard, my children.—And yet one word
Makes all those difficulties disappear:
That word is love. You never shall have more
From any man than you have had from me.
And now you must spend the rest of life without me."   20

That was the way of it. They clung together
And wept, all three. But when they finally stopped,
And no more sobs were heard, then there was
Silence, and in the silence suddenly
A voice cried out to him—of such a kind   25
It made our hair stand up in panic fear:
Again and again the call came from the god:
"Oedipus! Oedipus! Why are we waiting?
You delay too long; you delay too long to go!"

Then, knowing himself summoned by the spirit,   30
He asked that the lord Theseus come to him;
And when he had come, said: "O beloved one,
Give your right hand now as a binding pledge
To my two daughters; children, give him your hands.   35
Promise that you will never willingly
Betray them, but will carry out in kindness
Whatever is best for them in the days to come."

And Theseus swore to do it for his friend,
With such restraint as fits a noble king.
And when he had done so, Oedipus at once
Laid his blind hands upon his daughters, saying:
"Children, you must show your nobility,   5
And have the courage now to leave this spot.
You must not wish to see what is forbidden,
Or hear what may not afterward be told.
But go—go quickly. Only the lord Theseus
May stay to see the thing that now begins."   10

This much every one of us heard him say,
And then we came away with the sobbing girls.
But after a little while as we withdrew
We turned around—and nowhere saw that man,
But only the king, his hands before his face,   15
Shading his eyes as if from something awful,
Fearful and unendurable to see.
Then very quickly we saw him do reverence
To Earth and to the powers of the air,
With one address to both.   20
                              But in what manner
Oedipus perished, no one of mortal men
Could tell but Theseus. It was not lightning,
Bearing its fire from God, that took him off;
No hurricane was blowing.   25
But some attendant from the train of Heaven
Came for him; or else the underworld
Opened in love the unlit door of earth.
For he was taken without lamentation,
Illness or suffering; indeed his end   30
Was wonderful if mortal's ever was.

Should someone think I speak intemperately,
I make no apology to him who thinks so.[1]

---

[1] Sophocles, *Oedipus at Colonus*, translated by Robert Fitzgerald, lines
1579–1667.

MOSES

Judaic

For Moses, too, death becomes atonement. God takes his soul with a kiss.

In the meanwhile Moses' time was at an end. A voice from heaven resounded, saying: "Why, Moses, dost thou strive in vain? Thy last second is at hand." Moses instantly stood up for prayer, and said: "Lord of the world! Be mindful of the day on which Thou didst reveal Thyself to me in the bush of thorns, and be mindful also of the day when I ascended into heaven and during forty days partook of neither food nor drink. Thou, Gracious and Merciful, deliver me not into the hand of Samael." God replied: "I have heard thy prayer. I Myself shall attend to thee and bury thee." Moses now sanctified himself as do the Seraphim that surround the Divine Majesty, whereupon God from the highest heavens revealed Himself to receive Moses' soul. When Moses beheld the Holy One, blessed be His Name, he fell upon his face and said: "Lord of the world! In love didst Thou create the world, and in love Thou guidest it. Treat me also with love, and deliver me not into the hands of the Angel of Death." A heavenly voice sounded and said: "Moses, be not afraid. 'Thy righteousness shall go before thee; the glory of the Lord shall be thy reward.'"

With God descended from heaven three angels, Michael, Gabriel, and Zagzagel. Gabriel arranged Moses' couch, Michael spread upon it a purple garment, and Zagzagel laid down a woolen pillow. God stationed Himself over Moses' head, Michael to his right, Gabriel to his left, and Zagzagel at his feet, whereupon God addressed Moses: "Cross thy feet," and Moses did so. He then said, "Fold thy hands and lay them upon thy breast," and Moses did so. Then God said, "Close thine eyes," and Moses did so. Then God spake to Moses' soul: "My daughter, one hundred and twenty years had I decreed that thou shouldst dwell in this righteous man's body, but hesitate not now to leave it, for thy time is run." The soul replied: "I know that Thou are the God of spirits and of souls, and that in Thy hand are the souls of the living and of the dead. Thou didst create me and put me into the body of this righteous man. Is there anywhere in the world a body so pure and holy as this is? Never a fly rested upon it, never did leprosy show itself upon it. Therefore do I love it, and do not wish to leave it." God replied: "Hesitate not, my daughter! Thine end hath come. I Myself shall take thee to the highest heavens and let thee dwell under the Throne of My Glory, like the Seraphim, Ofannim, Cherubim, and other angels." But the soul replied: "Lord of the world! I desire to remain with this righteous man; for whereas the two angels Azza and Azazel when they descended from heaven to earth, corrupted their way of life and loved the daughters of the earth, so that in punishment Thou didst suspend them between heaven and earth, the son of Amram, a creature of flesh and blood, from the day upon which Thou didst reveal Thyself from the bush of thorns, has lived apart from his wife. Let me therefore remain where I am." When Moses saw that his soul refused to leave him, he said to her: "Is this because the Angel of Death wishes to show his power over thee?" The soul replied: "Nay, God doth not wish to deliver me into the hands of death." Moses: "Wilt thou, perchance, weep when the others will weep at my departure?" The soul: "The Lord 'hath delivered mine eyes from tears.'" Moses: "Wilt thou, perchance, go into Hell when I am dead?" The soul: "I will walk before the Lord in the land of the living." When Moses heard these words, he permitted his soul to leave him, saying to her: "Return unto thy rest, O my soul; for the Lord hath dealt bountifully with thee." God thereupon took Moses' soul by kissing him upon the mouth.

Moses' activity did not, however, cease with his death, for in heaven he is one of the servants of the Lord. God buried Moses' body in a spot that remained unknown even to Moses himself. Only this is known concerning it, that a subterranean passage connects it with the graves of the Patriarchs. Although Moses' body lies dead in its grave, it is still as fresh as when he was alive.[1]

[1] Louis Ginzberg, *The Legends of the Jews*, vol. 3, pp. 471–473.

ABRAHAM

Judaic

Abraham is taken to paradise and enthroned in a state of immortality. For him death is apotheosis.

So Michael turned the chariot, and brought Abraham to the place of judgment of all souls. Here he saw two gates, the one broad and the other narrow, the narrow gate that of the just, which leads to life, they that enter through it go into Paradise. The broad gate is that of sinners, which leads to destruction and eternal punishment. Then Abraham wept, saying, "Woe is me, what shall I do? for I am a man big of body, and how shall I be able to enter by the narrow gate?" Michael answered, and said to Abraham, "Fear not, nor grieve, for thou shalt enter by it unhindered, and all they who are like thee." Abraham, perceiving that a soul was adjudged to be set in the midst, asked Michael the reason for it, and Michael answered, "Because the judge found its sins and its righteousness equal, he neither committed it to judgment nor to be saved." Abraham said to Michael, "Let us pray for this soul, and see whether God will hear us," and when they rose up from their prayer, Michael informed Abraham that the soul was saved by the prayer, and was taken by an angel and carried up to Paradise. Abraham said to Michael, "Let us yet call upon the Lord and supplicate His compassion and entreat His mercy for the souls of the sinners whom I formerly, in my anger, cursed and destroyed, whom the earth devoured, and the wild beasts tore in pieces, and the fire consumed, through my words. Now I know that I have sinned before the Lord our God."

After the joint prayer of the archangel and Abraham, there came a voice from heaven, saying, "Abraham, Abraham, I have hearkened to thy voice and thy prayer, and I forgive thee thy sin, and those whom thou thinkest that I destroyed, I have called up and brought them into life by My exceeding kindness, because for a season I have requited them in judgment, and those whom I destroy living upon earth, I will not requite in death."

When Michael brought Abraham back to his house, they found Sarah dead. Not seeing what had become of Abraham, she was consumed with grief and gave up her soul. Though Michael had fulfilled Abraham's wish, and had shown him all the earth and the judgment and recompense, he still refused to surrender his soul to Michael, and the archangel again ascended to heaven, and said unto the Lord: "Thus speaks Abraham, I will not go with thee, and I refrain from laying my hands on him, because from the beginning he was Thy friend, and he has done all things pleasing in Thy sight. There is no man like him on earth, not even Job, the wondrous man." But when the day of the death of Abraham drew nigh, God commanded Michael to adorn Death with great beauty and send him thus to Abraham, that he might see him with his eyes.

While sitting under the oak of Mamre, Abraham perceived a flashing of light and a smell of sweet odor, and turning around he saw Death coming toward him in great glory and beauty. And Death said unto Abraham: "Think not, Abraham, that this beauty is mine, or that I come thus to every man. Nay, but if any one is righteous like thee, I thus take a crown and come to him, but if he is a sinner, I come in great corruption, and out of their sins I make a crown for my head, and I shake them with great fear, so that they are dismayed." Abraham said to him, "And art thou, indeed, he that is called Death?" He answered, and said, "I am the bitter name," but Abraham answered, "I will not go with thee." And Abraham said to Death, "Show us thy corruption." And Death revealed his corruption, showing two heads, the one had the face of a serpent, the other head was like a sword. All the servants of Abraham, looking at the fierce mien of Death, died, but Abraham prayed to the Lord, and he raised them up. As the looks of Death were not able to cause Abraham's soul to depart from him, God removed the soul of Abraham as in a dream, and the archangel Michael took it up into heaven. After great praise and glory had been given to the Lord by the angels who brought Abraham's soul, and after Abraham bowed down to worship, then came the voice of God, saying thus: "Take My friend Abraham into Paradise, where are the tabernacles of My righteous ones and the abodes of My saints Isaac and Jacob in his bosom, where there is no trouble, nor grief, nor sighing, but peace and rejoicing and life unending."

Abraham's activity did not cease with his death, and as he interceded in this world for the sinners, so will he intercede for them in the world to come. On the day of judgment he will sit at the gate of hell, and he will not suffer those who kept the law of circumcision to enter therein.[1]

---

[1] Louis Ginzberg, *The Legends of the Jews*, vol. 1, pp. 304–306.

BUrDHA

Indian

*The death of the Buddha is like that of Oedipus, Moses, and
Abraham in that it represents a final release from the restric-
tions of the body. Death is the Buddhist's gateway to Nirvana
or perfect atonement with all things.*

This was the manner of Buddha's death, called *Parinirvana*,
or Final Release. In the forty-fifth year of his ministry the Buddha
suffered from a severe illness, and declared that he would not live
long. While residing in the city of Pawa he was entertained by a
good smith named Chunda. He prepared an offering of pork,   5
which was the cause of a sickness resulting in death. Buddha
became very faint, and though he set out for Kushinagara, had to
rest many times on the way. All this was endured that others
might be reminded that none are exempt from old age, decay, and
death. At last the Buddha reached the city, and there he addressed   10
Ananda as follows: "Inform the smith Chunda that his offering
will bring a great reward, for it will be the immediate cause of
my attaining *Nirvana*. There are, indeed, two offerings which will
bring great reward: one was given by the lady Sujata before I
reached the supreme wisdom, the other has just now been made   15
by Chunda. These are the two foremost gifts." The Buddha spoke
thus lest Chunda should feel remorse, or should be blamed by
others; but he had given strict orders that the remainder of the
offering was to be buried. Buddha lay down on a couch in a grove
of sal-trees near Kushinagara. He sent a message informing   20
the Malwa princes of his arrival, knowing that their regret, if he
died without their once more beholding him, would be very great.
Thus it was that a great company of kings and princes, nobles and
ladies of the court, beside innumerable priests, and the devas and
brahmas of the ten thousand worlds, assembled about the Bud-   25
dha's death-bed. All these wept and wrung their hands, and bowed
themselves to the ground in their grief. This occasion has been
made the subject of countless pictures, similar in sentiment to
the Christian *Pietas*.

Buddha inquired if the priests had any last questions to put to   30
him; but as they had no doubts on any point they remained silent.
A Brahman of Kushinagara, however, arrived, and desired to

316

argue certain matters; Buddha would not have him denied, and in the end he became a disciple. None of his disciples was more stricken with grief than Ananda. Buddha had given him instructions about his burial and about the rules to be observed by the monks and nuns. Then he said: "Now I depart to Nirvana; I leave with you my ordinances; the elements of the all-knowing one will indeed pass away, but the three gems will remain." But Ananda broke down and wept bitterly. Then Buddha continued: "O Ananda, do not let yourself be troubled; do not weep. Have I not taught you that we must part from all that we hold most dear and pleasant? No being soever born or created can overcome the tendency to dissolution inherent in itself; a condition of permanence is impossible. For a long time, Ananda, your kindness in act and thought and speech has brought you very near to me. You have always done well; persevere and you, too, shall win to perfect freedom from this thirst of life, this chain of ignorance." Then he turned to the other mourners and commended Ananda to them. He said also that the least of those present who had entered the path to Release should never entirely fail, but should at last prevail and reach Nirvana. After a pause he said again: "Mendicants, I now impress it upon you that the parts and powers of man must be dissolved; work out your salvation with diligence." Shortly afterward the Buddha became unconscious and passed away.

The Malwa princes, after they had a little recovered from their sorrow, wrapped the body in fold upon fold of finest cloth, and for six days the body lay in state. Then it was burnt on a magnificent pyre in the coronation hall of the princes. They were unable to set fire to the pyre, but in the end it ignited spontaneously. The body was entirely consumed, leaving only the relics like a heap of pearls. The chief of these, afterward enshrined in glorious monuments, were the four teeth, two cheek-bones, and the skull.[1]

[1] A. K. Coomaraswamy and Sister Nivedita, *Myths of the Hindus and Buddhists*, pp. 283–285.

HERACLES (HERCULES)
Greek

In his final act Heracles resembles the phoenix, the animal representative of resurrection. Out of the flames of Heracles' funeral pyre emerges a new body, which ascends immediately to heaven.

And now Hercules himself cut down the trees on high Oeta, and with their trunks made a great funeral pyre. He was aided by his friend Philoctetes, who lit the pyre and to whom, as a reward, Hercules gave the famous bow which later was to go to Troy. Now, at the point of death, with burnt and withered flesh, Hercules grew calm again. On top of the pyre he spread the skin of the Nemean lion. He rested his head on his club as on a pillow, and lay down among the flames with peaceful face, as if, after cups of fine wine and crowned with garlands, he were lying on a couch at a banquet.

The gods from heaven looked down and saw that the defender of the earth was dying. Even Juno at last pitied him, and to all the gods and goddesses Jupiter spoke: "Fear not. Hercules has conquered everything, and he will conquer those flames. Part of him is immortal, and, as an immortal, he will live with the gods for ever."

So indeed it happened. As a snake changes its old skin, so Hercules, as the flames consumed his body, seemed to put on a new body, stronger, more heroic, more beautiful and more stately even than before. Thunder pealed, and through the hollow clouds Jupiter sent his four-horsed chariot which bore him to Heaven, where he was welcomed among the shining stars and in the assembly of the gods.[1]

---

[1] Rex Warner, *The Stories of the Greeks*, pp. 106–107.

QUETZALCOATL
Toltec and Aztec

Fire plays a role in the death and apotheosis of Quetzalcoatl.
In this the Aztec hero resembles Heracles and the Buddha.

It ended on the beach
It ended with a hulk of serpents formed into a boat
& when he'd made it, sat in it & sailed away
A boat that glided on those burning waters, no one knowing when
    he reached the country of Red Daylight 5
It ended on the rim of some great sea
It ended with his face reflected in the mirror of its waves
The beauty of his face returned to him
& he was dressed in garments like the sun
It ended with a bonfire on the beach where he would hurl him- 10
    self
& burn, his ashes rising & the cries of birds
It ended with the linnet, with the birds of turquoise color, birds
    the color of wild sunflowers, red & blue birds
It ended with the birds of yellow feathers in a riot of bright gold 15
Circling till the fire had died out
Circling while his heart rose through the sky
It ended with his heart transformed into a star
It ended with the morning star with dawn & evening
It ended with his journey to Death's Kingdom with seven days of 20
    darkness
With his body changed to light
A star that burns forever in that sky[1]

---

[1] Jerome Rothenberg, ed., *Technicians of the Sacred*, p. 97.

KING ARTHUR
European

The apotheosis of King Arthur is implied in the miraculous events of his death. He is taken away, like Oedipus and Quetzalcoatl, as if to another world.

Arthur said unto Sir Bedivere, "take thou Excalibar, my good sword, and go with it to yonder waterside; and when thou comest there, I charge thee throw my sword in that water, and come again and tell me what thou there seest." "My lord," said Sir Bedivere, "your commandment shall be done." So Sir Bedivere departed, and by the way he beheld that noble sword, that the pommel and the haft were all of precious stones; and then he said to himself, "If I throw this rich sword into the water, no good shall come thereof, but only harm and loss." And then Sir Bedivere hid Excalibar under a tree. And so, as soon as he might, he came again unto the king. "What sawest thou there?" said the king. "Sir," he said, "I saw nothing." "Alas! thou hast deceived me," said the king. "Go thou lightly again, and as thou love me, spare not to throw it in." Then Sir Bedivere went again and took the sword in his hand to throw it; but again it beseemed him but sin and shame to throw away that noble sword, and he hid it away again, and returned, and told the king he had done his commandment. "What sawest thou there?" said the king. "Sir," he said, I saw nothing but waters deep and waves wan." "Ah, traitor untrue!" said King Arthur, "now hast thou betrayed me twice. And yet thou art named a noble knight, and hast been lief and dear to me. But now go again, and do as I bid thee, for thy long tarrying putteth me in jeopardy of my life." Then Sir Bedivere went to the sword, and lightly took it up, and went to the waterside, and he bound the girdle about the hilt, and then he threw the sword as far into the water as he might. And there came an arm and a hand out of the water, and met it, and caught it, and shook it thrice and brandished it, and then vanished away the hand with the sword in the water.

Then Sir Bedivere came again to the king and told him what he saw. "Help me hence," said the king, "for I fear I have tarried too long." Then Sir Bedivere took the king on his back, and so went with him to that waterside; and when they came there, even fast by the bank, there rode a little barge with many fair ladies in it, and among them was a queen; and all had black hoods, and they wept and shrieked when they saw King Arthur.

"Now put me in the barge," said the king. And there received him three queens with great mourning, and in one of their laps King Arthur laid his head. And the queen said, "Ah, dear brother, why have ye tarried so long? Alas! this wound on your head hath caught overmuch cold." And then they rowed from the land, and Sir Bedivere beheld them go from him. Then he cried: "Ah, my lord Arthur, will ye leave me here alone among mine enemies?" "Comfort thyself," said the king, "for in me is no further help; for I will to the Isle of Avalon, to heal me of my grievous wound." And as soon as Sir Bedivere had lost sight of the barge, he wept and wailed; then he took the forest, and went all that night, and in the morning he was ware of a chapel and a hermitage.

Then went Sir Bedivere thither; and when he came into the chapel, he saw where lay a hermit on the ground, near a tomb that was newly graven. "Sir," said Sir Bedivere, "what man is there buried that ye pray so near unto?" "Fair son," said the hermit, "I know not verily. But this night there came a number of ladies, and brought hither one dead, and prayed me to bury him." "Alas!" said Sir Bedivere, "that was my lord, King Arthur." Then Sir Bedivere swooned; and when he awoke, he prayed the hermit he might abide with him, to live with fasting and prayers. "Ye are welcome," said the hermit. So there bode Sir Bedivere with the hermit; and he put on poor clothes and served the hermit full lowly in fasting and in prayers.

Thus of Arthur I find never more written in books that be authorized, nor more of the very certainty of his death; but thus was he led away in a ship, wherein were three queens; the one was King Arthur's sister, Queen Morgane le Fay; the other was Viviane, the Lady of the Lake; and the third was the Queen of North Galis. And this tale Sir Bedivere, knight of the Table Round, made to be written.

Yet some men say that King Arthur is not dead, but hid away into another place, and men say that he shall come again and reign over England. But many say that there is written on his tomb this verse:

> *Hic jacet Arthurus, Rex quondam, Rexque futurus.*
> Here Arthur lies, King once and King to be.[1]

---

[1] Thomas Bulfinch, *Bulfinch's Mythology: The Age of Chivalry,* "Morte d'Arthur," pp. 188–190.

DIONYSOS (DIONYSUS)
Greek

Dionysos, having completed his mission on earth and in the underworld, is free to ascend to heaven.

Thus men perceived that he was a god and honoured him; and having brought up his mother from Hades and named her Thyone, he ascended up with her to heaven.[1]

[1] Apollodorus, *The Library*, translated by James G. Frazer, vol. 1, bk. 3, p. 3.

MARY

Christian

A tradition that developed in the early days of Christianity and was eventually accepted as dogma by the Church held that Mary, as **prima materia** *— the womb for the Word — must have been assumed bodily into Heaven to reign there as Queen.*

The dogma of the Assumption maintains that, after her death, the Virgin Mary was assumed bodily into heaven, where she was subsequently crowned — "more glorious than the Cherubim and Seraphim" — to reign with Christ for ever and ever.

The most ineffable Trinity itself applauds her with unceasing dance, [5] and since its grace flows wholly into her, makes all to wait upon her. The most splendid order of the apostles extols her with unspeakable lauds . . . unwilling Hell itself howls to her, and the wanton demons shriek her praise.[1]

The mysterious and altogether peculiar nature of the Assumption [10] is still clearer in the following passage from St. John of Damascus:

O Blessed Virgin, thou hast not gone to heaven as Elias did, or as Paul, who went up to the third heaven; thou hast mounted even to the kingly throne of thy Son! The death of the other saints is blessed because [15] it brings them to blessedness, but this is not true of thee: for not thy death . . . has bestowed upon thee the security of thy blessedness, since thou art the beginning and the middle and the end of all the blessings that surpass the mind of man! Hence death has not beatified thee, but thou hast glorified death, dispelling its sadness and turning it to joy![2] [20]

We are here within sight of the recognition that the Assumption is the revelation of what the Virgin was from the beginning — the one who reigns eternally with Christ, Sophia as the consort of Logos, divine Matrix of the universe. All the honours and symbols of this estate are present and the only thing lacking is the precise [25] theological definition.[3]

---

[1] From the *Homilies* of Gerardus in Jacobus De Voragine, *The Golden Legend*, vol. 2, pp. 458–464.
[2] Ibid.
[3] Alan Watts, *Myth and Ritual in Christianity*, pp. 111–112.

AGNES
Italian

As a Christian martyr, Saint Agnes, a virgin, is claimed by God and carried off to Heaven as — like Mary herself — a spouse.

Aspasius had the young girl thrown into a raging fire, but the flames, dividing, consumed the pagans and left Agnes untouched. Then, by order of Aspasius, a dagger was thrust into her throat, and in this manner her heavenly Spouse claimed her for His bride, having decked her with the crown of martyrdom. All [5] this is believed to have taken place under the reign of Constantine the Great, who reigned about the year 309. And the parents of Saint Agnes, with the other Christians, buried her with great joy; and they barely escaped the shower of stones which the pagans hurled at them. [10]

Agnes had a foster-sister whose name was Emerentiana, a virgin full of sanctity, who was preparing to receive baptism. This young maiden stood before Agnes' tomb, and began to inveigh against the pagans who had slain her, until these killed her also, by stoning her. At once the earth trembled, and God's thunder fell [15] upon the spot, taking the lives of many of these people, so that thereafter the faithful were allowed to draw near to the tomb without being molested. And the body of Emerentiana was buried beside that of Agnes.

Eight days later, as Agnes' kin watched around the tomb, [20] they saw a choir of virgins in robes of gold; and among them was the blessed Agnes, with a lamb whiter than snow at her right side. And she said to them: 'Look upon me, in order that ye may not mourn me for dead, but may rejoice and be glad with me; for I have been admitted henceforth to sit in the midst of this company [25] of light!' By reason of this vision the Church, eight days after the feast of Saint Agnes, celebrates the Octave of the feast.[1]

[1] Jacobus De Voragine, *The Golden Legend*, p. 112.

JESUS
Christian

Like Dionysos, Jesus ascends to heaven upon completion of his mission. He returns to God, of whom he is a part, in the ultimate act of atonement.

Then the eleven disciples went away into Galilee, into a mountain where Jesus had appointed them. And when they saw him, they worshipped him: but some doubted. And Jesus came and spake unto them, saying, All power is given unto me in heaven and in earth. Go ye therefore, and teach all nations, baptizing them in the name of the Father, and of the Son, and of the Holy Ghost: teaching them to observe all things whatsoever I have commanded you: and, lo, I am with you alway, even unto the end of the world.[1]

And he led them out as far as to Bethany, and he lifted up his hands, and blessed them. And it came to pass, while he blessed them, he was parted from them, and carried up into heaven. And they worshipped him, and returned to Jerusalem with great joy: and were continually in the temple, praising and blessing God. Amen.[2]

As to the third question, namely in what manner He ascended. First, with power, because He ascended by His own power. Thus Isaias: 'Who is this that cometh from Edom, with dyed garments from Bosra, this beautiful one in his robe, walking in the greatness of his strength.' So also John: 'No man hath ascended into Heaven (that is, by his own power), but he that descended from Heaven, the Son of man who is in Heaven.' And although He was lifted up in a globe of clouds, this was not done because He had need of the help of a cloud, but that it might thereby be made manifest that every creature is ready to serve its Creator. For He ascended by the power of His godhead, and in this is seen His power and lordship. For Henoch was taken by God, and Elias went up into Heaven by a whirlwind, but Jesus ascended by His own power: and the first of these, according to

[1] Matthew 28.
[2] Luke 24.

Saint Gregory, was engendered and did himself engender, the second was engendered but himself engendered not, and the third neither engendered nor was engendered. Secondly, He ascended visibly, in the sight of His disciples, whence it is said: 'While they looked on, He was raised up.' And in John: 'I go to him that sent Me, and none of you asketh Me, whither goest Thou?' to which the *Gloss* adds: 'Openly therefore, that no one might need to question what was seen with the eyes of the flesh.' He willed to ascend in the sight of His disciples, in order that they might be witnesses to His Ascension, and might rejoice that a human being was carried up into Heaven, and might yearn to follow Him thither. Thirdly, He ascended joyously, because the angels rejoiced, whence the Psalm says: 'God is ascended with jubilee, and the Lord with the sound of trumpet.' And Augustine says: 'Christ ascends: and the whole heaven trembles, the stars stand in awe, the heavenly hosts applaud, the trumpets resound and mingle their dulcet harmonies with the joyful choirs.' Fourthly, He ascended swiftly, as the Psalm says: 'He hath rejoiced as a giant to run the way'; and He traversed this great distance as in a moment.[3]

[3] Jacobus De Voragine, *The Golden Legend*, pp. 288–289.

THE DISCOVERY OF THE UNKNOWN:
Commentary on Part 8

Forty days after Easter, as the sun approaches mid-heaven following the vernal equinox, Christians celebrate the bodily ascension of Jesus into heaven. Mithras, Elijah, Saint Francis, and, in some stories, Faust, too, are carried off. And in a later addition to the Christian story the Virgin Mary is physically assumed into heaven to reign there with Christ.

The myth of the apotheosis is the logical conclusion to the hero's adventures. He is taken out of the cycle of life and given a permanent status in recognition of his inherent divinity—his real self. As he had been miraculously conceived of the void, so must he be returned to the creator and to that void. Thus Jesus carries back to heaven the body he had received through the Virgin. The historical hero vanishes into eternity and becomes all-present in the cosmos forever. It is as if the hero by this act were warning us to concentrate not on his historical qualities but on his role as world hero who is significant only when free of the local, the material, and the sectarian. To tie the hero to the historical is to kill him and all that he represents. If myth is to speak to man's inner life, it must emanate from the void—from the nonhistorical, timeless unknown. "Ascended into heaven," writes Alan Watts, "Christ is no more Jesus but 'all-in-all.'"[1] He is reborn again in God.

When he ascended up on high, he led captivity captive, and gave gifts unto men. Now that he ascended, what is it but that he also descended first into the lowest parts of the earth? He that descended is the same also that ascended up far above all heavens, that he might fill all things.[2]

The myth of apotheosis is psychologically as valid today as it ever was. The process of self-realization leads the individual in the direction of the universally valid human norms, freedom and unity. To achieve individuation is to achieve freedom from fear and from the limitations of time and to find unity in all opposites. Thus apotheosis is frequently expressed in the androgynous being in whom what has been separated in time and history returns

[1] Alan Watts, *Myth and Ritual in Christianity*, p. 188.
[2] Ephesians 4:8–10.

to the state of oneness free in the cosmos. In the androgyne, the Yin and the Yang combined in the Chinese holy woman T'ai Yuan, the Zuñi Indian chief god Awonawilona who is he-she, the child of Hermes and Aphrodite, Hermaphrodite, and in Eros himself, who is both male and female, we have the symbol of the final achievement of the essential self through loss of the illusion of local and personal self. "This is the release potential within us all," writes Joseph Campbell, "which anyone can attain – through herohood."[3] The hero of the apotheosis is the individual at his last threshold. As he is carried off to heaven, he is acting out the final event in the great process of losing the self to find the self. The hero is the symbol here of the individual who has achieved the mythical consciousness, in which the divine within is active in relation to all things and events. To realize the self in its total reality is to repossess the soul – the world soul of the collective unconscious.

A fuller understanding of the apotheosis myth will be achieved through a reading of Joseph Campbell's chapter on apotheosis in *The Hero with a Thousand Faces*. A penetrating consideration of the androgyne aspect and the ascent motif is contained in Mircea Eliade's *Mephistopholes and the Androgyne: Studies in Religious Myth and Symbol*.

---

[3] Joseph Campbell, *The Hero with a Thousand Faces*, p. 151.

APPENDIX 1

C. G. JUNG AND THE MAKING
OF A MYTHICAL CONSCIOUSNESS

The life and ideas of Carl Gustav Jung furnish concrete examples of ways in which myth can be applied to the needs of today. Jung felt that modern, rational, technocratic man has lost contact with the "inner center"—with the *daimon* or real "self," which is revealed in dreams and in myth. Only by reestablishing contact with that center—by creating a mythical consciousness—can Western civilization hope to achieve psychic balance. As an individual endowed with keen extrasensory perception, Jung was particularly sensitive to the "unknown." To him the world of myth was as real as that of matter. And as a man of science—a successful, practicing psychiatrist—he believed that the two worlds need not be mutually exclusive; in their interrelationship lay the power to heal. Like the hero of the monomyth, Jung was a pathfinder in search of the elixir of life, the answer to the "darkness of the Creator, who needs man to illuminate his Creation."[1] He boldly employed his visionary powers in conjunction with those of his profession, made the dangerous voyage to the depths, and returned to teach of what he had found there.

It is in the autobiography, *Memories, Dreams, Reflections,* that Jung records most fully the mythic events in his own life. As he traces his psychological development, it becomes clear that from his earliest years he had been destined to the lonely but heroic life of the seer. At the age of eighty-three he writes of himself as an old man and as a child: "Today as then, I am a solitary, because I know things and must hint at things which other people do not know, and usually do not even want to know."[2]

As a three-year-old, Jung had a significant dream, which he carried in his mind for the rest of his life. In the dream he found himself in a meadow staring into a stone-lined hole:

Then I saw a stone stairway leading down. Hesitantly and fearfully, I descended. At the bottom was a doorway with a round arch, closed off by a green curtain. It was a big, heavy curtain of worked stuff like

---

[1] Quoted from a letter from Jung to Miguel Serrano in Serrano's *C. G. Jung and Hermann Hesse: A Record of Two Friendships,* p. 88.

[2] Carl Gustav Jung, *Memories, Dreams, Reflections,* pp. 41–42.

brocade, and it looked very sumptuous. Curious to see what might be hidden behind, I pushed it aside. I saw before me in the dim light a rectangular chamber about thirty feet long. The ceiling was arched and of hewn stone. The floor was laid with flagstones, and in the center a red carpet ran from the entrance to a low platform. On this platform stood a wonderfully rich golden throne. I am not certain, but perhaps a red cushion lay on the seat. It was a magnificent throne, a real king's throne in a fairy tale. Something was standing on it which I thought at first was a tree trunk twelve to fifteen feet high and about one and a half to two feet thick. It was a huge thing, reaching almost to the ceiling. But it was of a curious composition: it was made of skin and naked flesh, and on top there was something like a rounded head with no face and no hair. On the very top of the head was a single eye, gazing motionlessly upward.[3]

This phallic dream of early childhood was Jung's introduction to the mysterious duality which was to form an important part of his overall philosophy. To achieve wholeness, man must confront the darkness which is in himself and which is usually associated with evil and sin. Jung expresses this mythically as he interprets the dream. The phallus was a "subterranean God," the "underground counterpart" of Jung's naïve childhood view of Jesus. The grave was an "underground temple" of the Earth "with her covering of green vegetation."

Through this childhood dream I was initiated into the secrets of the earth. What happened then was a kind of burial in the earth, and many years were to pass before I came out again. Today I know that it happened in order to bring the greatest possible amount of light into the darkness. It was an initiation into the realm of darkness. My intellectual life had its unconscious beginnings at that time.[4]

From his adolescence Jung felt increasingly the call of the part of himself represented by this dream — of the inner center and the unknown.

There were times when the demands of this "self number two" became nearly overwhelming. In 1912 Jung's major work on the hero and myth, *Symbols of Transformation,* led to his final break with Freud and to a consensus among his colleagues that he was not a scientist but a mystic. For Jung this was a major crisis. A dialogue between the two selves took place, and a dilemma arose. Would the path to myth really lead anywhere?

[3] Ibid., pp. 11–12.
[4] Ibid., pp. 12–13, 15.

"Now you possess a key to mythology and are free to unlock all the gates of the unconscious psyche," said one side. "Why open all gates?" answered the other.

And promptly the question arose of what, after all, I had accomplished. I had explained the myths of the peoples of the past; I had written a book about the hero, the myth in which man has always lived. But in what myth does man live nowadays? In the Christian myth, the answer might be. "Do *you* live in it?" I asked myself. To be honest the answer was no. "For me it is not what I live by." "Then do we no longer have any myth?" "No, evidently we no longer have any myth." "But then what is your myth—the myth in which you do live?" At this point the dialogue with myself became uncomfortable, and I stopped thinking.[5]

But not for long. Like the hero of the monomyth, Jung withdrew into himself in preparation for the inevitable search for the modern myth. He recalled a period of his childhood when he had been fascinated with building blocks, stones, and mud-mortar. The memory struck a chord, stirred an emotion: "There is still life in these things. The small boy is still around, and possesses a creative life which I lack." To return to that primitive but creative stage of his own existence Jung began "playing" with stones and mud-mortar. He built a whole play village including a church in which he placed a small altar. The church brought back to mind the phallus dream of his childhood and "this connection gave me a feeling of satisfaction." Naturally enough one side of the successful psychiatrist was disturbed by what he was doing: "Now, really, what are you about? You are building a small town, and doing it as if it were a rite!" The second self had no answer to this question—"only the inner certainty that I was on the way to discovering my own myth. For the building game was only a beginning."[6] It stirred fantasies "underground" which Jung knew he must eventually give himself up to. If the "underground" was to provide him with useful material for an understanding of his own myth and the myths of his patients, he must have direct experience of that "underground." Thus Jung did what all shaman-heroes must do; he let himself drop.

Suddenly it was as though the ground literally gave way beneath my feet, and I plunged down into dark depths. I could not fend off a feeling of panic. But then, abruptly, at not too great a depth, I landed on my feet in

[5] Ibid., p. 171.
[6] Ibid., pp. 174–175.

a soft, sticky mass. I felt great relief, although I was apparently in complete darkness. After a while my eyes grew accustomed to the gloom, which was rather like a deep twilight. Before me was the entrance to a dark cave, in which stood a dwarf with leathery skin, as if he were mummified. I squeezed past him through the narrow entrance and waded knee deep through icy water to the other end of the cave where, on a projecting rock, I saw a glowing red crystal. I grasped the stone, lifted it, and discovered a hollow underneath. At first I could make out nothing, but then I saw that there was running water. In it a corpse floated by, a youth with blond hair and a wound in the head. He was followed by a gigantic black scarab and then by a red, newborn sun, rising up out of the depths of the water.[7]

Anyone who has read the myths and commentaries in this volume will realize as Jung did that this vision contains the myths of death, descent, and rebirth.

The rebirth myth is further expressed along with that of atonement in Jung's tower at Bollingen. The tower, built over the years according to his material and psychic needs by Jung himself, was a record in stone of the voyage to and return from the unknown.

From the beginning I felt the Tower as in some way a place of maturation —a maternal womb or a maternal figure in which I could become what I was, what I am and will be. It gave me a feeling as if I were being reborn in stone. It is thus a concretization of the individuation process . . . —a symbol of psychic wholeness. . . . At Bollingen I am in the midst of my true life, I am most deeply myself. Here I am, as it were, the "age-old son of the mother." That is how alchemy puts it, very wisely, for the "old man," the "ancient," . . . is personality No. 2, who has always been and always will be. He exists outside time and is the son of the maternal unconscious. . . . At times I feel as if I am spread over the landscape and inside things, and am myself living in every tree, in the splashing of the waves, in the clouds and the animals that come and go in the procession of the seasons. There is nothing in the tower that has not grown into its own form over the decades, nothing with which I am not linked. Here everything has its history, and mine; here is space for the spaceless kingdom of the world's and the psyche's hinterland.[8]

Jung at Bollingen succeeded in creating a mythical consciousness—in establishing meaningful contact with the life force which is everywhere and in everything.

Mythology, said Jung, is made up of archetypes or norms

[7] Ibid., p. 179.
[8] Ibid., pp. 225–226.

which spring from a collective unconscious common to us all. Although these norms—paradise, the underworld, the great mother, God—are not provable, they are real in the sense that they have been a part of human life from the beginning. And, most of all, they are real because "they give meaning to the life of man" by making him a part of a coherent whole. Man can endure any hardship as long as he is not forced to see himself "taking part in a 'tale told by an idiot.'" The person who lives without myth lives without roots, without links to the collective self which is finally what we are all about. He is literally isolated from reality. The person who lives with a myth gains "a sense of wider meaning" to his existence and is raised "beyond mere getting and spending."[9] The modern individual and modern man as a group must be willing, like the hero, to put aside the illusory and temporary veil of the purely rational. He must be willing to search for, recognize, and accept the real forces behind that veil. Alienated and disoriented now, he must regain his ability to respond to numinous symbols and ideas—to myth. Jung's "desire," writes Miguel Serrano, "was to project the light of the consciousness into the bottomless sea of the Unconscious, which is to say, into God himself."[10] This is the desire of the hero of the monomyth in whose adventures are mirrored the real Self. The beginning of the path to psychic wholeness is the recognition that the hero's voyage is in reality the voyage of each and all of us.

[9] Carl Gustav Jung, M.-L. von Franz, et al., *Man and His Symbols*, pp. 76–78.
[10] Miguel Serrano, *C. G. Jung and Hermann Hesse: A Record of Two Friendships*, p. 109.

APPENDIX 2

MYTHS OF CREATION*

THE MAORI COSMOGONY
Polynesian

Io dwelt within the breathing-space of immensity.
The Universe was in darkness, with water everywhere.
There was no glimmer of dawn, no clearness, no light.
And he began by saying these words,—
That He might cease remaining inactive:

    'Darkness become a light-possessing darkness.'

And at once light appeared.
(He) then repeated those self-same words in this manner.
That He might cease remaining inactive:

    'Light, become a darkness-possessing light.'

And again an intense darkness supervened.
Then a third time He spake saying:

    'Let there be one darkness above,
    Let there be one darkness below,
    . . . .
    Let there be one light above,
    Let there be one light below,
    . . . .
    A dominion of light,
    A bright light.'

And now a great light prevailed.
(Io) then looked to the waters which compassed him about,
    and spake a fourth time, saying:

    'Ye waters of Tai-kama, be ye separate.
    Heaven, be formed.'

Then the sky became suspended.

    'Bring forth thou Tupua-horo-nuku.'

And at once the moving earth lay stretched abroad.

* See also Genesis 1, 2.

Those words (of Io) (the supreme god) became impressed on the minds of our ancestors, and by them were they transmitted down through generations, our priest joyously referred to them as being:

The ancient and original sayings.
The ancient and original words.
The ancient and original cosmological wisdom (wananga).
Which caused growth from the void,
The limitless space-filling void,
As witness the tidal-waters,
The evolved heaven,
The birth-given evolved earth.

And now, my friends, there are three very important applications of those original sayings, as used in our sacred rituals. The first occurs in the ritual for planting a child in the barren womb.

The next occurs in the ritual for enlightening both the mind and body. The third and last occurs in the ritual on the solemn subject of death, and of war, of baptism, of genealogical recitals and such like important subjects, as the priests most particularly concerned themselves in.

The words by which Io fashioned the Universe—that is to say, by which it was implanted and caused to produce a world of light—the same words are used in the ritual for implanting a child in a barren womb. The words by which Io caused light to shine in the darkness are used in the rituals for cheering a gloomy and despondent heart, the feeble aged, the decrepit; for shedding light into secret places and matters, for inspiration in song-composing, and in many other affairs, affecting man to despair in times of adverse war. For all such the ritual to enlighten and cheer includes the words (used by Io) to overcome and dispel darkness. Thirdly, there is the preparatory ritual which treats of successive formations within the universe, and the genealogical history of man himself.[1]

---

[1] Hare Hongi, "A Maori Cosmogony," *Journal of the Polynesian Society* (1907): 113–114. Quoted in Eliade, *Gods, Goddesses, and Myths of Creation*, pp. 86–87.

THE YAUELMANI YOKUT CREATION
Californian Indian

At first there was water everywhere. A piece of wood (wicket, stick, wood, tree) grew up out of the water to the sky. On the tree there was a nest. Those who were inside did not see any earth. There was only water to be seen. The eagle was the chief of them. With him were the wolf, Coyote, the panther, the prairie falcon, the hawk called *po'yon*, and the condor. The eagle wanted to make the earth. He thought, 'We will have to have land.' Then he called *k'uik'ui*, a small duck. He said to it: 'Dive down and bring up earth.' The duck dived, but did not reach the bottom. It died. The eagle called another kind of duck. He told it to dive. This duck went far down. It finally reached the bottom. Just as it touched the mud there it died. Then it came up again. Then the eagle and the other six saw a little dirt under its finger nail. When the eagle saw this he took the dirt from its nail. He mixed it with *telis* and *pele* seeds and ground them up. He put water with the mixture and made dough. This was in the morning. Then he set it in the water and it swelled and spread everywhere, going out from the middle. (These seeds when ground and mixed with water swell.) In the evening the eagle told his companions: 'Take some earth.' They went down and took a little earth up in the tree with them. Early in the morning, when the morning star came, the eagle said to the wolf: 'Shout.' The wolf shouted and the earth disappeared, and all was water again. The eagle said: 'We will make it again,' for it was for this purpose that they had taken some earth with them into the nest. Then they took *telis* and *pele* seeds again, and ground them with the earth, and put the mixture into the water, and it swelled out again. Then early next morning when the morning star appeared, the eagle told the wolf again: 'Shout!' and he shouted three times. The earth was shaken by the earthquake, but it stood. Then Coyote said: 'I must shout too.' He shouted and the earth shook a very little. Now it was good. Then they came out of the tree on the ground. Close to where this tree stood there was a lake. The eagle said: 'We will live here.' Then they had a house there and lived there.[1]

---

[1] A. L. Kroeber, *Indian Myths of South Central California*, University of California Publications, American Archeology and Ethnology no. 4 (1906–1907): 229–231. Quoted in Eliade, *Gods, Goddesses, and Myths of Creation*, pp. 90–91.

A BANTU COSMOGONY
African

In the beginning, in the dark, there was nothing but water. And Bumba was alone.

One day Bumba was in terrible pain. He retched and strained and vomited up the sun. After that light spread over everything. The heat of the sun dried up the water until the black edges of the world began to show. Black sandbanks and reefs could be seen. But there were no living things.

Bumba vomited up the moon and then the stars, and after that the night had its light also.

Still Bumba was in pain. He strained again and nine living creatures came forth; the leopard named Koy Bumba, and Pongo Bumba the crested eagle, the crocodile, Ganda Bumba, and one little fish named Yo; next, old Kono Bumba, the tortoise, and Tsetse, the lightning, swift, deadly, beautiful like the leopard, then the white heron, Nyanyi Bumba, also one beetle, and the goat named Budi.

Last of all came forth men. There were many men, but only one was white like Bumba. His name was Loko Yima.

The creatures themselves then created all the creatures. The heron created all the birds of the air except the kite. He did not make the kite. The crocodile made serpents and the iguana. The goat produced every beast with horns. Yo, the small fish, brought forth all the fish of all the seas and waters. The bettle created insects.

Then the serpents in their turn made grasshoppers, and the iguana made the creatures without horns.

Then the three sons of Bumba said they would finish the world. The first, Nyonye Ngana, made the white ants; but he was not equal to the task, and died of it. The ants, however, thankful for life and being, went searching for black earth in the depths of the world and covered the barren sands to bury and honour their creator.

Chonganda, the second son, brought forth a marvellous living plant from which all the trees and grasses and flowers and plants in the world have sprung. The third son, Chedi Bumba, wanted something different, but for all his trying made only the bird called the kite.

Of all the creatures, Tsetse, lightning, was the only trouble-maker. She stirred up so much trouble that Bumba chased her into the sky. Then mankind was without fire until Bumba showed the people how to draw fire out of trees. 'There is fire in every tree,' he told them, and showed them how to make the firedrill and liberate it. Sometimes today Tsetse still leaps down and strikes the earth and causes damage.

When at last the work of creation was finished, Bumba walked through the peaceful villages and said to the people, 'Behold these wonders. They belong to you.' Thus from Bumba, the Creator, the First Ancestor, came forth all the wonders that we see and hold and use, and all the brotherhood of beasts and man.[1]

---

[1] Maria Leach, *The Beginning* (New York, 1956), pp. 145–146; translated and adapted from E. Torday and J. A. Joyce, *Les Boshongo*, pp. 20 f. Quoted in Eliade, *Gods, Goddesses, and Myths of Creation*, pp. 91–92.

THE MAYA-QUICHÉ GENESIS
Mexican and Central American

Admirable is the account — so the narrative opens — admirable is the account of the time in which it came to pass that all was formed in heaven and upon earth, the quartering of their signs, their measure and alignment, and the establishment of parallels to the skies and upon the earth to the four quarters thereof, as was spoken by the Creator and Maker, the Mother, the Father of life and of all existence, that one by whom all move and breathe, father and sustainer of the peace of peoples, by whose wisdom was premediated the excellence of all that doth exist in the heavens, upon the earth, in lake and sea.

Lo, all was in suspense, all was calm and silent; all was motionless, all was quiet, and wide was the immensity of the skies.

Lo, the first word and the first discourse. There was not yet a man, not an animal; there were no birds nor fish nor crayfish; there was no wood, no stone, no bog, no ravine, neither vegetation nor marsh; only the sky existed.

The face of the earth was not yet to be seen; only the peaceful sea and the expanse of the heavens.

Nothing was yet formed into a body; nothing was joined to another thing; naught held itself poised; there was not a rustle, not a sound beneath the sky. There was naught that stood upright; there were only the quiet waters of the sea, solitary within its bounds; for as yet naught existed.

There were only immobility and silence in the darkness and in the night. Alone was the Creator, the Maker, Tepeu, the Lord, and Gucumatz, the Plumed Serpent, those who engender, those who give being, alone upon the waters like a growing light.

They are enveloped in green and azure, whence is the name Gucumatz, and their being is great wisdom. Lo, how the sky existeth, how the Heart of the Sky existeth — for such is the name of God, as He doth name Himself!

It is then that the word came to Tepeu and to Gucumatz, in the shadows and in the night, and spake with Tepeu and with Gucumatz. And they spake and consulted and meditated, and they joined their words and their counsels.

Then light came while they consulted together; and at the moment of dawn man appeared while they planned concerning

339

the production and increase of the groves and of the climbing vines, there in the shade and in the night, through that one who is the Heart of the Sky, whose name is Hurakan.

The Lightning is the first sign of Hurakan; the second is the Streak of Lightning; the third is the Thunderbolt which striketh; and these three are the Heart of the Sky.

Then they came to Tepeu, the Gucumatz, and held counsel touching civilized life; how seed should be formed, how light should be produced, how the sustainer and nourisher of all.

'Let it be thus done. Let the waters retire and cease to obstruct, to the end that earth exist here, that it harden itself and show its surface, to the end that it be sown, and that the light of day shine in the heavens and upon the earth; for we shall receive neither glory nor honour from all that we have created and formed until human beings exist, endowed with sentience.' Thus they spake while the earth was formed by them. It is thus, veritably, that creation took place, and the earth existed. 'Earth,' they said, and immediately it was formed.

Like a fog or a cloud was its formation into the material state, when, like great lobsters, the mountains appeared upon the waters, and in an instant there was great mountains. Only by marvellous power could have been achieved this their resolution when the mountains and the valleys instantly appeared, with groves of cypress and pine upon them.

Then was Gucumatz filled with joy. 'Thou art welcome, O Heart of the Sky, O Hurakan, O Streak of Lightning, O Thunderbolt!'

'This that we have created and shaped will have its end,' they replied.[1]

---

[1] *The Popol-Vuh*, chap. 1. Translation by H. B. Alexander in his *Latin-American Mythology* (Boston, 1920), pp. 160–162. Quoted in Eliade, *Gods, Goddesses, and Myths of Creation*, pp. 92–94.

AN EGYPTIAN COSMOGONY AND THEOGONY

The Lord of All, after having come into being, says: I am he who came into being as Khepri (i.e., the Becoming One). When I came into being, the beings came into being, all the beings came into being after I became. Numerous are those who became, who came out of my mouth, before heaven ever existed, nor earth came into being, nor the worms, nor snakes were created in this place. I, being in weariness, was bound to them in the Watery Abyss. I found no place to stand. I thought in my heart, I planned in myself, I made all forms being alone, before I ejected Shu, before I spat out Tefnut,[1] before any other who was in me had become. Then I planned in my own heart, and many forms of beings came into being as forms of children, as forms of their children. I conceived by my hand, I united myself with my hand, I poured out of my own mouth. I ejected Shu, I spat out Tefnut. It was my father the Watery Abyss who brought them up, and my eye followed them (?) while they became far from me. After having become one god, there were (now) three gods in me. When I came into being in this land, Shu and Tefnut jubilated in the Watery Abyss in which they were. Then they brought with them my eye. After I had joined together my members, I wept over them, and men came into being out of the tears which came out of my eyes.[2] Then she (the eye) became enraged[3] after she came back and had found that I had placed another in her place, that she had been replaced by the Brilliant One. Then I found a higher place for her on my brow,[4] and when she began to rule over the whole land her fury fell down on the flowering (?) and I replaced what she had ravished. I came out of the flowering (?), I created all snakes, and all that came into being with them. Shu and Tefnut produced Geb and Nut; Geb and Nut produced out of a single body Osiris, Horus the Eyeless One,[5] Seth, Isis, and Nephthys, one after the other among them. Their children are numerous in this land.[6]

[1] Shu the air, Tefnut the moist.

[2] Same myth in the *Book of Gates*, division 4 (*The Tomb of Ramesses* VI, p. 169).

[3] An allusion to the myth of the Eye of the sun god which departs into a foreign land and is brought back by Shu and Tefnut. Another aspect of this myth is to be found in the *Book of the Divine Cow*.

[4] The fire-spitting snake, the uraeus on the head of the god.

[5] The Elder Horus of Letopolis.

[6] Translation and notes by Alexandre Piankoff, in his *The Shrines of Tut-ankh-amon* (New York, 1955), p. 24 [Eliade's note]. Quoted in Eliade, *Gods, Goddesses, and Myths of Creation*, pp. 96–97.

THE MAORI CREATION OF WOMAN
Polynesian

To produce man it was therefore necessary for the god Tane, the Fertilizer, to fashion in human form a figure of earth upon the Earth Mother's body, and to vivify it. This event transpired in the following way. (The account, according to Best, is 'rendered as given by an old native'):

Tane proceeded to the *puke* (*Mons veneris*) of Papa [the Earth] and there fashioned in human form a figure in the earth. His next task was to endow that figure with life, with human life, life as known to human beings, and it is worthy of note that, in the account of this act, he is spoken of as Tane te waiora. It was the sun light fertilizing the Earth Mother. Implanted in the lifeless image were the *wairua* (spirit) and *manawa ora* (breath of life), obtained from Io, the Supreme Being. The breath of Tane was directed upon the image, and the warmth affected it. The figure absorbed life, a faint life sigh was heard, the life spirit manifested itself, and Hine-ahu-one, the Earth Formed Maid, sneezed, opened her eyes, and rose – a woman.

Such was the Origin of Woman, formed from the substance of the Earth Mother, but animated by the divine Spirit that emanated from the Supreme Being, Io the great, Io of the Hidden Face, Io the Parent, and Io the Parentless.[1]

---

[1] E. S. Craighill Handy, *Polynesian Religion*, Bernice P. Bishop Museum Bulletin 34 (Honolulu, 1927), p. 39; quoting Elsdon Best, "Maori Personifications," *Journal of the Polynesian Society* 32 (1923): 110–111. Quoted in Eliade, *Gods, Goddesses, and Myths of Creation*, p. 130.

THE ZUÑI CREATION OF MAN
New Mexican Indian

Before the beginning of the new-making, Awonawilona (the Maker and Container of All, the All-father Father), solely had being. There was nothing else whatsoever throughout the great space of the ages save everywhere black darkness in it, and everywhere void desolation.

In the beginning of the new-made, Awonawilona conceived within himself and thought outward in space, whereby mists of increase, steams potent of growth, were evolved and uplifted. Thus, by means of his innate knowledge, the All-container made himself in person and form of the Sun whom we hold to be our father and who thus came to exist and appear. With his appearance came the brightening of the spaces with light, and with the brightening of the spaces the great mist-clouds were thickened together and fell, whereby was evolved water in water; yea, and the world-holding sea.

With his substance of flesh outdrawn from the surface of his person, the Sun-father formed the seed-stuff of twain worlds, impregnating therewith the great waters, and lo! in the heat of his light these waters of the sea grew green and scums rose upon them, waxing wide and weighty until, behold! they became Awitelin Tsita, the 'Four-fold Containing Mother-earth,' and Apoyan Tä'chu, the 'All-covering Father-sky.'[1]

---

[1] F. H. Cushing, *Outlines of Zuñi Creation Myths* in Thirteenth Annual Report, Bureau of Ethnology (Washington, D.C., 1896), pp. 325–326. Quoted in Eliade, *Gods, Goddesses, and Myths of Creation*, pp. 130–131.

APPENDIX 3

MYTHS OF THE FLOOD*

THE GRECO-ROMAN FLOOD

Then Jove raised thunderbolt against the earth—
And checked the blow. Would heaven break in fire,
And flames pour over earth from pole to pole?
He then remembered that the Fates had scored
A certain distant hour when sea and land,
Earth and the vault of heaven would be consumed
In universal fire. He put aside
The lightning spear Cyclopean hands
Made as his weapon to assert his will:
Another doom for man came to his mind
A death that stormed beneath the waves, and fell
From air; and then dark rain began to fall.

As straight as rain, quicker than thought Jove locked
The North Wind in the island-drifting cave
Of Aeolus and with him winds that harried
Clouds, but Auster he released, its dark
Wings over earth, the Nubian darkness
Deeper than midnight, beard and long grey hair
In fall of rain, black forehead in wild clouds,
Its great clapping hands thunder in the dark.
And as rain fell Iris, handmaid of Juno,
In rainbow dress drew water from earth's streams
Replenishing the clouds. Nor did rain cease.
Wheat fell before the storm, the uncut harvest
Drifting in rivers as the waters turned;
The farmers' prayer unheard within the tempest,
The heavy labour of long years undone.

Nor was Jove's rage appeased by pouring heavens.
Neptune arrived with armies of the waters,

* See also Genesis 6–9 and the Gilgamesh tale in Part 4.

Rivers assembled at his ocean's floor
To hear his orders: "The hour is all short
For long orations, open your locks and dykes,
Your streaming walls, and springs, unleash the horses
Riding in foam through waterfalls and waves."
At his command the mouths of fountains opened
Racing their mountain waters to the sea.
Under the blow of Neptune's fork earth trembled,
And way was open for a sea of waters:
Where land was the great rivers toppled orchards,
Uncut corn, cottages, sheep, men, and cattle
Into the flood. Even stone shrines and temples
Were washed away, and if farmhouse or barn
Or palace still stood its ground, the waves
Climbed over door and lintel, up roof and tower.
All vanished as though lost in glassy waters,
Road, highway, valley, and hill swept into ocean,
All was a moving sea without a shore.

And in flood's desert one saw a creature,
Perhaps a man, swim toward a vanished hill
That once he knew; another rowed a boat
Over the acres of his plough; another sailed
The fields that were to be his harvest,
Over the roofs of his sea-buried home.
Another caught fish from the floating branches
Of the tallest elms; ships' anchors dropping
In grass-grown meadows and swift keels sped
Over green hill and vineyard. Where yesterday
Thin-legged goats stepped on their way to pasture,
The bearded seal dozed through the deep sea hours,
And mermaids drifting with new-opened eyes
Gazed into cities that were walked by men.
The leaping dolphins dashed through grove and covert
Splashing their sides against oak bough and tree
Till the dim forest swayed beneath the waters;
Over them pursuing wolf swam with the sheep.
The exhausted lion drifting with the tiger,
The plunging thrust of the wild boar, the lightning
Step of the deer perished within the vortex
Of the waters; wing-spent, the circling bird

Wheeled his slow flight into unceasing waves.
Green hills then joined the valleys of the sea
And mountain peaks were islands in strange waters;
And almost every being that breathed on earth
Drowned as it met the flood; those who survived
Died of starvation on the shores of mountains.

Within the happy fields of fertile valleys,
Before all turned to sea, lay peaceful Phocis
Where the twin-horned Parnassus pierced the clouds.
There, in a little boat young Deucalion
And his bride sailed to the mountaintop that
Now was island and stepped ashore. Their first
Thought was to pray, to praise the Delphic nymphs,
To give their thanks to Pan and most to Themis
Who from her grottoes was the voice of Fate;
She in that day was queen of oracles.
Deucalion had been the best of men;
His wife, his heart devoted to the gods.
When Jove looked down on earth all that he saw
Was a stilled ocean and on a mountain shelf
One man, one woman. Of many thousands sent
To untimely death, only this gentle innocent
And his bride were left to praise the fortunate
Will of God, Jove swept the clouds aside and made
A channel where the North Wind opened heaven:
And earth again looked upward to the sky,
Again the heavens showered earth with light.
Then even the distant reaches of the seas
Fell quiet and to soothe the rocking waters
Neptune let fall his triple-headed spear.
Then ocean's master called to sea-wreathed Triton
Who at echo of Neptune's voice came from the sea
Like a tower of sea-green beard, sea creatures,
Sea shells, grey waters sliding from his green shoulders
To sound his horn, to wind the gliding rivers
Back to their sources, back to rills and streams.
At Neptune's order Triton lifted up
His curved sea shell, a trumpet at his lips
Which in the underworld of deepest seas
Sounds Triton's music to the distant shores

Behind the morning and the evening suns;
And as his voice was heard through land and ocean
The floods and rivers moved at his command.
Over all earth the shores of lakes appeared
Hillsides and river banks, wet fields and meadow,
As floods receded and quays came into view:
A cliff, then a plateau, a hill, a meadow,
As from a tomb a forest rose and then
One saw trees with lean seaweeds tangled
Among their glittering leaves and wave-tossed boughs.
It was a world reborn but Deucalion
Looked out on silent miles of ebbing waters.
He wept, called to his wife, "Dear sister, friend,
O last of women, look at loneliness;
As in our marriage bed our fears, disasters
Are of one being, one kind, one destiny;
We are the multitudes that walk the earth
Between sunrise and sunset of the world,
And we alone inherit wilderness.
The living are lost beneath a dwindling sea.
Even the ledge of mountain where we stand
May drop to darkness; and even the brief shadow
Of clouds that drift and fade is the return
Of midnight to the terror in my heart.
And you, dear soul, what if the Fates had swept
You on these pale rocks alone, to whom would you
Confess your grief, your tears? For if wild sea
Had claimed you then I would have followed after;
O had I Father's gift I would breathe life
Into the lifeless earth, but who are we
To recreate mankind? It is the will
Of heaven to bring us here and we the last
Of human creatures on this earth." They wept,
Yet promised to raise further prayers to God,
To know his will, to hear his oracles.
And hand in hand they came to Cephisus,
Whose waters, scarcely clear, still ran in freshets
Between its grassy sides. They dipped their hands
Into the sacred stream, in priestly fashion
Scattered living waters on bowed head and tunics.
And from the river they walked to Themis' shrine

Whose fires were ashes and where wall and cornice
Still dripped with seaweed and the creeping moss.
Then falling to their knees they kissed the stones
Where sea-washed altar turned their tears to ice
And trembling lips to speech: "O Themis, hear us.
How shall we please the gods? Can piety
In prayer, can goodness still wake pity in
The gods' anger that destroys mankind?
O merciful lady, how can we save
Our brothers, the very race of man from hell,
From eternal nothingness now and forever?"

Themis was moved and like an oracle
Answered their prayer: "Walk from the temple
With covered head, with girdled tunic open
At breast and shoulder, and as the wind flows
Scatter your mother's bones." Deucalion
Could not believe his ears and silent Pyrrha
Could not obey the voice. Then Pyrrha spoke
Her words in tears: "How can I desecrate
My mother's spirit? O forgive me, Goddess."
"But what did the voice say?" turned in their hearts
And waked their souls until Prometheus' son,
Mild Deucalion, said to the troubled girl
Who stood beside him, "Either I've gone mad
(Yet sacred voices never lead to sin)
Or our Great Mother is the Earth, her bones
Are guiltless stones we throw behind us."

Though wavering Pyrrha heard her husband's voice,
Both were in doubt, shaken with fear, with hope.
But what harm could be done? They left the temple
With floating robes and veiled heads, then furtively
Dropped pebbles in their trail and as they ran
(Some find this fable more than fabulous,
But we must keep faith with our ancient legends)
Pebbles grew into rocks, rocks into statues
That looked like men; the darker parts still wet
With earth were flesh, dry elements were bones,
And veins began to stir with human blood—
Such were the inclinations of heaven's will.

The stones that Deucalion dropped were men,
And those that fell from his wife's hands were women.
Beyond, behind the years of loss and hardship
We trace a stony heritage of being.

Within the weed-grown swamps left by the flood
The animal kingdoms of the earth appeared.
The seeds of earth swelled in the heat of noon
As in a mother's womb—as when the seven-lipped
Nile shrinks to its source, so sun's heat wakens
The moss-green river side, and there the peasant
As he turns the soil finds under it a world
Of things that live, half-live, or creep or run
As though one body of earth were alive,
Half dead, so in all things
And in a single body, half motionless,
Inert, yet half alive. As heat and water
Become one body, so life begins; though fire
And water are at war, life's origins
Awake discordant harmonies that move
The entire world. Therefore when fires
Of newly wakened sun turned toward the earth
Where waters still receded from her sides,
All living things in multitudes of being
Became her progeny once more. Some were
Of ancient lineage and colors
And others were mysterious and new.[1]

---

[1] Ovid, *The Metamorphoses*, Horace Gregory translation, book 1, pp. 37–43.

1. In the morning they brought to Manu water for washing, just as now also they (are wont to) bring (water) for washing the hands. When he was washing himself, a fish came into his hands.

2. It spake to him the word, 'Rear me, I will save thee!' 'Wherefrom wilt thou save me?' 'A flood will carry away all these creatures: from that I will save thee!' 'How am I to rear thee?'

3. It said, 'As long as we are small, there is great destruction for us: fish devours fish. Thou wilt first keep me in a jar. When I outgrow that, thou wilt dig a pit and keep me in it. When I outgrow that, thou wilt take me down to the sea, for then I shall be beyond destruction.'

4. It soon became a *ghasha* (a great fish); for that grows largest (of all fish). Thereupon it said, 'In such and such a year that flood will come. Thou shalt then attend to me (i.e. to my advice) by preparing a ship; and when the flood has risen thou shalt enter into the ship, and I will save thee from it.'

5. After he had reared it in this way, he took it down to the sea. And in the same year which the fish had indicated to him, he attended to (the advice of the fish) by preparing a ship; and when the flood had risen, he entered into the ship. The fish then swam up to him, and to its horn he tied the rope of the ship, and by that means he passed swiftly up to yonder northern mountain.

6. It then said, 'I have saved thee. Fasten the ship to a tree; but let not the water cut thee off whilst thou art on the mountain. As the water subsides, thou mayest gradually descend!' Accordingly he gradually descended and hence that (slope) of the northern mountain is called 'Manu's descent.' The flood then swept away all these creatures, and Manu alone remained here.[1]

---

[1] "Shatapatha-Brāhmana," I, 8, 1–6. Translation by Julius Eggeling, in *Sacred Books of the East*, vol. 12 (Oxford, 1882), pp. 216–218. Quoted in Eliade, *Gods, Goddesses, and Myths of Creation*, p. 151.

SELECTED BIBLIOGRAPHY

This bibliography contains a selection of works of importance to the student of mythology. It includes among others books used in the preparation of this volume. It is not intended as a complete list of works on the subject.

Aarne, A. A. *Types of the Folktale: A Classification and Bibliography.* Translated and enlarged by Stith Thompson. Helsinki: Suomalainen Tiedeakatemia, 1961.

Alexander, H. B. *Latin-American Mythology.* Boston: Marshall & Jones Company, 1920.

Andersen, Johannes C. *Myths and Legends of the Polynesians.* Rutland and Tokyo: Charles E. Tuttle, 1969.

Apollodorus. *The Library.* Translated by James G. Frazer. London: W. Heinemann, 1921.

Apollonius of Rhodes. *The Voyage of the Argo.* Translated by E. V. Rieu. Baltimore: Penguin Books, 1959.

Ballou, R. O., ed. *The Bible of the World.* New York: The Viking Press, 1939. Available in paperback as *The Viking Portable World Bible,* abridged.

Bastian, Adolf. *Ethnische Elementargedanken in der Lehre vom Menschen,* Berlin: F. Dümmler, 1895.

Boas, Franz. *Race, Language, and Culture:* [1940], New York: Free Press, 1966.

Boer, Charles, trans. *The Homeric Hymns.* Chicago: Swallow Press, 1970.

Branston, Brian. *Gods of the North.* New York: Vanguard Press, 1955.

Brown, Norman O. *Love's Body.* New York: Random House, 1966.

Budge, Wallis. *Osiris and the Egyptian Resurrection.* 2 vols. [1911] New York: Dover, 1973.

Bulfinch, Thomas. *Bulfinch's Mythology.* 2 vols. New York: Mentor Books, 1962.

Campbell, Joseph. *The Flight of the Wild Gander: Explorations in the Mythological Dimension.* New York: Viking, 1969.

——. *The Hero with a Thousand Faces:* [1956] Princeton: Princeton Univ. Press, 1968.

——. *The Masks of God.* 4 vols. New York: Viking Compass Books, 1970.

——. *The Mythic Image.* Princeton: Bollingen Series C, 1974.

——. *Myths to Live By.* New York: Viking Press, 1972.

Carpenter, Rhys. *Folk Tale, Fiction, and Saga in the Homeric Epics.* Berkeley: University of California Press, 1962.

Cassirer, Ernst. *Language and Myth*. Translated by Susanne Langer. New York: Dover, 1946.

Chase, Richard. *Quest for Myth*. Baton Rouge: Louisiana State Univ. Press, 1949.

Coffin, T. P., ed. *Indian Tales of North America*. Philadelphia: American Folklore Society, 1961.

Colum, Padraic. *Myths of the World (Orpheus)*. New York: Universal Library, 1972.

Coomaraswamy, Ananda, *Buddha and the Gospel of Buddhism*. London: G. G. Harrap, 1928.

———. *The Dance of Shiva*. [1918], New York: Noonday, 1957.

———. *Hinduism and Buddhism*. Westport, Conn.: Greenwood, 1971.

Coomaraswamy, Ananda, and Nivedita, Sister. *Myths of the Hindus and Buddhists* [1914] New York: Dover, 1967.

Cushing, F. H. *Outlines of Zuñi Creation Myths*. Washington, D.C.: Thirteenth Annual Report, Bureau of Ethnology, 1896, pp. 325–447.

Dante. *Divine Comedy*.

———. *Vita Nuova*. Translated by R. W. Emerson. Chapel Hill, N.C.: Univ. of N.C. Press, 1960.

De Santillana, Giorgio, and von Dechend, Hertha. *Hamlet's Mill: An Essay on Myth and the Frame of Time*. Boston: David Godine, 1977 (orig. 1969).

De Voragine, Jacobus. *The Golden Legend*. London: Longmans, Green & Co., 1941.

Durkheim, Emile. *The Elementary Forms of the Religious Life*. Translated by Joseph Ward Swain. London: Allen & Urwin, 1915.

Eggeling, Julius. *Sacred Books of the East*. Oxford: Oxford Univ. Press, 1882.

Eliade, Mircea. *Birth and Rebirth*. Translated by W. R. Trask. New York, 1958.

———. *Gods, Goddesses, and Myths of Creation*. New York: Harper & Row, 1974.

———. *Mephistopheles and the Androgyne: Studies in Religious Myth and Symbol*. Translated by J. M. Cohen. New York: Sheed & Ward, 1965.

———. *Myths, Dreams, and Mysteries*. Translated by P. Mairet. New York: Harper & Row, 1960.

———. *Myth and Reality*. New York: Harper & Row, 1963.

———. *The Myth of the Eternal Return*. Translated by W. R. Trask. New York: Pantheon, 1954.

Eliot, T. S. "The Waste Land."

Euripides. *The Bacchae*. Translated by F. L. Lucas, *Greek Tragedy and Comedy*. New York: Viking Compass Books, 1968.

Fiske, John. *Myths and Myth-Makers: Old Tales and Superstitions Interpreted by Comparative Mythology.* Boston: Houghton Mifflin, 1885.

Frazer, Sir James. *The Golden Bough.* 12 vols. London, 1907–1915.

———. *The New Golden Bough.* 1 vol. Edited by Theodor H. Gaster. New York: Mentor Books, 1964.

Freud, Sigmund. *Totem and Taboo.* Translated by A. A. Brill. New York: Moffat, Yard & Co., 1918.

Frobenius, Leo. *African Genesis.* New York: Stackpole & Sons, 1938.

Frye, Northrop. *Anatomy of Criticism.* New York: Atheneum, 1970.

———. *Fables of Identity: Studies in Poetic Mythology.* New York: Harbinger Books, 1963.

Gaster, Theodor H. *The Oldest Stories in the World.* New York: Viking, 1952.

———. *Thespis: Ritual, Myth, and Drama in the Ancient Near East* [1950], Garden City: N.Y.: Doubleday [Anchor], 1961.

Ginzberg, Louis. *The Legends of the Jews.* Philadelphia: The Jewish Publication Society of America, 1913.

Goethe. *Faust.*

Graves, Robert. *The Greek Myths.* 2 vols. Baltimore: Penguin, 1955.

Gray, Louis, ed. *The Mythology of All Races,* 13 vols. Boston: Marshall Jones Co., 1916–1932.

Grimal, Pierre, ed. *Larousse World Mythology.* New York: Hamlyn, 1973.

Grinnell, George B. *Blackfoot Lodge Tales: The Story of a Prairie People.* Lincoln: University of Nebraska Press, 1962.

Hamilton, Edith. *Mythology.* New York: Mentor Books. 1969.

Handy, E. S. Craighill. *Polynesian Religion.* Honolulu: Bernice P. Bishop Museum Bulletin 34, 1927.

Harrison, Jane. *Epilegomena to the Study of Greek Religion and Themis: A Study of the Social Origins of Greek Religion.* Hyde Park, N.Y.: University Books, 1962.

———. *Mythology.* New York: Harbinger Books, 1963.

Henderson, Joseph L., and Oakes, Maud. *The Wisdom of the Serpent: The Myths of Death, Rebirth, and Resurrection.* New York: Collier Books, 1971.

Holy Bible. King James version.

Homer. *Iliad.* Translated by Richard Lattimore. Chicago: Phoenix Books, 1961.

———. *The Odyssey of Homer.* Translated by T. E. Shaw (T. E. Lawrence). New York: Oxford University Press, 1932.

———. *The Odyssey of Homer.* Translated by Robert Fitzgerald. Garden City, N.Y.: Doubleday (Anchor), 1963.

Hongi, Hare, "A Maori Cosmogony." *Journal of the Polynesian Society* 16, (1907): 113–114.

Hultkrantz, Ake. *The North American Indian Orpheus Tradition.* Stockholm: Statens Etnogra Fiska Museum, 1957.

Joyce, James. *Ulysses.*

Jung, Carl Gustav. *Answer to Job: The Problem of Evil: Its Psychological and Religious Origins.* Translated by R. F. C. Hull. Cleveland: Meridian Books, 1960.

———. *The Archetypes and the Collective Unconscious.* Princeton: Bollingen Series, 1959.

———. *Memories, Dreams, Reflections.* Edited by Aniela Jaffe, translated by Richard and Clara Winston. New York: Vintage Books, 1961.

———. *Modern Man in Search of a Soul.* London: K. Paul, Trench & Truoner, 1933.

———. *Symbols of Transformation.* Princeton: Bollingen Series, 1956.

Jung, Carl Gustav, and Kerényi, C. *Introduction to a Science of Mythology: The Myth of the Divine Child and the Mysteries of Elensis.* London: Routledge & Kegan Paul, 1951.

Jung, Carl Gustav, von Franz M.-L., et al. *Man and His Symbols.* New York: Dell. 1968.

Kazantzakis, Nikos. *The Odyssey: A Modern Sequel.* Translated by Kimon Friar. New York: Simon & Schuster, 1958.

Kerényi, C. *The Gods of the Greeks.* London: Thames and Hudson, 1951.

———. *The Heroes of the Greeks.* New York: Grove Press, 1960.

Kramer, S. N., ed. *Mythologies of the Ancient World.* Garden City, N.Y.: Doubleday (Anchor), 1961.

———. *Sumerian Mythology.* New York: Torchbook, 1961.

Kroeber, A. L. *Indian Myths of South Central California.* University of California Publications, American Archeology and Ethnology (1906–1907): 229–231.

Leach, Maria. *The Beginning.* New York: Funk & Wagnalls, 1956.

Leeming, David A. *Mythology.* New York: Newsweek Books World of Culture Series, 1976.

Lévi-Strauss, Claude. "The Structural Study of Myth." *In Myth: A Symposium.* Edited by A. Sebeok. Bloomington, Ind.: Univ. of Indiana Press, 1958.

Malinowski, Bronislaw. "Myth in Primitive Psychology." *In Magic, Science and Religion and Other Essays.* Edited by Robert Redfield. Boston: Beacon Press, 1948.

Marlowe, Christopher. *Doctor Faustus.* New York: New American Library, 1969.

Mooney, James. *Myths of the Cherokee.* [1900] New York: Johnson Reprint Corp. 1970.

Morgan, Edwin, trans. *Beowulf.* Berkeley: University of California Press, 1967.

Muir, Sir William. *The Life of Mohammad.* Revised by T. H. Weir. [1923], New York: AMS Press, 1975.

Narasimhan, C. V., trans. *The Mahabharata*. New York: Columbia University Press, 1965.

Neumann, Erich. *The Great Mother: An Analysis of the Archetype*. Translated by Ralph Manheim. New York: Pantheon Books, 1955.

——. *Mystical Man*. Eranos-Jahrbuch XVI, 1959.

Nietzsche, Friedrich. *The Philosophy of Nietzsche*. New York: Modern Library, 1927.

Nivedita, Sister. See Coomaraswamy.

Oakes, Maud. See Henderson.

Oldfather, C. H., trans. *Diodorus of Sicily*. London: W. Heinemann, 1933–1967.

Otto, Walter F. *Dionysus. Myth and Cult*. Translated by R. B. Palmer. Bloomington: Univ. of Indian Press, 1965.

Ovid. *Metamorphoses*. Translated by Horace Gregory. New York: Mentor Books. 1958.

Piankoff, Alexandre. *The Shrines of Tut-ankh-amon*. New York: Pantheon Books, 1955.

Quinn, E. C. *the Quest of Seth: For the Oil and Life*. Chicago: Univ. of Chicago Press, 1962.

Radin, Paul. *The Trickster: A Study in American Indian Mythology*. [1956], New York: Greenwood Press, 1969.

Radin, Paul, and Sweeney, James J. *African Folktales and Sculpture*. New York: Bollingen Series 32, 1952.

Raglan, Lord Fitzroy. *The Hero: A Study in Tradition. Myth, and Drama*. [1937], New York: Vintage Books, 1956.

Rank, Otto. *The Myth of the Birth of the Hero and Other Writings*. Edited by Philip Freund. New York: Vintage Books, 1959.

Róheim, Géza. *The Origin and Function of Culture*. New York: Nervous and Mental Disease Monographs, 1943.

Rothenberg, Jerome ed. *Technicians of the Sacred: A Range of Poetries from Africa, America, Asia, and Oceania*. Garden City, N.Y.: Anchor Books, 1969.

Sahagún, Fray Bernardino de. *Florentine Codex*. Translated by A. J. O. Anderson, Santa Fe: School of American Research, 1951.

Schoolcraft, H. R. *The Myth of Hiawatha and Other Oral Legends Mythologic and Allegoric of the North American Indians*. Philadelphia: J. B. Lippincott & Co., 1856.

Serrano, Miguel, *C. G. Jung and Hermann Hesse: A Record of Two Friendships*. Translated by Frank MacShane. New York: Schocken Books, 1968.

Smith, W. Ramsay. *Myth and Legends of the Australian Aboriginals*. London: George G. Harrap, 1970 (reprint).

Sophocles. *Oedipus at Colonus*. Translated by Robert Fitzgerald. *Sophocles I*. Edited by David Grene and Richard Lattimore. New York: Washington Square Press, 1967.

Thompson, Stith. *The Folktale*. New York: The Dryden Press, 1946.
————. *Motif-Index of Folk Literature*. Copenhagen and Bloomington: Indiana Univ. Press, 1955–1958.
————. *Tales of the North American Indians*. Bloomington: Midland Books, 1971.
Thurston, Herbert and Attwater, Donald, eds. *Butler's Lives of the Saints*, vol. 2. New York: P. J. Kennedy and Sons, 1963.
Tripp, Edward, ed. *Crowell's Handbook of Classical Mythology*. New York: Crowell, 1970.
Turville-Petre, E. O. G. *Myth and Religion of the North: The Religion of Ancient Scandinavia*. New York: Holt, Rinehart & Winston, 1964
Tylor, E. B. *Primitive Culture*. 2 vols. London: J. Murray, 1871.

Underhill, Evelyn. *Mysticism: A Study in the Nature and Development of Man's Spiritual Consciousness*. [1911], London: Methuen & Co., 1949.

Vermaseren, M. J. *Mithras, the Secret God*. New York: Barnes & Noble, 1963.
Vickery, John B., ed. *Myth and Literature: Contemporary Theory and Practice*. Lincoln: University of Nebraska Press, Bison Books, 1969.
Vickery, John B., and Sellery, J. M., eds. *The Scapegoat: Ritual and Literature*. Boston: Houghton Mifflin, 1972.
Virgil. *Aeneid*.

Wägner, W. *Romances and Epics of Our Northern Ancestors: Norse, Celt, and Teuton*. Translated by W. S. W. Anson. London: Norroena Society, 1907.
Warner, Rex. *The Stories of the Greeks*. New York: Farrar, Straus & Giroux, 1967.
Warren, Henry Clarke, trans. *Buddhism in Translations*. Cambridge, Mass., 1896.
Watts, Alan. *Myth and Ritual in Christianity*. Boston: Beacon Paperback, 1968.
Weston, Jessie L. *From Ritual to Romance: An Account of the Holy Grail from Ancient Ritual to Christian Symbol*. Garden City, N.Y.: Doubleday (Anchor), 1957.
————. trans. *Sir Gawain at the Grail Castle*, London: D. Nutt, 1903.

Yeats, William Butler. *The Collected Poems of William Butler Yeats*. New York: Macmillan, 1957.

Zimmer, Heinrich. *The King and the Corpse: Tales of the Soul's Conquest of Evil*. New York: Pantheon Books, 1948.

INDEX

Aaron, 79, 98, 99
Abaddon, 265
Abantes, 59
Abhidhamma Pitaka, 91
Abihu, 98
Abinadab, 67
Abner, 70
Abraham, 79, 96, 237, 249, 314–315, 316
Absolute knowledge, 149–153
Abu Beker, 114, 115
Abydos, 212
Achaea, 269
Achates, 271
Achelous, 189, 218
Acheron, 218, 272
Achilles, 124, 125, 144
Acoetes, 81, 82
Acropolis, the, 145, 148
Actaeon, 133
Adam, 48, 172, 177, 232, 248, 249, 275, 276
Adonis, 213, 231, 232, 233
  birth of, 40, 48
  death of, 205–206, 232
  rebirth of, 199, 283–284, 301
Adopted parent, 22–29
Aegean islands, 194
Aegean Sea, 148
Aegeus, 12, 59, 145, 148
Aegle, 147
Aeneas, 266
  descent into underworld by, 271–274
  quest for the Golden Bough by, 197
Aeneid (Virgil), 197
Aeolus, 344
Aethra, 12–13, 59
Aetna, Mount, 215
Aetolia, 195
Africa, 81
African myths
  Bantu, 37, 337–338
  Tanzanian, 154
  Wanjiru, 223–224, 246, 303
Agamemnon, 11, 124, 125, 269
Agave, 188, 193
Agdistis, 203
Agdos rock, 29
Agnes, 324
Agon, 185, 198
Agrippa, 180
Aisinokoki (Wind Sucker), 253
Aissa, 124
Ajax, 124, 146, 282
Akhaians, 116
Albanus, 181

Alcaeus, 55
Alcmene, 55, 56
Alcyonian Lake, 247
Alençon, Duke of, 75
Ale-nu-haha channel, 242
Allah, 113
All-Athenian Festival, 12
Almain rutters, 180
Almo, 298
Alpheus, 216
Alpheus River, 134
Altar of Strong Zeus, 12
Althaea, 195
Alukah, 264
Ama no uzume, 289
Amaterasu, 288–289
Amathus, 205
Amazons, 135, 195
America, 180
American Indian myths
  Blackfoot Indian, 33–35, 149–153, 222, 253, 294
  Californian Indian, 336
  Cherokee Indian, 295–297
  Comanche Indian, 258
  Gitksan Indian, 100–102
  Ojibwa Indian, 103–106
  Tewa Indian, 30–32
  Zuñi, 343
Ammon, 195
Amphithea, 57
Amphitrite, 146
Amphitryon, 55–56
Amram, 79, 263, 313
Anahuac, 174
Analytics, 177
Ananda, 316, 317
Anapis, 214
Anat, 231
Anaxagoras, 194
Anchises, 271, 273
Andrew, 183
Androgeus, 145
Androgyne motif, 328
Angel of Death, 312, 313
Angel of Hell. *See* Nasargiel
Angels of Destruction, 263–265
Anna (mother of Mary), 41
Anna (prophetess), 76–77
Annas, 226
Anotatta Lake, 14
Answer to Job (Jung), 127, 276
Anthony, Saint, 125
Anticleia, 267
Antipater, 121
Antwerp bridge, 179

357

Hero, The (Raglan), 49
Hero with a Thousand Races, The (Campbell), 49, 84, 199, 276, 328
Hesperides, garden of, 138
  golden apples of the, 137–138
Hesperus, 214
Hiawatha, 103
Hidden places, 22, 23–24, 25, 30, 39, 40, 42, 44, 48
Hiera, island of, 12
Hiiaka', 166–171, 198, 239–245
Hilaria. See Festival of Joy
Hilo, 169
Himalaya Mountains, 14
Him Buto, 38
Hine-ahu-one, 342
Hippolyte, 136
  girdle of, 135
Hippolytus, 136
Hipta, 219, 231
Hira, Mount, 113
Hispania, 22
Hittite Myth, Telipinu, 231, 285–287
Holy Ghost, 42, 76, 96, 325
Holy Grail, search for, 155–159, 198, 199
Homer, 186, 197
Honoipi, 170
Honolulu (Kou), 170
Honua-mea, 242
Hopoe, 168, 169, 239
Horeb, Mount, 78, 79
Horse Mesa Point, 31
Horus, 210, 292
  birth of, 38, 39, 341
Hou, 243
Huitzilopochtli, birth of, 36
Hula drum (pahu-hula), 167
Hunger, 272
Hur, 99
Hurakan, 340
Hyacinth, rebirth of, 281–282, 283, 305
Hyades, the, 81
Hydra, destruction of, 132
Hymen, 254
Hyperippe, 118
Hypolipnus, 247

Icaria, island of, 81
Icarius, 194–195
Icelandic myth, Hermodr and Balder, 259–260
Iliad (Homer), 186
Ilios, city of, 267, 269
Immortal Gods, 268
Immortality, 126
"Impetuous Male," 288–289
Inanna. See Ishtar
Incest motif, 39, 40

India, 179, 195-196, 198, 247
Indian myths
  Buddha, 14–18, 71–72, 87–92, 290–291, 316–317
  Indian Deluge, 350
  Karna, 23–24
  Krishna, 53–54
Indra, 17, 23–24
Ino, 186
Introduction to a Science of Mythology (Jung and Kerényi), 49, 84
Io, 335, 342
Iolaus, 132
Iphianassa, 118, 194
Iphicles, 56
Iphigeneia, 124
Iphinoe, 194
Iphis, 254
Iris, 344
Irish myth, Cuchulainn, 62–63
Isaac, 79, 315
Isaac Tens, communion with the unknown by, 100–102
Isaiah, 96, 183
Isaias, 325
Ishtar (Inanna), 207–208, 213, 231
  descent into underworld by, 237–238, 239, 275, 276
Isis, 38, 209–212, 213, 231, 292–293
Israel, children of, 26, 45, 79, 98, 99, 265, 341
Israel, land of, 46
Israel, men of, 7, 68, 70
Israelites, 264
Issachar, 26
Italian myths, Agnes, 324
Italy, 136, 137, 275
Ithaca, 57–58, 266, 267
Ithakans, 116
Ixion, 255
Izanagi and Izanami, 288
  descent into underworld by, 261–262

Jacob, 26, 79, 315
  house of, 42
James, 183, 225, 300
Japanese myths
  Amaterasu and Susanowo, 288–289
  Izanagi and Izanami, 261–262
Jason, 131
  quest for the Golden Fleece by, 197
Jeremiah, 46
Jericho, 182
Jerome, Bible of, 178
Jerome, Saint, 41
Jerusalem, 45, 70, 73, 76, 77, 96, 182, 183, 249, 300, 301, 302, 325
  Daughters of, 228
Jesse, 67–68, 70

80 81 82 83 84 9 8 7 6 5 4 3 2 1